ID0858340

Whaddaya Got, Loran?

MERCER UNIVERSITY PRESS

Endowed by

TOM WATSON BROWN
and
THE WATSON-BROWN FOUNDATION, INC.

Whaddaya Got, Loran?

DISPATCHES FROM GEORGIA

Loran Smith

MERCER UNIVERSITY PRESS
Macon, Georgia

MUP/ H1013

25 24 23 22 21   5 4 3 2 1

Books published by Mercer University Press are printed on acid-free paper that meets the requirements of the American National Standard for Information Sciences—Permanence of Paper for Printed Library Materials.

Printed and bound in the United States.

This book is set in Adobe Caslon Pro and Georgia display.

Cover/jacket design by Burt&Burt.

ISBN   978-0-88146-797-0
eBook   978-0-88146-816-8

Cataloging-in-Publication Data is available from the Library of Congress

For
Alex and Zoe Smith, Sophie and Penny Martin;
Grandchildren are never overrated.

Contents

Acknowledgments

First, the highest of high fives to Bill Stembridge, a nice man who advanced the notion to Mercer University Press to consider publishing a book of my columns for which I am deeply grateful. Bill has ties with Mercer, the University of Georgia and the entire state, always glossing the positives.

To my wife, Myrna, whose proofing and management of weekly columns for years, has been a godsend for one who, with a demanding day job, is often guilty of "writing on the run."

To Claude Felton, the University of Georgia's genial sports information director who is never too busy to help a staff member with fact checking; to Tim Hix, Claude's MVP associate whose counsel and sounding board conversations are not only helpful and insightful, but elevating and fun.

To Sarah Garner and Katie Durden, student assistants for typing, fact checking, and proofing—efficient and eager to underscore details; most of all their command of technology for an author who is sorely lacking in that realm. And Sarah, again, who also compiled the index.

To Marc Jolley and Marsha Luttrell at Mercer University Press: thanks for guiding and managing the process which brought the manuscript to printed pages. Happy to be on your team.

PART I

Georgia Will always Be on My Mind

There are times, even with the influence of the aging process, when I would really enjoy a spur-of-the-moment opportunity to pack a few essentials and embark from Hartsfield-Jackson International Airport on a flight to Paris. Or London. Or Rome. Or anywhere I could afford to go to enjoy a new destination or settle in with an encore.

After all, you never tire of the Eiffel Tower, Big Ben, or the Sistine Chapel.

However, home and its offerings are just as warm, uplifting, and inviting. Seeing the Bulldogs play in Sanford Stadium; following my favorite team from Athens to New Orleans to Pasadena—every road address for well over fifty-eight years; fishing the Chattahoochee and the intercostal rivers and streams within view of the Marshes of Glynn.

I can never get enough of my home state. The Empire State of the South has had some forgettable times in its history, but it has navigated its troubled waters better than most Southern states. Georgia has more accomplished people, stimulating places, and arresting things to enjoy than a native son could ever find time to absorb.

When I think of Georgia and its pleasures to soak up, I think of the unspoiled hills, pristine beauty, roasting ears, lakes, and cool nights of the northern part of our state, and the fields and farms in the southern half, highlighted by fishing opportunities that abound in each part.

Then there are the quail hunting options that are there for avid hunters, an exercise highlighted by the best in the world at Thomasville. Hunting quail is accompanied by the most gratifying of outdoor highs when you see a bird dog on a point.

There's a wide range of choices to seek out, such as enjoying a meal with an exalted scientist or learned professor, spending time with an accomplished person in any field, or interviewing the blue-collar working man who doggedly found a way to get his daughters through college.

Some highlights include Barbecue, corn on the cob, strawberry ice cream pie at the Georgia Center for Continuing Education, and hearing Erk Russell, the memorable Bulldog coach, tell a story as good or better than Jerry Clower. Walking the fairways of the Augusta National Golf Club during a pre-tournament practice round with Jack Nicklaus. Tape-recording an interview in the Clubhouse with Arnold Palmer when he had missed the cut but was still on the premises to participate in the televising of the ceremony introducing the new Masters champion. Seeing the Braves win a World Series game at home, hoping the Falcons would find a way to win the big one someday, and never tiring of seeing Georgia play for the SEC championship at Mercedes-Benz stadium.

Remembering my God-fearing parents, who never did anything of the sort. Salt-of-the-earth country folk. I love them and their type. Gospel music, country music, from Hiawassee to Hahira, Chickamauga to Tybee Island Light, and unforgettable stops in between.

My cup runneth over and I am button-popping proud to call Georgia home.

Accidental President

Politics seems to turn people off more often than not these days. It is fashionable to bash those in office, giving them the back of the hand with the same negative emotional thrust we would give a Ponzi schemer. This being an election year, I let a book bring about an eager reflection regarding the subject of politics.

Do you know a high-level politician? If you do, you might hold a different view. You may find that they are not such bad characters, although I do admit that we were once advised by a soothsayer from Stratford-upon-Avon that politicians sometimes make for strange bedfellows.

Presidential history has always maintained an eager fascination in this corner. A good book on any president, regardless of the author's take, is usually worthwhile. Such books are usually thick in size and are on the expensive side. However, I have found that they are well worth the investment.

We all have favorite presidents. One of mine is Harry Truman. A few years ago, I was connected with an annual event in Kansas City and could not wait to tour the Truman Library in nearby Independence. This led to engaging encores. Lately, I have spent time with a fine book, *The Accidental President: Harry S. Truman and the Four Months That Changed the World*.

The author is A. J. Baime, whose research reminds you that a biography is a lot of hard work, requiring the finessing of a multitude of details. After having read several books by Truman or about him, I found this one the most stimulating of all.

First of all, Truman admittedly did not want to be president. He did not enjoy living in the White House and he did not like the attention that came with him holding the highest office in the land. Imagine how different it is today for a president.

If you peruse Truman's record, appreciating the things he accomplished and recognizing that he went into high office in debt and died a man of modest assets, you recognize that Truman achieved what most of us would want from elected officials—he took the oath of office to serve his country. He finally escaped the jaws of debt with the help of friends after he left Washington.

Plainspoken, this treatise on his presidency confirms that he was a regular Joe. When the day was done, he enjoyed a bourbon or two and found great emotional comfort by playing poker.

His times were different, but it is mind boggling to think that, even in his day, he could slip out of the White House and walk a few blocks to church on Sunday mornings with a chagrined Secret Service detail wondering where he was. Once, when he was invited to a weekend jamboree at Burning Tree, one of the most prestigious golf clubs in the country, the guests were suddenly shocked to hear piano music being played with gusto. It was the President who was providing the entertainment. Again, a regular Joe.

Although Truman won an election with the support of the Tom Pendergast machine, no one has uncovered anything illegal or sinister with regard to their relationship.

While I am not a historian, I am an American who appreciates the right to vote and never misses an election. Candidates can be disappointing. Reading the latest book about Harry S. Truman confirms certain basics that are illuminating and uplifting:

Truman was a modest man who was elected as a commoner and who had no interest in bettering himself financially.

He was a workhorse, not a show horse.

It saddened him when his wife, Bess, was not with him in the White House.

He was as much of a common-sense president as any who had ever resided in the White House.

He did his "damndest" to live up to the oath of office.

He could make the tough decision, such as dropping the atomic bombs on Japan, with reasoned deductions based on his war department's estimates of the loss of life projected by invading the island nation. He knew the Nation and the world did not want to "study war no more."

He could parry with Stalin, the murderer, and Churchill, the ally who was rightfully concerned about Europe's future with the brutal Stalin looking over its shoulder.

There are no rules in politics, but if all candidates were required to read *Accidental President*, perhaps we would be blessed with more statesmen than self-serving advocates. Selah!

Agnew Peacock, My Neighbor and Friend

Agnew Peacock was a rock of a man in the days of yore. The passing years, however, brought about a decline in his health that made him compatible with the notion that sometimes it is better to leave this discordant world than to remain with agony, riding shotgun in your life.

Likely, there are many who will take in the following personal ruminations without knowing my neighbor and close friend who lost a battle with lymphoma and other complications a few days ago. Agnew died in a hospital, longing to be home.

You did not have to know my altruistic friend to appreciate his remarkable selflessness and modesty. Perhaps there is one in your circle of friends. One in your neighborhood. I wish for every precinct, every street, every neighbor an Agnew Peacock.

In his youth, Agnew was one who seemed physically indestructible. He could build and fix with the best. Nobody could make do better than Agnew. He gloried in being able to work. It was as if God had said to him, "I have given you two hands. Let them never be idle."

Those who knew my friend were keenly aware that never in his life did Agnew keep company with idleness. When the sun came up, he joined ole Sol for a long day of manual labor, glorying in earning his bread by the sweat of his brow. He went through life with a sobering half-smile, half-grin that emanated from the kindest and gentlest heart. He could not have brought himself to do bodily harm to another human being unless his family or his property were threatened. Had that ever come about, the perpetrator would have soon realized he had made a very foolish mistake.

My guess is that Agnew moved across the street from my wife and me at least thirty-five years ago. It wasn't long before I began singing his praises as the "World's Greatest Neighbor." We were always pleased to host a party and include Agnew and his wife, Hilda. I would introduce him with the aforementioned sobriquet, which brought about a blushing moment for Agnew, but it really was true. We loved introducing our friends to the "World's Greatest Neighbor."

He was always pitching in. For shrimp cookouts, he would eyeball the boiling water in the cooker and pronounce it just right to dump a carton of frozen shrimp into the pot. Sometimes he would put the tip of a weathered finger into the water which brought a nod of approval.

He was always inspecting our house in a good, neighborly way. "Your gutters need cleaning. I've got somebody who can do that for you. I will call him." The next thing you know, I would come home from work and my wife would announce that Agnew's friend had cleaned the gutters. When a bill was not forthcoming, we would call the gutter cleaner and he would say, "Agnew took care of the bill."

I would walk across the street and protest to my friend and he would say, "You can get the next one." Further engagement would lead Agnew to say, "Well I didn't pay for any football tickets last fall, so we are even." Agnew had a friend who had excess firewood. When the first dip on the thermometer came about in October, I would come home and my side porch reflected a becoming state. A truck load of firewood was neatly stacked and ready for use.

About suppertime, there would be a knock on the door and there would be Agnew, grinning and handing over a small box of kindling wood. "Here," he would smile, "you will need some of this."

Agnew played for Athens High in the Fran Tarkenton era. He was older than Fran and was a very good player. As you might expect, he played in the line, never seeking any praise but forever bent on being a good teammate.

Following high school graduation, Agnew went to work with Georgia Power, which never had a more loyal and dedicated employee. In his downtime, he bought and spruced up houses that he would sell for a profit. No man ever was more enterprising. He would find a good house on an attractive street, give it a makeover, move in, and live in it for a while. Hilda had very good taste, and the house, as they say, "looked lived-in."

Before long, some prospective buyer would make an offer. Agnew would call the moving van and the "World's Greatest Neighbor" would soon upgrade another neighborhood, turning a tidy profit in the process. There was pure joy in working. It brought about fulfillment for him.

Agnew had no vices. He abstained when it came to alcohol. He preferred a vegetable diet, and although that does not guarantee greater longevity, he left behind a legacy that could be envied by the pope.

I don't know if St. Peter needed a carpenter when Agnew Peacock showed up last week, but if heaven needs any "fixing-up," the right man is now on the scene.

Alex, Our First Grandchild

DALLAS—Reflecting back on the holidays, this Cowboys' town is where we have spent Christmas for sixteen years. We have two grandchildren living here, which makes for the "rest of the story." Grandkids spark an allure that makes one change and alter plans no matter the challenge.

Sometimes a Georgia bowl game has made Christmas travel complicated, but it seems to have always worked out. Charlotte, the other grandkids' habitat, is a little more convenient and easier to get to, although for years those grandchildren lived next door, which made Christmas really easy.

Dallas is an exciting place with a lot of activity to spike emotions and curiosities, but this last trip there was joyfully highlighted by a milestone birthday. Alex, our oldest grandchild and only grandson, turned sixteen.

Naturally, the focal point of the weekend, for him, was talk of a car. He was conditioned to accept that there would be a process involved. No new car to begin with. He was okay with that. In January, there would be an ongoing survey of used car lots, and at some point a deal would be struck.

Alex was amenable to the plan and was not disappointed. But wily, ole Santa just happened to have a friend in the car business; and he just happened to have a used Chevy Tahoe with an odometer reflecting a hundred thousand miles of seasoning. Just right for a teenage boy's first car. Alex hangs with a circle of friends who have parents given to similar thinking. Learn to drive something that if stricken with a fender bender, damage control is not so consequential and/or impactful on the budget.

Grandchildren, as you have probably heard, are not overrated. Alex and his sister, Zoe, have been the beneficiaries of quality education principles. They have been exposed to balanced views and selfless conduct. Music is enduringly relevant in Alex's life, and before entertaining thoughts about becoming the beneficiary of a car, he wanted a nice guitar. He finds solitude in his room even when he is causing the walls to shake with his ensemble.

Church is a part of Alex's life. He has learned the importance of making time for Mass on Sunday. He and his sister engage in athletic competition at school. Track is their choice of sports. Camp in the summer has become an invaluable ritual where they meet new friends and renew old friendships. In a year, Alex will be moving into a leadership role as a counselor.

All of this suggests that he will enjoy his forthcoming college experience and be prepared for the future. While there are no givens in life with regard to success—the inevitable pitfalls can lead to pratfalls that can spoil and interfere—it is good to see that he has the compatibility of good training and leadership at home as he has reached that milestone birthday.

I can remember when he was born on Christmas Eve 2002. He came into this world with a shock of thick, black hair on a cold day in Dallas. His father, maternal grandfather, and I puffed on cigars in the garage of the hospital—the only place where we were allowed to celebrate in such fashion—making toasts to his good fortune of starting life with robust health, nothing that should ever be taken for granted.

As Alex began his life on a bitterly cold afternoon, there were thoughts about the survival of mankind. Humans have survived the toughest of times. Alex was born in a state-of-the-art hospital that provided him with the greatest of care. What was it like for the Native Americans, for example, giving birth on the high plains in the dead of winter? Eskimos on the frozen tundra? Rural folk with little or no modern conveniences and the nearest doctor fifty miles, or more, away?

This year as Alex opened his birthday presents two days before Christmas, there was an emphasis on music-related gifts and tee shirts (does any teenager ever get enough tee shirts?), and there was a shyness in his demeanor. Being the center of attention with a gift largesse is nice but emotionally overwhelming.

Soon it was dinnertime at a nearby restaurant. With celebrating at a peak, there was silverware rapping on a water glass, bringing pause to the evening. Alex, on his own, chose to speak. He thanked everybody in the room and allowed us to hear how fortunate he felt.

While I am not sure of his career path, I simply hope for responsibility, accountability, integrity, and selflessness to accompany him on his journey. My hope is that he will always appreciate the humility that comes with driving a used Chevy Tahoe.

Allan Armitage, a Man for All Seasons

It is a good thing that the dastardly COVID-19 pandemic has brought about a tsunami of lawn and garden patronage, a reminder that sometimes dark hours are required to bring about the realization that energy and industry can be powerful game changers in our lives, especially in times of challenge. Whatever your burdens, whatever your issues—getting outdoors can make a telling difference.

Just ask Allan Armitage, a retired University of Georgia horticulturist. It would be difficult to imagine a man who has enjoyed more fulfillment in life. Much of that comes from having been a proponent of digging in the dirt. Gardening, he says, will help enable us to get through COVID-19.

In the last fortnight or two, maybe more, I have read two of his books, *Of Naked Ladies and Forget-Me-Nots* and *It's Not Just About the Hat*, which made me appreciate his work and his life story. With an engaging and inquiring mind, he has a resume that overwhelms. He has always had a bent for reaching out and touching life and its treasures. His hallmark is adapting to life's vicissitudes. He gets up every day, expecting to learn something new, which makes him a beacon in a sedentary world.

Beholding the spectacular gardens of the earth, which became an abiding passion, meant that he would also connect with the Vatican, the Parthenon, the Louvre, Pompeii, the Alhambra, the Great Barrier Reef, the Great Wall, and great vineyards in between. He and his family had the good fortune to live for a spell in New Zealand, a gardener's wonderland.

Born in Mount Royal, a suburb of Montreal, Allan experienced a normal, middle-class life with parents underscoring enterprise, insightful research, and motivation, as well as daily bread.

Allan and his brother Howard played games as the seasons dictated: baseball, basketball, and as you would expect, hockey. What Canadian kid did not? That affinity for the outdoors, even when snow was knee-deep on the landscape, segued into a love of gardens and brought about a green thumb pastime, which both coddled and sustained him.

Born with an extra helping of wanderlust, Allan's life has become an exciting journey in which he has made things grow, gained inspiration from travel, and visually ingested varied landscapes. With the help of his lovely wife, Susan, he has connected with people and places that have enabled them—from the date of their marriage in December 1968—to live happily ever after.

The Armitages arrived in Athens in 1980, a very good year. While Allan identified with big-time football and basketball at Michigan State as a graduate student (he witnessed Magic Johnson's prime years as a student-athlete), Allan never could have imagined what an experience game day between the hedges would be like, especially when he saw grandmothers barking approval following a Herschel Walker jaunt to the end zone.

As a tennis aficionado, Allan was honored with an introduction to Georgia's iconic coach, Dan Magill, who in turn introduced him to Vince Dooley, whose love of gardening was as intense as Allan's if not as seasoned and studied. (A member of the Clarke Oconee Tennis Association, Allan's over-the-hill gang won the National Seniors Championship in 2018, which was also the year his brother Howard won the World Masters Squash Championship.) I'm sure his high school annual had "Best All Around" stenciled under his photograph.

The "publish or perish" dictum fits compellingly in Allan's wheelhouse. He has written over seventy academic papers, five hundred industry papers, and sixteen books. You get the drift that he could type with one hand while digging in a flowerpot with the other.

One of his most rewarding initiatives was developing a trial garden behind Snelling Hall on UGA's South Campus, a signature outdoor laboratory where invaluable research has taken place and that has brought immeasurable value to the horticultural industry. However, Allan fears that some dean or administrator will someday deem it the perfect place for a parking deck.

If you don't identify him by his works, look for his hat. He wears broad brim Tilley hats, which are almost as good as a cloud when the sun is bearing down on resourceful horticulturists. Allan is an international personality, universally regarded for his plant and garden expertise, and of course, the hat. That hat, a Canadian product, helped him conquer Georgia's heat, which led him and Susan to abandon their plan to try the South for only a couple of years.

Canada's deep-freeze weather that Allan grew up in was not always a bother, but five months of it every year! When is enough, enough? He has found a home where he can dig in the dirt when it is the coldest in Georgia. In Canadian winters, to dig in the dirt, you need a pickaxe.

The Armitages took a run-down shack in the Five Points community in Athens and gave it a botanical face-lift, added bird houses, and are exhilarated by the changing of the seasons, all in full view of a small Canadian flag that features the maple leaf in familiar red. Wine and conversation on their deck in the late afternoon is a rich experience.

The perfect sign-off for this treatise is that Allan Armitage is most appreciative of having been a loyal and devoted teacher for decades, appreciating what Henry Adams, an accomplished educator, once said: "A teacher affects eternity; he can never tell where his influence stops."

Georgia Journalist Makes It to the Top

NEW YORK—Anyone who makes it to the top more often than not experiences a few pratfalls along the way, enduring the slings and arrows of competition, jealousy, and envy. You might agree with the many who say that it is more difficult to stay at the top than to get there.

There has always been an unabated curiosity about those who climb the mountain, how they function, and how they view life from an elevated station. It is always inspiring to interact with those who are the best at what they do.

At schools of journalism across the country, there are countless young women who aspire for lofty network status, but few are chosen. This is about one who has made it big.

You observe Amy Robach, the Good Morning America news anchor, and you see talent, poise, and comportment that confirms she performs before the camera as effortlessly as a brickmason who has been at his craft for decades; a concert pianist who is flawless on the keyboard at Carnegie Hall; a pilot landing a jetliner for the three hundredth time at Heathrow.

There is a savory regard and seasoned respect for her on-the-air presence and compelling delivery of the morning news. She is good at what she does, very good, but when her workday is done, she takes time to be a homemaker and a mother. In some ways, she is an everyday mom as much as anything. Her work is important. Her homemaking responsibilities are equally important. She is a big deal, but she doesn't think so. How refreshing!

Born in Michigan, Amy spent her teenage years in Gwinnett County and was educated at the Henry Grady College of Journalism at the University of Georgia. It was in Athens that she came to appreciate the beauty of the campus, the fun between the hedges of Sanford Stadium on Saturday afternoon, and the intellectual motivation of a journalism faculty who underscored a noteworthy blueprint for success—principally, to use your brain for the ultimate achievement in life and roll up your sleeves and go to work expecting no free lunch.

She has been the reporter who worked in the field in the most chal-lenging of conditions which required that she "get her hands dirty." She takes professional fulfillment in a job well-done, even when the task was emotionally unpleasant, such as interviewing a father who had come to a dormitory to gather his daughter's belongings after the daughter had com-mitted suicide.

There is fervid praise for her alma mater in that while her undergrad-uate days were an over-the-top experience, she was also the beneficiary of a "phenomenal education." She majored in broadcast journalism with a minor in political science. "I felt that I walked away [from campus] after those four wonderful years with what I needed to go out in the real world and succeed," Amy says.

> My senior year, we put on, at that time, a show called University News, and we actually had to go out and produce pieces every day for our newscast at 5:00 p.m., typically the time most students take to their dorm rooms to relax. I still had to juggle classes and get everything managed to be able to go out and shoot the stories and put them together. And the deadline pressure with professor [Da-vid] Hazinski on your butt, telling you your work wasn't good enough...was challenging. When I went to my first assignment months later, I knew exactly what I was supposed to do and how to handle the stress of someone yelling at me because that's what takes place in your first newsroom. I can't speak highly enough about the journalism school at the University of Georgia and how it exposed me to the ethics involved, how to manage media law, and all the things you need to know when you're writing a story—and making sure you're being objective as much as you can. I felt like I had street smarts to be successful when I walked into my first newsroom as the result of the education and experience I got at the University of Georgia.

Travelers on Delta in October took note of Amy's cover story in SKY Magazine recapping her poignant journey with breast cancer. As a favor to her colleague, Robin Roberts, Amy underwent a mammogram on net-work television. The results were positive, alarming her and her family. "I thank God for it [mammogram]. Time was not on my side," she says. Treatments were successful, and now she is cancer-free. This amazing story has resulted in countless women becoming proactive by scheduling a mammogram posthaste. They write her every day about her influence. Her story has made them reach out to their doctor for an appointment without delay.

The result is that Amy is saving lives every day and simply says, "The reaction has been overwhelming." With abundant humility and gratitude, she doesn't seem aware that the most important life she saved was her own.

Belle Meade Bourbon:
Try It and You Will Like It

GREENBRIER, Tennessee — Nelson's Green Brier Distillery has the elements that would arouse the curiosity of a connoisseur, historian, and traditionalist. Owners Charlie and Andy Nelson, phoenix-like, reconnected to their ancestral roots to reestablish a bourbon recipe that once reached such lofty status that it overshadowed Jack Daniels as the world's leading and preferred Tennessee whiskey.

Every roaring success along the way, however, was followed by tragedy of some sort, which was a riches-to-rags saga that would be sensational fodder for a business-oriented novel. The story has no murder or steamy romance to spice it up, but it is a remarkable tale.

It all began with Charlie and Andy's great, great, great grandfather, Charles Nelson, who was born July 4, 1835 in a small town in northern Germany. Charles was fifteen years old when his parents sold their soap and candle factory in Germany in order to emigrate to the United States.

Charles' father sewed the family fortune, which he had converted into gold coins, in the lining of his clothes. On the way across the Atlantic, their ship encountered storms that swept several passengers overboard, including the patriarch, whose coin-lined garment caused him to sink with the greatest of alacrity.

The other members of the family survived but arrived in New York with only the clothes on their backs. This meant that teenage Charles became the head of the house. He and his brother naturally began making soaps and candles so the family could survive. A couple of years later, the Nelsons moved to Cincinnati to enter the grocery business but serendipitously learned to make high-end whiskey.

After the Civil War, Charles moved to Nashville, where his business became the place for anyone interested in buying meat, coffee, and whiskey. He was especially accomplished at making whiskey, which influenced him to concentrate on producing and marketing his fine product. In 1885, Charles sold over 380,000 gallons of whiskey in the US and Europe. Jack Daniels sales totaled 23,000 gallons, according to company archives.

Charles was a young man of fifty-six when he passed away in 1891, with his wife Louisa assuming control of the business, the only woman of the time to run a distillery. The business flourished, but another downturn loomed. Prohibition, which officially began in 1909 in the state of Tennessee, brought about the demise of the family's distilling business.

Six generations later, a funny thing happened to the Nelson descendants while on the way to a butcher shop in the summer of 2006. Charles, Andy, and their father Bill had purchased a cow and were taking the beef to a butcher shop to be cut into steaks for their freezer, an act of enterprise that many families underscore today.

The Nelson boys had heard the stories about the family's distilling history. While in conversation with the butcher about their heritage, he pointed to a warehouse across the street, noting that the spring on the property had never stopped running and that it was "pure as can be." This is where the "original" Nelson made his fortune.

Next move? The Greenbrier Historical Society. The curator had come in possession of two original bottles of Nelson's Green Brier Tennessee Whiskey. From a company handout, there is this reference: "For a moment time stood still. It was love at first sight. Charlie and Andy then looked back at one another, knowing what the other was thinking: 'This IS our destiny,'" they concluded.

The only better way to appreciate this story is to sit down in the warehouse with a bottle of Belle Meade Bourbon, which Charlie and Andy make today just like their ancestors did a century ago. It took them three years of research, planning, and hard work to resurrect the brand that had spawned aficionados for years. That original recipe would enable the Nelsons to gain traction in distilling and is now central to marketing and sales.

With a long history of affiliation in the wine and spirits business, Mike Cheek, a University of Georgia graduate, became chairman of the board. Other potential investors are eagerly taking note.

What's the significance of all this? That ingenuity, enterprise, and an appreciation for history remind us that the Great American dream survives today. The original Charles Nelson was an unflagging advocate of the work ethic. His word was his bond, and his business integrity connected with the man in the street.

The rest of the story—the current distilling of Belle Meade Bourbon—is as appealing as the celebrated drink that Charlie and Andy's great, great, great grandfather originally produced.

Bill Griffin
The Consummate Gentleman

The University of Georgia once had a colorful and unforgettable character by the name of William Tate, who hailed from the North Georgia mountain town of Tate that was named for his ancestors. He was as much a fixture on the campus as the Chapel Bell and the hedges of Sanford Stadium.

As dean of men, an office that no longer exists (on any campus), William Tate was in charge of discipline, which meant that his powers were absolute. He could kick you out of school for any offense, great or small. Yet he did not relish that he sometimes had to be the enforcer. He preferred to wax insightfully with sage wit. He loved his alma mater like no other.

He once said, "There is nothing finer than a Georgia boy with a Georgia education."

I thought of that line while enjoying a birthday party this past weekend—for a Georgia boy who grew up in Rutledge, matriculated in Athens, and is indelibly linked to his alma mater with a generous and undying love. Never demonstrative about his affection, he is a loyalist who gives back to his family, his university, and his friends.

With a business degree from the Terry College, he set about making his way in the world of finance, which has had him living in places that are far from the down-home life he knew growing up in rural Morgan County. His work has always made him a man on the go.

I often get calls from him as he is on the way to some distant airport: Chicago, Denver, Dallas, Jacksonville, San Francisco—and places like Vidalia when he is driving from his home at Sea Island to Athens. You call him, he calls you back. You email him, he responds.

This is a man with a perpetual and polite smile, a kind word for everybody—from the eager executive to the chairman, but also the waiter, the caddie, and the parking lot attendant. He is about as well-connected as one could be. He holds membership in some of the most prestigious private clubs in America. Golf has introduced him to executives in high places where he is at ease when there is business to discuss, his insightfulness and modesty overwhelming.

I once had a conversation with Tom Osborne, Nebraska's longtime head football coach and athletic director, who said poignantly, "It is important to be nice to the big contributors to your program; you can't survive without their support. But it is just as important to be nice to the custodian and the maintenance worker who play a significant role in your program."

As soon as Osborne made his comment, I thought of Bill Griffin. Most of the time, depending on a number of circumstances, men have to work at being a gentleman. It comes naturally with Bill.

Bill is past president of the Oakmont Country Club in Pittsburgh. He held that position for six straight years. That, in itself, warrants the ultimate tribute. How can a man in an eastern establishment golf and country club keep getting reelected? Shows you what a small-town boy can achieve when he has the right stuff.

We had gathered for his birthday party. We were celebrating, making our toasts with Diet Coke. Bill's lovely wife, Lynn, had organized just what he prefers. He didn't want a dinner at an upscale restaurant in Manhattan, where he has dined often in the past. He didn't even want to go to the "in" place in Pittsburgh, where he has lived for years.

Lynn knew exactly what he wanted. She sent out the invitations for everybody to come to Athens to celebrate Bill's birthday. At the Varsity. Bill was overjoyed. He never comes to Athens without having a meal at the Varsity.

Suddenly the prose of Rudyard Kipling flashed through my consciousness as we enjoyed a chili dog at the world-famous fast-food emporium.

If you can talk with crowds and keep your virtue,
Or walk with kings and not lose the common touch…

I hope there is a Bill Griffin in your life.

Catherine Marti
The Renaissance Woman

In my neighborhood, there is an extraordinarily accomplished person, a renaissance woman with ties to her family and her job to which she has unbending loyalty and commitment, both which bring about lofty fulfillment and pure joy in living.

Catherine Marti expects herself to be a caring mother and a team-oriented wife when she is not sharing her medical expertise with her many patients, with whom she has a genial rapport that makes her practice conspicuously singular in the medical community. She is the only female cardiologist in Athens, a cosmopolis she adores. She and her husband Jon, also a physician, are University of Georgia graduates who are always shouting out *hosannas* for their beloved hometown.

"We just love it here," she says, and then checks off the resounding blessings of the classic city: UGA sports, Athens Academy, restaurant variety, concerts, pioneering professional opportunities, and vibrant atmosphere, among other extras.

All the while, she makes you aware that her unabridged compliment list on the quality of life where she lives and works is as expansive as Sanford Stadium, which she and Jon consider a second home in the fall.

The Martis, active in the Athens First United Methodist Church, lead a full life and swoon to sustaining it. Catherine plays tennis and enjoys antique searches and grocery shops. She cooks almost every night, and believe it or not, tries to read a novel when there are quiet moments. When it comes to accommodating her ambitious schedule, she does have a resourceful advantage down the street where her parents, John and Jean Norton, are always available to pitch in.

"My greatest accomplishment in life is being a mother," Catherine says. That bodes well for the future of her three children: Mary Reid, seven; Bennett, four; and Bright, two. When Bright was a babe-in-arms, five months old to be exact, the Martis took her to France for a week. If Bright had needed special attention, she could not have had better access. Their plan also meant that it would not bring about any undue stress for her babysitting parents, in whose custody she left the other two siblings. Catherine and Jon had the best of times enjoying the best of France.

Life for the Martis is an up-in-the-morning-out-on-the-job routine, resulting in abundant joy and reward for this husband-wife team—where the living is good and their work is personally and professionally rewarding. Theirs is a "no complaining" household. They are always letting the sunshine in.

Jon is the emergency medicine physician at St. Mary's Hospital, which requires frequent nighttime duty, but the Martis have fashioned a compatible regimen that takes the stress out of their daily lives. Jon works in a stimulating environment in which you never know who might come through the door. On his first night of ER duty at Grady Hospital a few years ago, the mother of Falcons owner Arthur Blank came to the emergency room with a broken hip. A short while later, the mother of a Washington Nationals pitcher, in town to play the Braves, was accompanied by her son for a medical assist. She had tripped and fallen, "busting up her face pretty bad."

Catherine is the director of the Magill-Miller Advanced Heart Failure Clinic, which is under the Piedmont umbrella. She also founded the Women's Heart Clinic. Having that opportunity is the primary reason that she was attracted to Athens professionally. She is an assistant professor at the University of Georgia Medical College and is constantly researching. The fruits of her voracious research are enhancing lives and saving them.

In an informal setting, Catherine will talk free-flowing with steadfast and immutable passion about her work and opportunity. There are alarming facts about heart disease in women of all races and ethnicities in the US. Too few females take heed. Heart disease death rates in women between the ages of thirty-five to fifty-four are increasing. Over four hundred thousand women die of cardiovascular diseases every year.

All too many women think that heart disease attacks mostly males, which means that education is part of Catherine's challenge. "Heart disease is so treatable," Catherine says. "Diet and exercise can be keenly impactful with regard to achieving good health."

One of the biggest liabilities for women with regard to heart disease is smoking. All too many women are puffing themselves to death. Poor diet and sedentary lifestyle also move women into the high-risk category.

Catherine's work and that of her colleagues are attracting more women to cardiology. In the US, about 12.6 percent of practicing cardiologists are women, as compared to 42.6 percent of the women physicians in internal medicine.

"Although you don't have to be a woman to treat women, sometimes listening to someone who gets it, who's been there, who has had children, who has gone through some of these things is helpful," Catherine says.

Another factor in locating to Athens was that she is not just another doctor following a typical office routine. She has the opportunity to build a close-knit rapport with her patients. "Getting to be their doctor and getting to see them from the beginning of their illness to the end and to be intimately involved the entire time is quite uplifting," she says. "We get to know our patients very well."

Just for the record, if there is a guy out there with a dysfunctional heart, she'll try her best to fix it.

Chattahoochee in Winter

ATLANTA—Those who live in Atlanta's Northside and within arm's reach of Georgia's most romantic river, the Chattahoochee, whose banks were once a playground for Native Americans, are treated with a daily view that makes one feel that their lives are prolonged by this geographical privilege.

The trees are stark and gray now but will soon be budding and flowering into a canopy of green that will stand sentry to the Chattahoochee's flowing waters, headed for the Gulf of Mexico. Down there, life is not as serene and peaceful, regarding the Chattahoochee, as it is in North Fulton County. Many in those parts think Atlanta's gulp from the Chattahoochee is way too generous. (A disclaimer is in order as we go forward. You are not hearing from a historian, but one who thinks that the fuss about oil wells going dry will pale if fresh water were to run out.)

In the meantime, the Chattahoochee can be enjoyed from numerous vantage points in the northern half of the state, from fly fishing at Helen (and beyond) to canoeing where the river flows past Roswell. Staying with friends Don and Barbara Hemrick, who live a little more than a stone's throw from Lovett School, I see the river in all its splendor with the change of seasons. The one exercise I need to get around to more often is fly fishing for a rainbow in the Chattahoochee where Scarlett O'Hara may well have skinny dipped.

Weekend mornings, when I am a guest of friends, allow for a leisurely rising—no matter the season. Usually, I am up when darkness prevails. Even so, there is the beauty of the moonlight glistening off the river. The peacefulness that calms the soul when you sip your decaf with the Chattahoochee sliding by in the moonlight is a tonic that inspires a toast of peace on Earth and goodwill toward men. It is at these times that I refuse to start my day without the morning paper. The headlines, which reveal hurt, hate, and gnashing of teeth around the world, are never allowed to ruin my reflective time in the company of the river. Here's to the Chattahoochee, balm for the soul.

As I finish my coffee, my mind's eye has an enjoyable flashback to the times I have stood in the Chattahoochee, an hour or so north, and tussled with a big rainbow with my friend, Jimmy Harris. The sounds of the river are so refreshing and uplifting. The current pressing against your waders makes you wish you could drop everything and let it magically take you to the Apalachicola in the Florida Panhandle. A three-pound trout grabs your San Juan worm and snatches you out of your daydreaming. Bringing him into the net takes priority in your mind at that point.

Those flashbacks usually give you inspiration when you arise in the company of the Chattahoochee. As daylight stealthily emerges, without haste or hassle, you open your computer and begin the day inspired and in a tranquil mood.

Down by the track at Lovett School, Canada geese, lumbering in flight and honking cacophonously, give character to the river but remain a menace. Canada geese, like pigeons at St. Mark's Basilica in Venice, have no manners. They leave their droppings anywhere and everywhere. I do like having the geese around, however.

As I take my designated laps around the track, I listen to the waters of the Chattahoochee as they merrily go their way, trumping the guttural offerings of the geese, and become fixated on the statue of the Lovett mascot, the lion. He's fake, but I think of what he represents. Lions are noble, whether they are ushering you, in stone, into a museum, giving you pause when they are documented on the Smithsonian channel, or confirming the movie you are about to see is brought to you by Metro-Goldwyn-Mayer.

A cup of coffee at daybreak on the Chattahoochee, a walk by its waters with Canada geese honking overhead, and reminiscing by the statue of a noble African beast—no better way to start your day. It too is a reminder that life in the city can be a pleasant thing.

Closing the Gate

Last week, we closed the gate.

You would need to know a few personal details to understand how emotional that was.

Robert Frost, the acclaimed New England poet, wrote that "Good fences make good neighbors." This prompted the question, which the great poet alluded to: Are you keeping someone in or keeping someone out?

When a real estate entrepreneur bought the property next door and began renting to students, the furor in the neighborhood ran deep. We bore the brunt of the unsightliness, the late partying after hours, and three cars for every occupant. Boy, girl in every room, you know—it soon adds up.

A fence kept them out, but not the noise, unsightliness, and the gnawing intimidation that our street had become a rental nook. Fortunately, the sale of the property to a good friend got rid of the rental problem. Amen!

In due time, my wife and I would be keeping out someone important to us. Our daughter and her husband bought the house next door, and we commissioned a carpenter to cut a gate in our fence for familial access. The gate was especially comforting when Sophie came along, and later her sister, Penny.

When Sophie and Penny grew big enough to walk and gained some measure of independence, we would hear a knock on the back door—more like a light tapping, yielding the sweetest sound. When we opened the back door, there in all their innocence and humility were two little girls who have enriched our lives.

The knock on the door was often to spend time with their grandmother, whom they adore. Sometimes they needed a popsicle. Sometimes they needed juice. Sometimes a cookie. Sometimes to use the stapler. Stapling paper until there are more staples than a sheet of paper can hold is a childhood delight.

They hardly knew a babysitter except their grandmother, whose patience is remarkable, allowing them free reign of the house. Meme was their waitress, their maid, and their confidante. Meme always cleaned up after them without sigh or complaint. Early on, when the knock on the door was audible and I would open the door, they seemed disappointed that it was not you-know-who. "Where's Meme?" they would ask anxiously.

They came to all our parties, sheepishly shying away from the attention, which caused a retreat to the den where they watched a movie to hold their attention.

The most amazing thing is that while they have their moments as all siblings do, they never really had any abiding conflicts. They are best friends, which made eavesdropping on their sensitive conversations something of a special memory to cherish.

Now that our extended family has moved away, the house will no longer be a wreck. There won't be any toys to trip over. Clothes will no longer be strewn hither and yon. The television will only be tuned to network programming. *60 Minutes* and CBS football won't be pre-empted anymore.

There will be orange juice in the refrigerator in the morning. Blueberries will no longer be squashed on the kitchen floor. Doors will no longer slam when the chase is on. The remote control will be visible, not stuffed out of sight in the bowels of the sofa.

Tea parties will no longer block the entrance to the den when there is the need to spend time at the computer. There won't be dolls in every chair and which cannot be disturbed. Cookie crumbs will no longer enhance an ant invasion. Now we will miss all that, just as we will miss the love and laughter, their keen interest in books, and the unending creative projects accommodated by the stapler, computer paper, Scotch tape, and scissors.

That space in the fence has always been soothing and comforting. For the better part of eight years, we have seen two smiling faces race through and make our day.

We like our new neighbors, but we respect their privacy. Gratefully, we recall our memories. We have seen robins and cardinals, blue jays and squirrels cavorting about our fence. They will remain, which we appreciate, but they don't smile and hug us. They won't jump in our arms when we open the back door. They won't tell us they love us.

In case you didn't know, it takes a lot of tears to close a gate.

Dan Jenkins
Hall of Fame Writer

FT. WORTH, Texas—When Texas Christian University named its press box at Amon G. Carter Stadium for alumnus Dan Jenkins recently, the honoree wouldn't let on how proud he was; but those who have knowledge of his passion and love of alma mater would conclude it was a highlight not to be taken lightly.

While Jenkins has always been able to invoke sarcasm and cynicism with a telling edge, he is a sentimentalist at heart. He just can't help it. Hearkening back to the good old days turns him on. For good reason. Those times were simply better. He'll take on anyone who wants to debate that.

Any soothsayer touting the fifties as the best of times would get little argument from those who experienced the days when only sailors showed off tattoos and earrings could only be found on women.

Likely the most knowledgeable person alive today when it comes to college football history, Dan could make irrelevant the most uppity player or coach on any campus, but he really got the most fun out of lionizing those who were champions and who stood the test of time. He knew Sammy Baugh. Davey O'Brien. Dutch Meyer, and later on, Darrell Royal and Bear Bryant. Bud Wilkinson. Barry Switzer, Bob Stoops, and Beebs Stallings. He supped with all of them.

His era was the "pull up a chair" era. Nobody took themselves seriously and no coach was too good to drink with a common sportswriter. Dan was more interested in an insightful story than he was a scoop. He was smart enough about the game that no coach ever thought any Jenkins questions could be labeled a "dumb" one. Woe be unto he who might have the temerity to advance that notion.

To Dan, you learned the game by bending an elbow with the head-liners. He listened, leaving the pontification to the principals. He always had a poignant story by cocking an ear and relying on his impeccable memory to take the reader on a classic journey.

Can you imagine his life in the fifties when the Southwest Conference was as good of a league as any in America? Except for Arkansas (Texas Tech had not been invited to join), you could virtually throw a blanket over the rest of the members of the conference. You could wake up on Saturday morning, and in a couple of hours drive to any campus where there was a big game, unless you preferred Arkansas versus whomever in Fayetteville.

Then there were Ben Hogan and Byron Nelson—two former caddies at the Glenn Garden Golf Club in Ft. Worth. Dan knew what they ate for breakfast and their view of the nuances of a 1-iron. All along Dan, without making a point of it, earned everybody's respect, mainly because they knew he respected the games he wrote about.

I have known and admired Dan since the sixties, when he was covering college football for Sports Illustrated. While Dan, a one-time scratch golfer who is a member of the World Golf Hall of Fame, has probably written more words about the four majors than any sportswriter in our time, he may be as passionate about college football as anyone you know.

In the prime years of Tiger Woods' career, ten years ago, the media at major championships flocked around Tiger as if he were Zeus "hisself." Dan would look my way, grin and say, "He won't have anything important to say. Let's go have some coffee and talk college football."

At Erin Hills in June for the US Open, we were having dinner one night at the media hotel; Dan was enjoying a hamburger (go to dinner with him at twenty-one in New York and he will order a burger) and said, "It won't be long now." I knew what that meant—the start of college football is just weeks away.

I was emotionally fulfilled to be in Ft. Worth when TCU did right by an alumnus who is perhaps more exalted as a writer than his one-time idol, Sammy Baugh, was as a quarterback. Dan, a gifted wordsmith, was honored with placards of many of his celebrated quotes. My favorite: "I married a homecoming queen, which means I know as much about college football as the next person, as long as the next person is not Darrell Royal or Bear Bryant."

Dan Jenkins has always enjoyed writing about his heroes, sanguine and insightful—never with rancor or fawning—but always leaving us, and them, laughing. I am pleased that TCU honored my friend, an abiding college football aficionado who has illuminated the game's great history better than anybody since Grantland Rice.

Piloting a Delta Big Jet

HAPEVILLE—Delta is my airline, I am proud to say. I am proudest when I fly some regional carrier from somewhere such as Budapest to an international hub like London, Paris, or Rome and see Delta's red and blue vertical stabilizer reaching skyward as I maneuver toward the departure gate. What a comforting view, what a sight to behold. Knowing Delta is going to take me home brings me soothing tranquility when I travel, especially when I am crossing a body of water like the Atlantic Ocean.

As the world changes, airlines, like everything else, change with it. Delta may not be the same airline it once was, but it still has a down-home family feel and a reassuring personal touch, which is a longtime Delta tradition. I have known several of the Delta chairmen, a plethora of the airline's executives, and a wide range of the personnel, from operations staffers to secretaries to flight attendants. Delta alumni are as passionate as college football aficionados are. They were and are proud to work for Delta, and there is no greater example of that than what took place in 1982 on an eventful day that underscored the ultimate employee loyalty.

The economy was down, fuel prices were up, but Delta friends and employees, led by three flight attendants, raised $30 million dollars to give Delta its first Boeing 767. The plane became known as "The Spirit of Delta." It was officially christened by Atlanta-born actress Jane Withers. She didn't bust a traditional bottle of champagne on the aircraft, but instead, and most appropriately, a bottle of Coca-Cola.

The Spirit of Delta is now retired, but it is one of the many attractions you can enjoy should you schedule a tour of the Delta Flight Museum. After a quarter century of service, the plane came home following its final voyage in 2006. Hangar 2 was its final destination, and Hangar 2 and The Spirit of Delta are part of the museum today. If you visit the Delta Flight Museum, you can also observe biplane crop dusters, which were once based in Monroe, Louisiana, where Delta originated.

The museum staff also located one of Delta's DC-3s, the first plane used for commercial passenger service. Although Delta originated passenger service back in 1929, utilizing a seven-seat Travel Air Curtiss-Wright

Travel Air 6B Sedan, the airline got serious for its inaugural flight with the DC-3 Ship 41 on Christmas Eve 1940. "That DC-3 is airworthy today," said a tour guide who beamed proudly as she hosted an informative and sprightly tour. Today's jets are big and imposing when you interact with them in a spacious hangar. All that power and thrust boggles at least one mind.

To take an ascendant voyage from crop dusting to the hubs of the four corners of the earth was more than being the beneficiary of good luck. Delta obviously has the "right stuff." Company loyalty is part of the magic potion that has benefitted from providential timing, cogent decisions on mergers and acquisitions, and insightful everyday management.

A longtime friend, Bob Somers, who has elevated passion for Saturday afternoons between the hedges of Sanford Stadium, has an assistant, Sabrina Cornelius, an Auburn aficionado, who introduced me to LaVerne Brown, who like Somers leans toward Red and Black. "You ought to let LaVerne take you through our flight museum," Sabrina said not long ago.

Next thing you know, I was doing just that. LaVerne said, "You should let me arrange for you to experience a tour of our flight simulator." Before you could say "Keep Climbing" LaVerne had arranged for me to "fly" with Paul Talbot, a retired Delta engineer with countless years in the flight simulator. From that session, I learned that all Delta pilots are trained via simulator. They graduate from simulator to maiden voyage.

Paul put me in the left seat, which meant that I immediately gained captain's status. There is an overwhelming emotion to be sitting where pilots sit. You are stationed high above, with the Atlanta skyline maintaining a calm peacefulness, as you prepare for your first takeoff. There is nothing like the sensation of thundering down the runway and feeling the thrust of the accelerated lift that takes your big ship up into the sky. As we reached cruising speed, I was silently humming the Air Force fight song: "Off We Go into the Wild Blue Yonder."

My first flight took us to Reagan National Airport in Washington, D.C. We also flew to Chicago and Boston. The best trip was taking off from Boston's Logan Airport and landing at LAX in Los Angeles. Flying into San Diego, Paul warned me about some outbuildings in the landing path. "Piece of cake," I thought as we landed smoothly. However, I slipped off the runway on the return trip to Atlanta, but made the correction to taxi uneventfully to the terminal. In real life, a brace of lawyers would have probably met me at the gate after the chief pilot finished chewing me out.

There were no flight delays, no turbulence, no baggage to claim on my voyages, but unfortunately, no pretty flight attendants, which Delta is noted for, to bring me a scotch and water.

If I were offered a ticket to go anywhere in the world of my choosing, my position would be that if Delta can't take me there and bring me home, I am not sure I would want to go.

Earl Leonard
Coca-Cola, and the Oval Office

BROOKHAVEN—Ongoing conversations with old friends are the renewal of a pastime that never abates or diminishes in appeal. Earl T. Leonard Jr. in winter is pretty much the same as he was yesteryear, except for limitations brought on by the calendar and COVID-19.

Earl pretty much spends his time reading, an old habit that dates back to his youth when he was the son of a weekly newspaper publisher, keeping up with the political scene and enjoying fireside chats at his Brookhaven residence with Bebe, his wife of fifty-five years.

Reflecting back on Earl's time at the University of Georgia, I have enjoyed a refreshing friendship with this man of letters who is a down-home sage and a seasoned pontificator. A conversation with him on any subject is likely to reveal that his intellect and widespread exposure, representing a US senator and the Coca-Cola Company, make him a very sagacious and enlightening conversationalist.

Following a brief teaching career at the Henry W. Grady College of Journalism and law school, he spent three-plus years as the press secretary for Senator Richard B. Russell, a job which whetted his appetite for the intoxicating environment of the Nation's Capital and the business of politics.

One day while in Washington in 1963, I went by the Senate office building to see my friend. He disclosed that he was leaving his job with Georgia's senior senator and would be going to work with the Coca-Cola Company. He would be succeeding Ovid Davis, who had been Coke's chief lobbyist for a number of years.

Well-read with a historical bent, Leonard became passionately informed about political history. He would often suggest book titles for friends to consider reading. The historical biographies he recommended over the years were enlightening and insightful. He knew several presidents and traveled much of the world.

When he retired from Coca-Cola, he underscored the priority of giving back to his alma mater. In addition to his support of the journalism school, he established, underwrote, and originated the "Leonard Leadership Scholars," a program in the Terry College of Business that is designed for selected students to gain practical leadership skills beyond the classroom. Leonard aspired for students to connect with real life experience and to meet established leaders in the field. As a result, he has opened doors for many future leaders in our society.

A vignette of his career that I have long enjoyed passing on came about in 1988 following the Summer Olympics in Seoul, South Korea. Leonard was invited to the White House for a reception honoring the US Olympic team. Coca-Cola has been a major corporate sponsor of the Olympics for years.

As he was in line going through security, a member of the White House staff came up and asked if he was Mr. Leonard. He nodded affirmatively. She then beckoned, "Please come with me." Wondering if he might have done something wrong, he soon learned that he was headed to the Oval Office at the behest of President Ronald Reagan.

When he reached the Oval Office, he found the president reading a paper, which he put down and then said, "Are you the man from Coca-Cola?" Leonard replied, "Yes, Mr. President."

Then Reagan said, "I have always wanted to ask someone from Coca-Cola this question. Why is it that Coca-Cola in a six and one-half ounce bottle tastes so much better than in a larger container?" Earl was happy to answer the question. "Well, Mr. President, that is a question that those of us at Coca-Cola often get," Leonard explained. "Coca-Cola was designed to be consumed ice-cold. In a larger container, larger than a six and one-half bottle, say twelve ounces, it takes a consumer longer to drink. The container warms up in their hands or when just sitting idle on a table. The flavor slightly changes."

Reagan responded by saying, "I never knew that. I have drunk Coca-Cola all my life in the small bottle, but you don't see them much anymore."

With that, Leonard offered to have a supply of six and one-half contour bottled Cokes delivered to the White House on a regular basis.

An appreciative president said, "That would be nice." He then added, "Could you put them on the airplane as well?" That meant Air Force One, which Earl was happy to make the arrangements for also. His Coca-Cola relationship with the president aside, Earl T. Leonard was and remains a Reagan fan. "Ronald Reagan was a genuine person who connected to people probably better than any president since Franklin Roosevelt," the former Coca-Cola executive says.

The rest of the story is that I have been a longtime fan of a friend with plentiful stories to tell from a distinguished career brought about by an association with a soft drink that is enjoyed worldwide.

Emily Giffin always Has a Story to Tell

Emily Giffin is an author—a very successful one, as many out there are aware of. She made my day last week when she told me that her latest novel, *The Lies That Bind*, was headed my way. While I am normally more into history and non-fiction, I enjoy Emily's work because she is a friend and because she is a seasoned and gifted storyteller. Her books bring about rapt attention.

When she comes out with another title, it won't be long before you will see it smiling at you from the New York Times Best Seller list. All nine of her novels have made that prestigious list. More than likely, that number will soon be ten. Not bad for the former manager of the Wake Forest men's basketball team with a law degree from Virginia and a survivor of the legal jungle of corporate Wall Street.

It didn't take Emily long to conclude that as soon as she paid off her education loans, she would leave the legalese world to follow her dream of being a writer. She envisioned that objective early in her teenage years and never let go. She has a natural love of books, handed down to her by her librarian mother.

One doesn't just "be a writer," however. You must take the plunge and sink or swim. More often than not, most would-be authors sink; few succeed as Emily has. Collectively, her novels have sold over twenty million copies worldwide in thirty-two languages, making her and her publisher Ballantine Books (an imprint of Random House) partners for life.

All the while, she co-managed the home front with an able assist from her husband, Buddy, with equanimity and measured balance. A reassuring mother of twin boys Edward and George, sixteen, and Harriet, who has just joined the teenage ranks, she finds time for family outings and school activities.

Living in Atlanta's upscale Buckhead neighborhood, Emily is immersed in the four seasons, from which she finds inspiration. There could not be a greater adrenaline rush than when spring and fall come to her wooded street.

A blonde with friendly green eyes, you would think Emily to be, if you did not know her story, a buttoned-down lawyer, which she once was, or a business executive. When she dresses up, she turns heads, but she prefers jeans, sweatshirts, and a baseball cap with her familiar ponytail protruding with verve and rhythmic bounce, depending on her mood. With her captivatingly good looks, she could have been a model. Once she published her first book, however, she found her briar patch and has never looked back.

"Her intellectual depth makes you understand why she is so good at her craft," says my Bulldog friend, Steve Fallon, who introduced us. Emily was accepted for admission at Harvard's law school but chose Virginia because of her love for the South. (Born in Baltimore, she moved about the country, which was dictated by her father, a Sears Roebuck executive, and calls Naperville, Illinois home.)

A Cavalier basketball fan growing up, Emily chose to become a Demon Deacon when Wake Forest coach Dave Odom answered her letter in which she asked if she could become the team manager. When he said yes, that became a lifetime highlight. The *hallelujah* emotion of that moment still makes her day.

When she travels, she monitors what people are saying and doing. She draws on her experiences wherever she has lived, including London, where she became a "royal watcher." Her characters are everyday people, just like you would find in your own neighborhood—flawed but real. "Good people just mess up in life," she says of the lifelike entanglements that take place in her books.

Understanding that women, whom statistics confirm buy ninety percent of all books sold in the US, primarily make up her doting audience, Emily describes her characters by telling you what they are wearing. Read her books and you will know about the latest fashions.

With her affinity for sports, she enjoys friendships with NBA stars Ralph Sampson (Virginia) and Tim Duncan (Wake Forest); but a quote from football coach Pat Dye of Auburn is one she happily flaunts: "How does a Yankee from Chicago know so much about football?" Emily took that as a "huge compliment," but she would remind the coach that she has become a devout Southerner-addicted-to-football, which is manifested in her book *The One & Only*, in which a widower coach falls in love with his daughter's best friend.

In the sports fraternity, her admirers include Roger Staubach's daughter, Michele Grimes, whose son Jeff is an upcoming senior at

Georgia. Michele, an author herself, finds Emily's story telling "stimulating and uplifting. She has enduring passion for her work and it shows in her books."

Coach Odom was confident that Emily would experience preeminent success professionally but did not suspect that she would become a best-selling author. "But then I reflected back to a stunning essay she wrote on the team bus returning home from Chapel Hill after a gut-wrenching loss to UNC, and I realized why she has enjoyed so much publishing success," he says.

Ralph Sampson, the Virginia and NBA star center, admires her writing, which "became her passion and has consumed her. She is committed and driven to succeed, but I respect her for her love of her family as much as I do her professional achievement."

Upon learning that her mother read to her as a young girl, I was eager to share with her these poignant lines:

> You may have tangible wealth untold;
> Caskets of jewels and coffers of gold.
> Richer than I you can never be—
> I had a Mother who read to me.

Father's Day Stimulates Good Memories

Today is a reminder of years far in the past, when we sang "Faith of Our Fathers" from the Broadman Hymnal at the little country church in the northeast section of Johnson County in Middle Georgia. Church was central to our lives. There was no television, and movies were bad for you unless they featured Roy Rogers, Gene Autry, and Johnny Mack Brown in big white hats, making miscreants pay for their misdeeds.

We sang "Faith of Our Fathers" slowly, almost funereal, which allowed for reflection. I always looked down front to see my father, tanned and weather-beaten from long hours in the sun, singing along reverently. He made a living, but life was a no-frills challenge for him and my mother. His assets were hard work, good health, and faith. He didn't want any handouts. Suggest welfare to him and he would have spit in your eye. He would have been embarrassed to accept a transfer payment.

All he wanted was his health and a shower of rain when the crops needed it most. There was no health insurance, which influenced his view that football was bad for me and my brother. A broken leg and the resulting medical bills would put stress on the family budget. He simply could not afford the cost of "fixing" a broken bone.

A good crop, and we are talking about cotton, would mean that he could pay off what he had borrowed in the spring to fund his annual operation. He could buy a few clothes for the kids, make an extra payment or two on our Chevrolet pickup, and put a few dollars in the bank. He paid rent on the farm where we lived and owned his first piece of land after I had finished college.

We never went out to dinner. My parents never took a vacation. Their goal was to see their children enroll in college and enjoy a better life than the one they had lived. The early life I experienced was austere, but we were never destitute. The rest of the family, my father's brothers and sisters and their families, along with our neighbors, experienced the same lifestyle—work, church, and radio. Eddy Arnold and Hank Williams were our best friends—at least emotionally.

It was important to listen to the weather forecast early in the morning. The weatherman might bring good news or bad. When the crops needed rain, there was always hope that he would say precipitation might be on the way. You kept your hopes up for rain all during the growing season. Then when it was harvesttime in the fall, you worried that the weatherman might bring the bad news that a hurricane was likely to come up from Florida and ruin the cotton harvest. There was always great urgency to get the cotton picked before the weather brought abundant rain, which we had prayed for in the spring and summer.

A prolonged drought never insulted my father. His faith was such that he believed every day of his ninety-two years on Earth that he had no quarrel with God's will. If He didn't want it to rain, we would suffer without contempt.

However, when a thunderhead came up and moved across our acreage, there was rejoicing in the form of humility that our prayers had been answered. At supper, as we enjoyed peas, corn, and butterbeans from the garden, which my father had grown with tender loving care, everybody bowed their head as my father offered thanks for the rain. Rain showers were showers of blessings. It was appropriate to give thanks for our good fortune.

On this day each June, I often think about my father and how he could make do. He gloried in putting up for the winter. First it was the Mason jars, which were sealed with painstaking care. One spoiled jar was a loss to be taken seriously. Then community canning came about, and finally the glorious deep freezer. The freezer enriched our lives. You could fill the freezer in the summer and it would sustain us all winter.

There were always fences to mend, firewood to cut, and something to repair. Hogs to slop and cows to milk. Martin gourds to hang and traps to be set for any unwelcomed varmint that might come sneaking around our chicken house.

When the day came that my father owned his own farm, it was a signature moment in his life. Never a day went by that he didn't think of his property as a gift from above. Life was hard for him, but in his mind, life was good.

My father always gave thanks for the blessings in his life, however small, and I give thanks for him and the lessons his example taught.

Fly Fishing, the Ultimate Fulfillment

HELEN—The poems of Sidney Lanier resonate with this Georgia cracker who finds the greatest pleasure in revisiting, often in the shower, the inspiring and fulfilling ruminations of Georgia's one-time poet laureate, whose lively poems involving two of the state's most celebrated natural habitats leave you feeling humbled: "The Marshes of Glynn" and the "Song of the Chattahoochee."

If you are a Georgian and have not wrestled with a spottail bass on Georgia's golden coast, if you have not hooked a three-pound rainbow while standing in the rushing waters of the Chattahoochee, you have denied yourself two of the simplest pleasures—both of which are within reach of most residents of our state. If you have been there and done that, you are remiss if you don't commit for an encore. If you are on the coast, you cast for that spottail with Sidney Lanier's sentimental verse touching your senses:

As the marsh-hen secretly builds on the watery sod,
Behold I will build me a nest on the greatness of God

While the marsh experience is something to revere, it could only be exceeded by an excursion to the Chattahoochee in that the North Georgia mountains remain virtually pristine, forever enhancing the outdoor experience. You are refreshed in summer even though the trout have run away to hide, but the shoal bass take their place in the interim. Then comes fall and you are mesmerized when you fish the Chattahoochee when the leaves are turning, the deer are peaking at you while standing in rhododendron up to their hindquarters, and the harmless black bear is getting ready for his winter's nap.

Jimmy Harris, who has multiple business interests—the centerpiece of which is Unicoi Outfitters, just south of Helen—is the unofficial mayor of the Chattahoochee, a gentleman with an altruistic bent, a generous laugh, and patience that would turn the head of Job. Jimmy gets as much pleasure out of seeing you catch a three-pound trout as you do. Helping you make your day makes his.

While you can enjoy this experience, by and large, any time of the year, no month offers more serenity and enrichment than October. Move onto the river when there is a reverberating chill in the air and feel the fresh waters of the Chattahoochee slapping against your waders as you are surrounded by fall color and the musings of Sidney Lanier. As the atmosphere implores you to reflect on the good things in life, you prepare to capture the moment by remembering the poet laureate's connect to our hearts:

> Out of the hills of Habersham,
> Down the valleys of Hall,
> I hurry amain to reach the plain,
> Run the rapid and leap the fall.

There are three species of trout in Georgia—rainbow, brown, and brook, the last being the only native trout. Browns and rainbows were introduced to Georgia streams in the 1880s and have been stocked for over a century, according to the Georgia Department of Natural Resources (DNR).

"The stocking of fish takes place from March through August," says Jeff Durniak, a wildlife expert with the DNR. "If you like to trout fish, you can hardly beat the streams in North Georgia. Trout live in pretty places and Georgia is blessed with a wonderful environment. We have this 750,000-acre playground, the Chattahoochee National Forrest, and the Forest Service has provided this playing field for this game we call trout fishing."

Georgia has more than 4,000 miles of trout streams that attract over 100,000 fishermen each year. Trout depend on clean, cold water, which is why the Chattahoochee and other streams in the state's northern half are so popular.

One Chattahoochee outing begets another and another. You go home and your mind's eye won't let go. You see yourself standing in the river while casting a wooly bugger upstream. The barely visible fly comes meandering by and suddenly there is tension as your line becomes taut; exhilaration segues into elation as a classic rainbow takes line off your reel with startling alacrity. Soon the trout tires and starts coming your way as you reel in the slack—suddenly he takes off again, but you are now in control. After fatigue subdues his will to resist, you thrill to his homecoming—

into your net, his gills expanding and contracting. He's winded and so are you, but what a trophy to hold and behold.

Nothing like letting him off the hook, setting him free to cavort again in the Chattahoochee and live to make someone else's day.

Harold Brewer
Old Friend, Enviable Lifestyle

KEY LARGO, Florida—At the Ocean Reef Club, the weather was just right—long sleeves in the morning and evening, something less during the day; the accommodations peaceful and tranquil—bringing about long slumbers; the hospitality unmatched and views unsurpassed—wildlife interrupting naked views of an island creek and mangroves, along with blue skies dripping with ambient atmosphere. And, not to be overlooked, a vintage cabernet within arm's reach.

As soon as bags were unpacked, there was the reality that the stay would be much too abbreviated. With all of the above, one would dare not insult the host, but the fleeting wish would not give up: how nice it would be to stay for the season!

Some out there in the circulation reach of this publication may know our hosts, Harold and Mona Brewer, and may well have been the beneficiaries of hospitality from this resourceful couple. They are well-traveled and muchly acquainted. Both have University of Georgia ties, both spent residency in the classic city of Athens, and both have experienced the vicissitudes of life. This has brought balance and modesty to their perspective.

While Ocean Reef is their home, they cross other borders with a preference for summers in Kennebunkport, which allow for civic and charity exposure to the Bush family—not bosom buddies, but not exactly strangers either.

If you put their lifestyle in dining perspective, it has been a surf-and-turf sojourn. They like golf, Harold likes hunting. They like the outdoors; Mona likes fishing and Harold is a seasoned ornithologist with over eight hundred species sighted—many having been photographed. Climbing aboard for an afternoon excursion into the bonefish flats makes their day.

It would not be apropos to chronicle the fun and games of their lives without remembering yesteryear when they met on a plane (they were never introduced in Athens) and eventually chose to incorporate as a couple. Harold was a consultant in the banking business during the industry's prime years in the 70s and 80s. Those were also the years when the computer was a necessary evil for most bankers. Nobody knew how to utilize technology. Harold showed 'em. Enterprise and industry have always been Harold's accomplices, dating back to when he became the first branch manager for the National Bank of Athens. Making friends and making money became his *modus operandi.*

With success owing primarily to energy, loyalty, insight, and honorable business principles, Harold and Mona have been able to grab a slice of the good life—without avarice, greed, or arrogance. They rub shoulders with millionaires and a billionaire or two, their Southern charm breaking down all social barriers.

This entire treatment could be about Mona, which would suit Harold just fine. She can tie a fly as expertly and succinctly as many of the seasoned guides who make big money, plying their trade in the Keys. If you want a fly casting lesson, you couldn't find a better certified teacher than Mona or one of her friends with the same fishing bent. They function under the name "Bonefish Bonnies" after the consummate lady bonefish advocate, named "Bonefish Bonnie Smith."

Their website confirms their threefold objective:

Gather together female members interested in fishing.

Provide knowledge about all aspects of the sport in the comfort of an all-female atmosphere.

Find fun in fishing, no matter the level (beginner or expert), technique (spin or fly), or location (flats or offshore).

Mona Brewer is the only "Bonefish Bonnie" I know, but the conclusion that holds sway is that if she were to fish for your supper, you would not go hungry.

On my next visit-with-old-friends-trip, Harold and Mona, be forewarned. I expect to go bird-watching with Harold and bonefishing with Mona. I'll do my part—I'll fetch a worthy Bordeaux. The foregone conclusion is that I'll more than likely catch bonefish with Mona's assist than spot a rare-winged species with Harold.

Harvest Moon
Highlight of Autumn

The harvest moon is nothing more than a full moon which appears nearest the start of fall. According to a modicum of research, the harvest moon coincides with the September full moon, although it can fall in early October, which is the case this year.

The harvest moon rose on October 5th at 2:40 p.m. You may ask, and I wasn't sure until I took to the internet, why is it called the harvest moon? The answer has such emotional capital for those of us who have special affection for the fall season.

Years ago, when life was simpler—when technology, poor manners, lack of common courtesy, and selfishness had not compromised our lives— the harvest moon brought about bright moonlight early in the evening and assisted farmers in harvesting their crops. The days were getting shorter and it was important to "get the hay in the barn."

Among the many songs to hold dear is "Shine On, Harvest Moon," the most golden of the golden oldies, which warms your heart even if you hear it in the dead of winter. Its resonating lyrics have stood the test of time, the song having a connection all the way back to the Ziegfeld Follies—real music, if you know what I mean.

Those were the days of melody and romanticism, as opposed to noise, yelling, and screaming, which we so often hear today. "Shine On, Harvest Moon" has been recorded by many legends of entertainment, including Kate Smith, Laurel and Hardy, Vaughn Monroe, the Four Aces, Mitch Miller, and Rosemary Clooney. Kate Smith singing "Shine On, Harvest Moon" made you feel that you should stand at attention and bow in reverence at its conclusion.

While I haven't committed them to memory, I often look up the lyrics in my computer this time of the year, just to bring them to life:

Oh, Shine on, shine on harvest moon, up in the sky;
I ain't had no lovin' since April, January, June or July.
Snow time, ain't no time to stay outdoors and spoon;
So shine on, shine on harvest moon, for me and my gal.

When you hear "Shine On, Harvest Moon" during the harvest season, you are usually visually swooning to displays of hay bales, cornstalks, and pumpkins, and you know that when the harvest moon comes up, there will soon be a fire in a wood-burning fireplace.

The fall is the best time of the year, with all of the aforementioned charming and inspiring us. We know that following the appearance of the harvest moon, fall color will soon give us further emotional sway and affection for the outdoors and nature.

There have been many times when it was possible to leave after a Georgia home game on Saturday afternoon, catch a flight to Albany, New York, and drive to Manchester, New Hampshire to emotionally invest in New England color, which knows no bounds when it comes to finding adjectives to describe the scene and setting.

Pancakes and maple syrup. The Vermont Country Store. The Battenkill River and a rainbow trout moving about carefree and slothfully, cocksure that no angler can get the best of him. The New England experience is awe-inspiring, but there are many compliments to be tossed about for October in our own state.

Fall in North Georgia is festival time—from apples to sorghum to moonshine. Oktoberfest in Helen practically lasts all fall, but the best that the northern half of our state has to offer is the Chattahoochee and an opportunity to trout-fish while the turning of the leaves takes first prize with your emotions.

Most places, rightly so, are catch-and-release rivers and creeks, but I have been able in times past to catch a nice rainbow with autumn leaves falling about—then filet the trout for the grill to be followed by dinner and a nice bottle of wine while the host played "Shine On, Harvest Moon" on the tape deck. That is ultimate fall fulfillment.

Is there some way we can make October last for at least sixty days?

Best Friend
Victim of Alzheimer's

A couple of years ago, there was a call from my best friend growing up with a bad news message. There were no good news possibilities as good news/bad news anecdotes often allow.

"They have confirmed that I have Alzheimer's," he said without strained emotion. Nothing could have been more troubling. That call had been preceded by one to say that he was going to have a diagnosis to determine whether or not he had that dreaded disease. "It runs in my family, you know," he said resignedly.

His call came without contempt or "woe is me." It was more like "que sera, sera." He then made his small-town life business as usual. Up to that point, we'd kept in touch—our conversations just as they always had been. Laughing about growing up in a nest of colorful characters. Cynical old men who were flummoxed by any teenage male who chose to wear Bermuda shorts. "Do y'all use the ladies room?" the lead cynic would say.

Those colorful characters were the motley prophets of doom who hold sway in any town or community, drinking "co-colers" at 10:00 a.m. and 3:00 p.m. at Sheppard's filling station instead of coffee, clandestinely gambling at the local pool room, offering preachments and gossip at the popular beer joint—the railbirds who view life though suspicious lenses.

Week before last, my friend's middle son, Greg, called from the hospital in Swainsboro to tell me his father wasn't doing well. My lifelong friend was compromised with debilitating stomach issues in addition to Alzheimer's. "He's not eating," Greg lamented, which I knew was a very bad sign.

When I spoke to Hodges Rowland from his hospital bed, I did not think that would be my last conversation with the best friend I had in yesteryear's halcyon days. He died on the weekend, and I was unable, due to the dastardly COVID-19 pandemic, to attend his funeral.

I have lost a relationship that has uplifted and delighted me for years. The precious memories will still linger. We were responsible and enterprising, for the most part, but every day was filled with unbridled laughter.

We told jokes, we made fun of our friends and ourselves. Makes you realize that the nonsensical lifestyle that made our days was something that came about naturally.

There was the time to let the drones—our colorless teachers—hold sway. There was a time for abundant laughter at recess, time for scrimmaging under a sardonic and colorful football coach named "Red," who had a bent for humor, but mostly sarcasm, that illuminated and amplified our clumsy mistakes—much to the delight of our teammates who were keenly cognizant that their time for caustic rebuke would come their way sooner than later.

My friend Hodges was friends with everybody. He might not have been their best buddy, but he treated them all with good-natured respect. There was an air of harmony and goodwill with all of his classmates, all of whom were attracted to his generous and congenial personality.

He was responsible for enhancing my social life. We doubled-dated, which meant that he was always the vehicular host. Back then, it was not fashionable to date in a pickup truck, which was all I had access to.

Fishing and hunting were constants in his life. We were attracted to golf at nearby golf clubs, mostly the "Twin Cities" course that served the communities of Tennille and Sandersville.

All it took to play was the green fee of seventy-five cents, a dime for a Coca-Cola, and a nickel for a pack of square cheese crackers…and the comportment to not be embarrassed when your mighty swing sent a golf ball screeching into the woods. If we shot a good score and lost two balls, it was a bad day. If we scored poorly but found two un-scuffed balls, it was a good day.

Driving home after golf was highlighted by a quart of Pabst Blue Ribbon, everybody in the car sipping away clandestinely, with all parties except the driver scouting the side roads to make sure we didn't imbibe in view of a state patrolman. Or a fundamental preacher who might pass us on Highway 15 and see to it that our parents would become privy to our miscreant behavior.

An alert and prudent student in law school at the University of Georgia, Hodges earned his degree, passed the bar, and took over the practice of his father, who also served in the Georgia House of Representatives. (Hodges was a relative of J. Roy Rowland, who spent twelve years in US Congress after retiring from his medical practice in Dublin.)

Hodges was intellectually alert, well-connected in the state, and could have flourished in a prestigious Atlanta law firm, but he preferred to live in the down-home environment that spawned and sustained him.

With plenty of golden memories for reflection on a bountiful life, I know that the years growing up with my best friend can't be relived. What I would give, however, if that were so.

Jack Davis
"Doggone" Great Cartoonist

In late July, among the moss-draped live oaks near the charming Christ Church on St. Simons Island, Jack Davis, the cartoonist extraordinaire who was all about tradition, the simple things in life, and Georgia football, was laid to rest.

You would have had to have known Jack to be aware that he was so proud of his final resting place that he would attend burial services at the Christ Church Episcopal Cemetery and say, "Isn't this a beautiful place? This is where I will be someday. My plot is right over there." He would take you over to the hallowed ground if you were interested.

The last thing on this great American's mind was that he, the reluctant celebrity, would become a focal point of upcoming tours for the more than 30,000 annual visitors at the cemetery. He will now be a member of the "Big Three" in the cemetery: Eugenia Price, the celebrated local novelist; Furman Bisher, longtime sports columnist of the *Atlanta Journal-Constitution*; and Jack.

For sure, Jack would be compatible with the viewpoint of noted Georgia historian Lucian Lamar Knight, also buried here, who said, he wished "to sleep in the long peace of eternity under the boughs of the Wesley oak and by the waters of the murmuring Altamaha."

The service in the packed, little Christ Church, which dates back to 1736 and survived the desecration by Union soldiers, was conducted with a simplicity that Jack Davis would have appreciated.

When the news of his death at age ninety-one came and I began preparing a eulogy, my first thought was that accomplished men are not always modest men. Jack Davis was the exception. The memories flooded forth and brought pause to my day. The emotional hurt was deep and abiding.

You probably know about his many successes: twenty-two *TV Guide* covers and thirty-six *Time* magazine covers, founding contributor of *Mad* magazine. In his world, that was like Ted Williams batting .400, Joe DiMaggio hitting in fifty-six consecutive games, or Georgia winning the national championship in football. However, Jack's success in the art world never turned his head.

From the first time I met him at his home in Scarsdale, New York in the mid-seventies, to up until his body went into decline, Jack functioned with sophomoric enthusiasm. In that first meeting, we had lunch at his club and then repaired to his drawing room at home where he said, "I would like to do a 'little something' for the University of Georgia."

He did more than a "little something." He and his work became iconic to the Bulldog fans. Football program covers. Posters by the thousands. We created a billboard campaign. You could see Jack Davis and his latest Bulldog creation all over the state in the late seventies and early eighties. And he never got paid. It was his contribution to his alma mater, "Just a little something for the University of Georgia."

I talked Coach Bill Hartman, then-chairman of the UGA Athletic Scholarship Fund, into paying Jack and Dena's way to the Georgia-Florida game every year. He would meet up with his lifelong pal, Charlie McMullen, and other good friends, like the late Dick Budd, for a weekend of golf and Bulldog fellowship.

He swooned with every first down, groaned with every play that misfired, but was never the critic. He never carped about any failed execution or coaching decision—even when he was surrounded by those given to castigation.

He often returned home to Westchester County from Atlanta and boarded many flights with Varsity hot dogs and Poss' barbecue. This was when the world was civil and you could do such things. I once asked him for a self-portrait for a story we were doing for the football programs. He sent a headshot of himself, then drew a cartoon body with big feet, spindly legs, and a big pot gut. On the pot gut, he wrote "Poss Barbecue."

A member of the Greatest Generation, Jack remembered being on the deck of the ship coming home from the Pacific, looking at the stars, offering thanks to the Almighty that he had survived, and looking ahead with great anticipation. We now know that a bountiful life awaited him.

At UGA, he was a member of the SAE fraternity. He created a one-page humor tabloid that he called the "Bull Sheet." He loved the campus social scene and considered the hedges of Sanford Stadium sacred. He rang the Chapel Bell as a freshman and upheld the greatest reverence for homecoming, the autumn leaves, silver britches, the Chapel Bell ringing into the night, and a keg party.

A man of good humor, the only evidence of any miscreant behavior was when he and his friends would catch opossums in North Atlanta and go turn them loose at the Varsity. Women shrieked, children screamed, and waiters flat-footed the hoods of cars—as he and his buddies stealthily stole away as police sirens confirmed they were on the way.

The greatest of sentimentalists, he was overwhelmed by one particular gift. In the eighties, Nike produced a shoe for UGA that had D. O. G. S. imprinted on the heel. Jack almost came to tears when I gave him a pair of those shoes.

The next artwork he sent to Athens included a note: "Hey man, I wear my Dog shoes every day." He would often call and say, "Man, I got my Dog shoes on."

Jack Davis was indeed a modest man. He was an altruistic man, a humble man, and a caring and giving man.

Now that he has moved on to those hedges in the sky, he would be proud that his doting family chose to send him on his heavenly journey wearing his Dog shoes.

Farewell to Jack Davis, a Great Dawg and a Great American. Selah.

Jack Kehoe
A Sculptor's Resounding Legacy

The flags in Cortona, Italy, were at half-staff last week when the citizens of a hilltop town in Tuscany mourned the passing of an American whom they considered their best friend.

It wasn't a government connection, or a financial connection—but an expression of friendship which was engendered by respect, goodwill, and enlightenment on the part of the founder of a program that would align the city with the oldest state-chartered university in the United States. When John "Jack" Kehoe settled in Cortona as the head of the UGA Art Department's Studies Abroad Program, the Cortonesi took note that he generously expected to be a good neighbor and become a part of the fabric of the community. He embraced the populace, and its inhabitants embraced him back.

If you recall the history of the University of Georgia, you remember that there was a small fraternity who—while exclusively male at the time, they have since come to include accomplished women—were so especial that they were soulful difference-makers. They didn't care about the way it was: modest pay and limited resources for the disciplines with which they were associated, among other trappings of austerity. They nonetheless became pacesetters who made life better for countless Georgians, even those who were so provincial that they couldn't comprehend what was being done on their behalf, and in many cases would have spoken out against intellectual gifts from learned men. A man of the arts often got no respect in those days.

And while Lamar Dodd, the distinguished artist who was the head of the UGA Art Department, supported Kehoe, he was also the bearer of bad news. In essence, "You are on your own." There would be no financial support. Nonetheless, the visionary Kehoe persevered.

A roll call of some of the luminaries who brought signature achievement includes: D. W. Brooks, who gave agriculture in our state a shot in the arm for over five decades; Gene Odum, father of modern ecology; the aforementioned Lamar Dodd, whose highly acclaimed art gave Georgia an accomplished image that knew no borders; Dean John E. Drewry, the journalism dean who founded the Peabody Awards, a distinction that the titans of broadcast television treasure as much as an actor does an Oscar; Glenn Burton, the genius scientist at Tifton whose research and development are legend in the development of agricultural grasses; O. C. Aderhold, former president who fought diligently to improve education in the state; Merton Coulter, the extraordinary historian; Dean Rusk, the former secretary of state under presidents Kennedy and Johnson who brought international prestige to the Georgia campus.

The name of Jack Kehoe should be added to that illustrious list. It was he who birthed the international classroom for Georgia. Universities across America have study abroad programs everywhere from south Samoa to Timbuktu these days, and Georgia has a plethora of such programs around the globe—but the first, and the inspiration for the rest, was Jack Kehoe's founding of the Cortona Program.

Talk about a bare-bones budget—none has ever been more depressing. Jack was forever pulling his program up by his bootstraps. He was a study in dogged determination. Buoyed by faith and by accentuating the positive, the Cortona Program not only became the model for future programs at UGA; other institutions adopted Jack's model as well.

When the Cortona Program became established, a couple of institutions made overtures to see if they could unseat the University of Georgia. They were quickly rebuffed by the Cortona town elders. The loyalty that existed between the citizenry and Kehoe was not suddenly available to the highest bidder. Jack's gentlemanly ways, subordinated ego, and intellectual but modestly driven insightfulness enabled him and Cortona to flourish even when there were communist mayors. Jack could get along with anybody.

Cortona would evolve from a summer program to a three-semester (plus a Maymester) curriculum. Students could study year-round. Then the University of Georgia purchased property there and appropriately named a building for him—the John D. Kehoe Cortona Center.

Jack and his charming wife, Marilyn, purchased a flat in Cortona. It was high up in the village, which kept him and Marilyn in peak physical condition. They always walked, never taking a taxi. Their flat afforded the most emotionally invigorating views.

An accomplished sculptor, Jack spoke near-fluent Italian. He was a well-rounded connoisseur of life—his idea of a good time was a fine piece of art, a seasoned bottle of Chianti, a Bulldog victory between the hedges, laboring with his beloved chisel and a block of Carrara marble, knowing he would be proud of the finished product.

Due to all he built, his death doesn't really leave a void, except emotionally. His legacy of Cortona will live on as one of the most truly remarkable contributions ever inspired by a Georgian, who gave of himself for the benefit of others, especially those who appreciated the arts.

Jenny and Guinness: A Love Affair

If you were to bump into a lady named Jenny Tucker Brinkley at Earth Fare grabbing a healthy snack for lunch, or at the Five and Ten, where she often goes for a fulfilling dining experience, you would likely think this pretty woman to be a sophisticate who is as far from a down-home aficionado as Kate Middleton.

Get to know her, however, and you quickly learn that she enjoys an upbeat lifestyle with an accent on immersing herself in all things in her daily life—from homemaker chores to monitoring the building of a new house on University Drive to racing over hill and dale on her beloved Irish thoroughbred, Guinness, or in her silver Ford F-350 off-road super duty pickup truck with all the bells and whistles.

She can drive that truck with aplomb for long distances with a three-ton trailer hitched to the back. She can back her beloved pickup into tight spaces. Reverse does not intimidate or flummox this ebullient brunette with an evergreen smile, one who enjoys Georgia football and basketball and any travel experience that is emotionally intoxicating and illuminating. An art museum or a new bestseller keep her in an anticipatory mood almost as much as a blue ribbon she and Guinness might claim in competition.

The thing her friends appreciate about her most is that she is a genuine person. She's the same in an evening gown as she is in her riding breeches or a pair of faded jeans as she stomps about the grounds of her new house-in-the-making—ensuring that contractor, Tyler Davis, keeps all bevels becoming and in sync.

Her horse trailer was tailored for lodging accommodation, which reflects that she has a wizened appreciation for economy, but mostly a deep and abiding affection for being awestruck by the heavens as she turns in for the evening and being exhilarated by the forthcoming sunrise. Landscapes, nature, and the great outdoors make her day.

When she enjoys a rarefied air sojourn over to Newton County to bond with Guinness and guide him through a workout, she will follow the backcountry roads in her silver pickup or in her vintage Triumph convertible. When she chooses her Triumph, she is energized by the elevated hum of the engine of her sassy sports car, her ponytail waving in the breeze, her spirits uplifted by the pleasure of the moment.

Nobody enjoys the journey more than Jenny, whether it is life in general, the forty-one-mile trek to Mansfield to be with Guinness, or "fixing" an appetizing meal garnished with stimulating conversation for her and her husband Matt, a wealth manager for Consolidated Planning Corporation. You could take her to Buckingham Palace or the Varsity and she would be the same. Enjoying the moment is what Jenny is all about.

A couple of summers ago, my wife and I invited the Brinkleys to accompany us on a trip to New York: Broadway, River Café, shopping, or whatever our off-the-cuff agenda called for. We then drove up US Route 1 to Maine, making stops of historical note along the way, satisfying our collective curiosities—touring the Yale campus at New Haven, having dinner at the seafood café that was the favorite of the first President Bush, getting a close-up view of the Bush compound at Kennebunkport, which was arranged by old friends Mona and Harold Brewer, but mostly just "lazying" our way through the seaside villages of Maine.

In New York, I asked my friend Aaron Boone, manager of the Yankees, for tickets, which he provided for a prime Yankee Stadium location. Matt and Jenny dressed in Yankee garb to express appreciation, which was followed up by the same display of home team loyalty when we got to Boston, where longtime Sox announcer David O'Brien arranged for Red Sox tickets. This outing allowed the Brinkleys, outfitted in home team Sox regalia, to swoon at baseball's antiquity, Fenway Park. Yankee fans for a day! You bet. Same with the Sox!

After shopping on Fifth Avenue in Manhattan, Jenny was just as eager to plunge into the shelves and racks of L. L. Bean when we got to Portland, Maine. After all, Fifth Avenue accommodates her sophisticate taste and L. L. Bean has the right stuff for an outing in Mansfield.

When fishing the Yampa River in Colorado during a Georgia open date last fall, Jenny could hardly contain her emotions when her tiny fly was sucked down by a twenty-two-inch brown trout, which will someday be an artifact that will greet guests when her new digs are finished.

Any treatise on the life and times of J. T. B. would be incomplete without a serious review of Guinness's trophy-grabbing history in association with the riding expertise of Jenny, her close friend and trainer Mary Bess Davis, and her only child, daughter Matilda.

Recently, we accompanied Jenny for a warm-up with Guinness at the home and stables of Mary Bess in Mansfield, six miles east of Covington. Guinness's ears perked up at the sound of Jenny's voice. His neighs and whinnies became a staccato symphony when she came into view. She caused his anxiety to subside by softly extending her hand with a sugar treat.

His nod of approval bespoke generous thanks but his glistening eyes reflected that "one treat is not enough." Next it was workout time. For the better part of an hour, Mary Bess spoke encouraging words while Jenny let her knees—gentle to Guinness' ribs—become like a conductor's semaphore to motivate Guinness over jumps and obstacles, all designed to help make him an accomplished show horse.

Although long in the tooth, Guinness still has a lot in the tank. When the day comes when he and Jenny can no longer claim championship ribbons, their bonding won't subside. Their love for each other will not abate and there will still be those rarefied-air drives over to Mansfield to make each other's day.

John Addison
Business Man, Motivational Speaker, and Football Junkie

GAINESVILLE—John Addison is a small-town boy who made good mainly because he was a good student, a good leader, and a good listener—although he can go toe-to-toe with the best of raconteurs and wax without restraint with the most garrulous and voluble of seasoned conversationalists.

Without question, John has affection for engaging in stimulating conversation that allows him to share his experiences and become engrossed in what you are willing to impart. If he has an idea, he is motivated to share it with others. He gives ideas away.

When Addison talks, he has something to say. He garnishes his conversations with fact, humor, and insight. He is evangelical in style and presentation. He would have been a good preacher. For sure, he would have kept everybody on the edge of his/her seat.

Talking business about Primerica—of which he became co-CEO in 1999 with his friend, Rick Williams—the University of Georgia, and Bulldog football are among his favorite topics. The late dean of men at UGA, William Tate, once said, "There is nothing finer than a Georgia boy with a Georgia education." John took that to heart and has been a loyal Dawg who relishes his alumnus role as a graduate of Terry College and a member of the Silver Circle, which is a key support group for athletics.

A native of Covington, Addison has a number of passions: good food, good humor, and good times on Saturday afternoons between the hedges of Sanford Stadium. He knows a thing or two about college football. He studies the game, and he is conversant with facts, history, and lore. Like a good football junkie, John has a depth of knowledge when it comes to Georgia football history.

Growing up in Covington, John was little more than arm's reach from Athens. He followed the 'Dogs, but his deep and abiding love didn't take root until he spent a weekend in Athens during his junior college days at Emory-at-Oxford, where he played tennis. His "can't live without the

Dogs" birthing came about the weekend of the Georgia-Alabama game in 1976. He journeyed over to Athens to visit friends, having no idea what he was in for.

Georgia defeated the Crimson Tide 21-0, and the town celebrated like it never had before. Milledge Avenue became an intense no-holds-barred party thoroughfare, traffic eventually coming to a complete stop. Fraternity houses ran out of booze—even the liquor stores were in danger of going dry. John took all this in, wondering if such a weekend could ever be trumped. He told his friend and host, "There is no doubt where I will spend my next four years."

He had grown up with unequaled love of UGA, but after that weekend, he was no longer "wet behind the ears." He enjoyed Bulldog football from the student section, arriving early to keenly observe warm-up drills in their entirety. He expected himself to be an ardent student of the game. That commitment has never abated.

As an undergraduate, Addison never missed a game between the hedges and maintained an affinity for the social life on campus—but he was also a very serious student. He embraced the notion of being a well-rounded matriculate.

He holds a bachelor's degree in economics from UGA and earned a master's degree at Georgia State while finding his way in the business world.

In 1979–80, he found himself a member of the "Railroad Track Fraternity," building a scaffold that gained a degree of recognition when it appeared in the book, *Glory, Glory*. He was in the Superdome for the national championship on New Year's Day, 1981. He and a buddy were the first down the aisle to claim the pole position to charge the field at the final gun. As the final seconds ticked off, he leapt over the wall and was on the turf seeing the Georgia players lift Vince Dooley on their shoulders for the victory ride out to accept congratulations from the Notre Dame Coach Dan Devine.

He was the first to reach the nearest goal post and was trying to scamper up to help bring it down but got knocked off as "about a thousand others had the same idea." Addison Bulldog credentials have been firmly established since.

When he isn't in Clermont, you can often find him at one of his three secondary homes in the Five Points section of Athens. He spends his home game weekends there, cooking for his legion of friends. "Thank goodness for Loveanne's patience," he says. "Our home after the games is party central. We love entertaining."

The author of the best-selling book, *Real Leadership*, John is the CEO of Addison Leadership Group and is the leadership editor of *Success* magazine, for which he writes a monthly column. He is a world-class speaker. You may find him wowing audiences by the thousands, from the capital cities of the United States to London and Singapore.

If you listen to the Georgia football broadcasts on Saturday, you hear John's commercial messages for Primerica, the company with which he was a Wall Street star for over fifteen years. He spearheaded his company's separation from Citibank in 2010, commuting weekly to New York to usher Primerica into exalted IPO status, which turned heads on Wall Street when the company went public.

Throughout most of his business career, John has maintained a residence in nearby Clermont, where his green thumb gets a thumbs-up from serious gardeners. While he was always comfortable in any setting while making big deals for his company, he has always been just as comfortable amid the multiple vegetables in his garden—peas, okra, squash, tomatoes, corn, and cucumbers. He also has an expansive blueberry patch and ten hives of bees (plus two hundred acres of wildflowers for pollination purposes), all surrounded by roses and flowering ornamentals, which satiate his affection for English-style gardens. He makes trips to the United Kingdom each year just to tour gardens in the land of his forebears. Just this past summer, he toured the Chelsea home of one of his favorite authors, Sir Thomas Carlyle, who wrote one of John's favorite books, *Sartor Resartus*.

The influence of John's mother, Ruth, when it comes to "putting up for the winter" has never lost its hold on her only son. He prefers the traditional canning process over the freezing process. He is a pickling aficionado who shares with his friends.

He and Loveanne winter in Vero Beach, Fla., where he interacts with former Dodgers pitcher Ron Perranoski, who hangs out at Bobby's, a popular local watering hole. Enjoying small talk with accomplished athletes has always been a passion of Addison's, which is why you will often find him visiting at Georgia football practices.

After having dinner with Kirby Smart, the Georgia coach noted that Addison, "probably asked me more questions in the shortest period of time than any fan I know."

"One of the things I enjoy about retirement," John says, "is that I can spend more time keeping up with the Dawgs." Loveanne is right in step with him. "She keeps up more than I do," he says. "I could be in a big corporate meeting and she might text me about a prized Georgia recruit who has just committed; that is, if our two sons, Kyle and Tyler, don't beat her to it."

Then with a grin he signs off with, "There is nothing like having the entire family engaged in Georgia football, and I can tell you—with Kirby Smart in charge, we are going to have some wonderful autumns in the days ahead."

John Parker
Home Sweet Home

The circle is almost complete for John Parker, who is a son of Athens and maintains a weekend residency in the house on Hampton Court where he grew up.

Talk about a local boy making good! You could keep adding exclamation points to that line. The story feels good but gets better the more you unravel it: each twist, from the time he graduated at the University of Georgia to a recent weekend when he took in a basketball game, a gymnastics meet, and walked to Five Points for a beer with his wife Kay—his son, John Reid Parker III, eagerly joining them.

This is a man who has risen high in the legal department of Coca-Cola and has traveled the world for the popular soft drink company. He has lived in London and Oslo among other distant addresses. Even now, he may jet off to Paris or Rome on a moment's notice. London or Brussels. Just for two or three days, maybe a half day, which is the way it is for an executive for a global company like Coke. John has seen, up close and personal, many of the places most of us only know about from travel magazines and television.

With a bent for history, John treasures the ancillary benefits that come from his work. With a small-town upbringing and an invigorating curiosity, he finds his pinch-me-is-it-real environment something he does not take for granted. The Tower of London, Big Ben, the Eiffel Tower, the Spanish Steps, the Coliseum, and countless other landmarks throughout the world have been focused in his camera—and he loves it. When it comes to having those kinds of travel and historical options, John's cup runneth over.

However, he also has an appreciation for the laid-back pace of Athens, which has an eclectic atmosphere that is brought about by energy from a student body that is triple the size of when he matriculated there in 1969–73.

John's attachment to Athens is understandably enduring. He wants to lounge on the same porch where his late father, Reid Parker, longtime member of the forestry faculty, hosted his closest friends Dick Copas and Bill Powell for late-afternoon Budweiser in a can. When he runs errands or just rambles about somewhere, he cranks up his father's '94 Chevy and moves about. He'd rather drive that old pickup than a new Lexus. That old truck reminds him of his days of yore, when he sold programs at home football games, crying if the Bulldogs lost. When he slid down the hillsides of the banks on each end of the stadium in the days when Sanford Stadium was about half its current size.

He could walk to all the sports venues. He could even walk to the Varsity for a chili dog. Today, the Varsity remains one of his treasured haunts.

After graduating from UGA in '73 with a degree in history, he began a longtime dream of being a coach. He absorbed the nuances of the games—football and basketball—quickly. He experienced the thrill of victory and the agony of defeat.

An opportunity with IBM came about for John's wife, Kay, in North Carolina in 1981. A graduate of Georgia Tech (she is now an honorary Bulldog), Kay's career options made sense for them to move. John gave up coaching and enrolled in law school at Chapel Hill. Those were the days. Michael Jordan was leading the Tar Heels to the NCAA championship, and John got to know basketball coach Dean Smith and was invited to watch Carolina practices.

Then his connection with Coca-Cola came about. The ride has been heady, but John— influenced by the balance in the lives of his parents, Cynthia and Reid, longtime campus loyalists—has never lost perspective. With his success, there has been an opportunity to give back to the institution that "made" him. He has endowed the athletic director's position at the University of Georgia in memory of his parents.

If you receive a letter from Greg McGarity—and his successors in perpetuity—it will carry the notation that the head Bulldog is the J. Reid Parker Director of Athletics.

A nice touch from a loving son and his family in memory of their parents—all underscoring the past and present with a deep and abiding love of alma mater.

Love to Lose, an Interesting Book.
We Love the Author

I have never been on a diet. If you were to stop by for a glass of wine or had an occasion to log in on a Zoom conference call, you might respond by saying, "Why yes, I can tell."

Years ago, I was considered skinny, and never consciously avoided any second helpings, including desserts. I can remember there were times, traveling in France in a charming town overlooking a picturesque stream in a setting that would have made Renoir reach for his palette, when I would listen to a waiter outline the dessert menu and say, not totally in jest, "I'd like one of each."

While I never went that far, I have been guilty of ordering two sweet-tooth confections on more than one occasion in bygone days. In France, it is not sinful to order extra desserts; it is a matter of being sinful NOT to do so.

And beer! There was once a time—as there is with all too many college incumbents—the notion that I could not get enough of this fulfilling beverage that can enhance laughter and bring about uplifting songfests. That is the joy in light-hearted socializing, even if it does endanger your waistline.

Fast forward, as the calendar does with all our lives, and I no longer drink beer unless I am somewhere like Speed's Kitchen at Shellman Bluff or the Frederica House on St. Simons, where fried shrimp only reach the ultimate in fulfillment when accompanied by a cold beer. Desserts I avoid with authority. No candy bar snacks, no tasty chocolate mints in those green wrappers that nice clubs and high-end restaurants bring with the check.

As these musings reach print, I can truthfully say that I have had only one dessert since the last week in February. My box score when it comes to beer consumption is two for this calendar year.

Guess what—with good habits and all that sugar and alcohol restraint, I have not lost a single pound. I walk every day, weather permitting. Acid reflux has curtailed wine consumption and it is a rare occasion that I go beyond one shot of Black Bush, the finest of Irish whiskey. (That requires a disclaimer. If I venture back to Northern Ireland anytime soon, Black Bush and I will have a rip-roaring good time. The setting, you know, does make a difference in your pace and habits.)

What I am saying is that diets usually don't work. What seems to work is pushing back from the table. Unless it becomes life-threatening, I plan to enjoy food with drinking in moderation and spending evenings with good friends toasting the good things and good people in life.

Lately, I have been reading a book, *Love to Lose*. It is about how to manage your weight and make the right choices to stay as trim and fit as possible. Normally, a book like that is not a genre for my reading habits, except that I am happily familiar with the author, Camille Martin.

She writes really well—not just with competent grammar, but with flowing sentences with refreshing nexuses, making sense from one phrase or one sentence to another. She provides graphic examples for each point she makes that enable the reader to understand her logic and perspicacity.

I never knew she fought a weight battle as she matured. She was never overweight to my naked eye. She was always jogging and could make a treadmill gasp for breath.

She has always been active and involved. Good student in school, with an affection for books, which brings about the conclusion that all that activity was good for her communication skills and for staying fit. Her discipline was the key to her success. She took a logical approach to managing her weight rather than quick fixes that are more often than not destined for File 13.

Mainly, she believes in what she has learned and is moved to pass it on to others who may be looking for a way out of life's weight-gain quicksand where they have become anchored.

I can remember her shyness as a young girl, her generous smile, and her curiosity. A book and a beer segued into a book and a glass of wine as she matured. Becoming immersed in a feel-good situation that stimulates the mind is something to be embraced, no matter your age.

There is good reason for me to be serenading this book and the author who has put so much into her insightful treatise. She is our firstborn.

Mike Cheek
Riding the Coattails of Enterprise

There are times when you are confronted with the reality that there are eminently accomplished friends and neighbors right under your nose. They might not have become a governor or a senator. They might not have won a PGA golf tournament or scored a critical touchdown for the Bulldogs in a big game or parlayed a novel idea into a fortune.

Just everyday folk from Middle America: those who capitalized on the American way, underscored the work ethic, and rose to the top in their professions, which brought about a better life for them and their families.

With hard-earned success, they became rich in experiences, enjoying memorable moments that made life fun, fascinating, and fulfilling. Mike Cheek is a Damn Good Dawg who has experienced a damn good business career. The upward mobility of his life's journey would bring pause to any career narrator.

His very beginning is intriguing and absorbing. He was born in Grantham, England, the birthplace of Sir Isaac Newton and Margaret Thatcher. Grantham is also the place that developed the diesel engine in the UK. Little did Mike know that there would be times in his life when he would push the envelope in business with a diesel-like thrust.

His mother was a war bride who had to leave her family and her homeland—not an easy decision—and travel across stormy seas on a crowded ship that offered nothing redeeming other than it could float. Mike often thought of the tender loving care his mother gave him on that difficult nine-day voyage, especially when he would later fly first class to the United Kingdom, where he still has cousins he often visits.

Mike's father, Verdon, was a soldier in the US Army and had to travel ahead without them in order to be mustered out of the military service following the war.

Mike was eighteen months old when he and his mother, Florence, boarded the *SS Argentina* in Southampton, England, along with 455 other wives and 169 babies bound for New York Harbor in January 1946. The ship became a bastion of seasickness, which overwhelmed Mike's mother.

The ship docked in New York, where they were processed through immigration at Ellis Island. Next they took a train south—destination: Winder, Georgia.

Naturally, Mike has no recollection of the voyage and has no idea how he and his mother were directed through Ellis Island, finding their way to Penn Station for the twenty-plus hour train ride to Winder. He now regrets that he did not glean more detail from the experience before his mother passed away.

Mike's picture, with his mother handing him over to a proud father, appeared on the front page of the Atlanta papers. It featured a screaming babe-in-arms. Mike reminded himself of his inauspicious arrival years later when he and his son-in-law, Tom Johnson, opened a Wendy's restaurant across US 29 in downtown Winder.

His new life began in Warner Robins. Albany was the next address, and then the family settled in Macon, where he would be graduated, with honors, from Willingham High School. It was a journey through austerity for the most part. Mike's father was a butcher who never made more than one hundred dollars a week. There were no frills or perks for Mike when he grew up; however, he was all about odd jobs, earning spending money, sports, and scholarship. His parents appreciated high marks, but Mike expected more of himself than to simply make passable grades.

His exposure to a familiar personality in high school coaching circles, Billy Henderson, brought about inspiration for him. "Coach Henderson made us all feel that we could succeed if we believed in ourselves and worked harder than the next guy," Mike recalls appreciatively.

With an abiding love of golf, Mike used this enterprising game to complement his sales and marketing skills, with consequential side benefits. He has played many of the leading golf courses in the world while serving as general sales manager (Southeast) for the Carnation Company, senior VP of marketing for Coca-Cola, president of Heublein Wines, president of North American Spirits Group, and president of Brown-Forman Global Spirits. He remains chairman of Finlandia Vodka Worldwide.

For the Kentucky Derby in 2000, George W. Bush, headed to the White House, and his father, George Herbert Walker Bush, were the guests of friends Mike and Brown-Forman. High cotton, indeed. Until he retired earlier this year, Mike flew to Sydney, Australia, once a quarter for board meetings.

Other than his wife, Runell, and his family, the University of Georgia and the Bulldogs take up the lion's share of Mike's interests today. He has been a generous supporter of his alma mater. He holds especial affection for the job Kirby Smart is doing. "I can tell you," Mike says, "Kirby has the right stuff to have been a super successful business executive."

Something that turns Mike on today, as he reflects on his past, is when "The Star-Spangled Banner" and the UGA alma mater are played pre-game. "I have learned to appreciate both of them deeply," he says.

Osceola High
You Need to Experience It More Than Once

PALMDALE, Florida—Here in the middle of the "Sunshine State," you are about two hours from either of Florida's coasts, where high-rise condominiums feature garages that showcase such luxury brands as Mercedes, Lexus, Jaguar, and a Bentley or two or four or more—a staple of resort living just as palmetto, palms, and scrub oak are staples in these parts.

Pickups and Polaris Rangers are best to ply the dirt roads and woods at Fisheating Creek hunting camp. There is beauty on the beaches, and I go for that, but outdoor aficionados bent on bringing down a ten-point buck or outwitting a wily Osceola turkey—named for the great Seminole chief—are the state's real people. I prefer it here.

Hosts Keith Beaty and Bill O'Leary are connected to the stock market and investment portfolios, among other pursuits. Lately they have been taking hits like everybody else, but in good times and bad, you will find them seeking respite where nature smooths out negative wrinkles, becomes a buffer for all of life's wayward flak, and inspires grateful feelings for all good deeds and good times.

Beaty hails from the South Georgia town of Moultrie. His modest upbringing spurred his ambition to succeed. He matriculated at Georgia Tech and ultimately produced and manufactured medical devices, specializing in dental implants. A nicer person you are not likely to meet.

O'Leary played tight end for Georgia, married into the Golden Bear family, and specialized in landscaping in the golf industry along with golf course design, eventually evolving into real estate entrepreneurship. All the while, he bagged big game in Africa (wake up in his guest suite, look around, and you might think you should run for your life with all the animal mounts staring at you); he became a wing-shooting and deer-hunting connoisseur across the South, but glories in his connect with the Osceola turkey. He is adept at iPhone video in the woods.

He and Keith lease the Fisheating Creek campgrounds, where the landlord inserted into the lease agreement that they should diligently try to kill a wild hog every day—if not legally binding, it would be keenly appreciated.

There was an unforgettable introduction to a local guide who knows the ways of the woods like Wyatt Earp knew gunslinging. Brandon Storey, blessed with rare woodsman's instincts, takes the greatest pleasure in seeing friends experience success in an Osceola stalking.

In the last fortnight before COVID-19 paralyzed our nation, Keith dropped Brandon and me off at an Osceola gathering place that had been scouted out before the season opened. I have never been more aware that it is truly darkest before the dawn. It was 5:30 a.m. Brandon, with flashlight in hand, put out the decoys that looked more turkey than a turkey itself, which is key to a successful hunt. Gobblers have been known to attack decoys with the same intent to destroy that moves a lion to bring down a wildebeest, but for different reasons.

It began to rain softly, not a good sign for an Osceola engagement; but after a quick rush, it slowed to a drizzle. Soon it disappeared altogether. We were ensconced in the solitude of pre-dawn. Birds began to sing, deer rustled in the brush as if to announce their presence. You could imagine them saying, "The season is over and you can't touch me now." Experiencing nature's wake-up call is one of life's rich gifts.

At first light, Brandon said, "I hear gobblers." I could not, but was aware that I was in a camouflaged pop-up tent with an expert who knows the woods as well as the wily Osceola.

Daybreak came and so did a hen. She dropped into view, talking. Brandon talked back to her. Coming off the roost an acre or two away, gobblers with a bent for romance heard the conversation, but everything soon went eerily quiet. Enveloped in all that outdoor solitude, I actually dozed off.

Brandon was on alert, however. He soon tapped me on the elbow. He could hear gobblers behind us, sashaying through the brush toward a rendezvous with the lone hen. A threesome of Osceola gobblers, fit for a Steve Penley portrait, strode confidently on the scene. "Let 'em separate," Brandon whispered.

The gobbler on the left, as if on cue, slid about three feet to his left and poked his head about, wary and alert, as gobblers are wont to do. Not being an expert marksman, I aimed where the gobbler's long neck met his well-fed body.

Suddenly, there was thunder in the woods and also in my racing heart as I was overcome with emotion seeing my bounty lie motionless. Brandon offered a fist bump. Photographs would come next. Keith and Bill, on the other side of the property, heard the shot. Keith came to ferry us back to camp, where they all helped me admire my Osceola prize.

That ride back to camp was more fulfilling than a ride in a ticker tape parade in Manhattan.

Fishing with Uga's Patriarch and Good Friend

SAVANNAH—History and tradition dominate Savannah, one of the oldest cites in the country. Having a river that reached inland, where export products abounded, and an ocean to connect with European ports gave Savannah remarkable economic advantage when this country was in its infancy—the markets in the mother country made for eager trading partners.

As Savannah grew, the state of Georgia grew with it. Early on there was a link to Athens. Ties with the University of Georgia became strong and passionate from economic influence, with latter-day Savannah becoming the domicile of Uga, the nation's No. 1 college football mascot.

Athens originally became a retreat for the wealthy Savannah planters who built colonial-style homes, many of which survive today. Savannah was not the place to be in the hottest days of summer; upland, Athens, with the cultural influence of the University of Georgia, enabled the planters to escape the miasma and intense heat of the Lowcountry and bask in the atmosphere of an intellectual environment.

Savannah remains an important port city today; tourism significantly stimulates the local economy, much of it brought about by "the book." That is what the locals call John Berendt's best-selling *Midnight in the Garden of Good and Evil*. The bestseller brought Clint Eastwood to town to produce a Hollywood movie in which Sonny Seiler starred as a judge.

Seiler, a highly regarded attorney, has been a local celebrity of note, beginning with the management—alongside his late wife, Cecilia, and family—of the Ugas, the Bulldog mascot dynasty, and his role in the movie and story of "the book." Over the years, I have driven to Savannah to spend time with the Seilers and Uga. I have fished with several of the Ugas on Sonny's boat, *Silver Britches*. Sonny is a keen fisherman, a man who dotes on the water and its outdoor options.

Competent swimmers, Seiler and his buddy Jack Schaaf, once swam the Savannah River from downtown Savannah to Tybee, a distance of twenty-one miles, which amused local citizens and is a reminder that

Sonny's love and affection for his hometown and the University of Georgia will always have priority in his life.

When the conditions are favorable, he glories in catching shrimp off his dock and then fishing for trout and bass, which he cleans and filets afterwards. Fish, prepared for dinner by Cecilia, was the most fulfilling meal I've ever had in Savannah. In her prime, Paula Deen should have done one of her cooking shows from Cecilia's kitchen. Cecilia's food was as good as what you might find at the Ritz.

Nothing has stirred Sonny's ire more over the years than someone castigating his beloved University of Georgia. Yet he could easily get his dander up over a coaching decision that was not propitious or successful. A swimming letterman at the University of Georgia, Sonny served on the Georgia Athletic Association board for decades and remains an emeritus member.

Here in the last fortnight, I repaired to Sonny's guest room after a seafood dinner up the inland waterway from Moon River, which inspired the genius of Johnny Mercer, the award-winning lyricist of the Chatham gallery of greats.

The next morning, I was in the company of another accomplished Savannah native, one Sam Peters, who is a man all about boats and boating fixtures and accoutrements, which are as classic as inspired verse from the aforementioned Johnny Mercer.

Sam's late father, Johnny Peters, was a Damn Good Dawg if there ever was one. Johnny's passion for Georgia football was off the charts. Sam is a chip off the old block. He is expert in dressing up your boat, fishing for intercostal bass and trout, and needling his elders. With him and Sonny, it doesn't matter your surname; you are always referred to as Bubba. Bait shrimp are worms. Their Geechee-influenced accents are charming but also biting. So when in their company, fasten your seat belt.

I don't have to tell you about Sam's boat—just imagine class and style. Can't tell you its brand name, but it would be like disembarking a BMW at an upscale restaurant. In boating circles, it would be fine art. Don't have to tell you about Sam's boatmanship or fishing expertise, except to say, don't be surprised if you see him in one of those Dos Equis "Most Interesting Man in the World" commercials—except that he drinks Budweiser when fishing.

Jack Nicklaus—whose son, Jack Jr., is a valued customer of Sam's—and Sam have something in common. Jack's ability to land approach shots within inches of the hole is akin to Sam dropping a baited shrimp between two clumps of marsh grass where a five-pound spottail bass might be lurking.

The rest of the story will have to incubate until I can find time to revisit my Dos Equis friends. They made my day and I hope I have made theirs in print.

"Unfinished State"
A Look at Georgia's Past

After an exercise in continuing education such as touring a museum, visiting a historical landmark, or reading a penetrating book with abundant lore and fact, you are often overwhelmed by what you don't know.

For decades, I have traveled my native state from Hiawassee to Hahira, Rabun Gap to Tybee Light—having set foot in each one of Georgia's 159 counties. Over the years, people who have written histories of their communities have shared their books and papers. I have read the works of local authors about their towns and colorful characters.

All this to say that I have long felt discerningly connected to the biggest state east of the Mississippi, not that there aren't places I have missed. One that I keep forgetting to commit to is the tree at St. Simons under whose limbs John Wesley once preached. I still have not seen Rock City but expect to go there when travel becomes uninhibited again.

With a book-buying habit, I am attracted to anything that connects with history and may well have purchased *Georgia: Unfinished State* somewhere along the way. However, I don't remember. It may have been a gift from a friend. Irregardless (this word has finally gained *Webster's* blessing), this book by a former writer with the Atlanta papers, Hal Steed, with a foreword by William Bailey Williford, is the best book I have ever read about our beautiful state that has but two physical blights: a preponderance of unsightly billboards, and roadside trash.

Steed, perhaps to write this book, drove up and down the state and enlighteningly chronicled the early development of the state, a history of the land, and its people. The book was first published in New York in 1942 and then in 1976 by Cherokee Publishing Co. in Atlanta. The following is the slightest glimpse of what I learned from the late Hal Steed.

Georgia was chartered as a dry state and also a non-slavery state. If someone suggested to you that Eli Whitney had a lot to do with slavery, you might think the purveyor of those words a damn fool. Giving credence to that notion, however, comes about when you consider that the revolutionary effect of Whitney inventing the cotton gin meant that cheap labor was needed in abundance. Cotton production flourished along with slavery, unfortunately.

Another interesting factoid that hits one between the eyes is that Robert E. Lee was opposed to slavery while General William Tecumseh approved of the idea.

When the Union general revisited Atlanta years after the war, he met with several prominent Atlanta citizens, including a Confederate captain, Evan P. Howell (father of Clark Howell, then a youngster in short pants), who owned the *Atlanta Constitution*. When the newspaper publisher asked Sherman why Atlanta was a military objective, the now-aging general said: "Atlanta was like my hand," and explained that the palm was the hub and the fingers the spokes that resembled the railroads. "I knew that if I could destroy those railroads, the last link of the Confederacy would be broken."

The Okefenokee Swamp, Hal Steed wrote, was once the home of Billy Bowlegs, a Seminole Indian chief who influenced his people to migrate to the Florida Everglades. In 1989, the state sold the swamp for twelve and a half cents per acre to a corporation which had the objective to drain the swamp to turn it into alluvial farmland. This is one time that nature prevailed. The Okefenokee refused to be drained.

Lumbermen stripped the timber from the Okefenokee. That and "unbridled" hunting and fishing resulted in several species becoming extinct. One species that disappeared was the ivory- billed woodpecker.

A group of scientists from Cornell University, led by Dr. W. D. Funkhouser, discovered a family of aborigines in the Okefenokee in 1912, which brought about national prominence for the swamp. Steed's account of that circumstance: "In many ways, the doctor said, these people were like wild animals. There was an old woman, three sons and two daughters. The children of these aborigines, he added, had intermarried and had eleven offspring of their own. All were characterized as degenerate weaklings, undernourished and full of hookworms.

"Tests showed that their blood was bad. A large graveyard nearby was filled. The family's shelter was a crude lean-to built against a tree. The elders wore no clothing to speak of and the children were naked," the author wrote.

Steed explained, "Their speech was unintelligible, but he [Dr. Funkhouser] and his associates made a dictionary of it. Consider their amazement when they discovered that many of the words the family used had come from Spenser, Chaucer and Shakespeare."

When John Wesley tried to convert the fabled Native American chief Tomochichi, the insightful old chief is supposed to have said to the minister: "Why talk Christian? Christian at Savannah, Christian at Frederica, Christian much drunk. Christian tell lies. Devil is a Christian, me no Christian."

Whisperin' Bill
Georgia Is Always on His Mind

NEW YORK—Here last week at the Marriott Marquis, the Songwriters Hall of Fame inducted three artists with Georgia ties. The event was a rousing affair in which there was laughter, tribute, and fun that turned into a festive evening in which the inductees performed live as an accompaniment to gathering a trophy.

The audience was treated to a concert that incorporated a mix of cultures, genres, and tastes—an occasional accent on unnecessary profanity and a "thanks for the memories." The Georgians inducted were Bill Anderson, Alan Jackson, and Steve Dorff. Whisperin' Bill and Dorff are University of Georgia graduates.

Others included in the induction were Kool & the Gang, Jermaine Dupri, John Mellencamp, and Allee Willis. Neil Diamond's live rendition of "Sweet Caroline" elevated the spirits of those in attendance and caused all to leap to their feet as if there was an electric charge underneath their seats.

Diamond was honored with the Johnny Mercer Award. Mercer, a native of Savannah, was the founder of the Songwriters Hall of Fame. His lyrics are legend, lighting up lives and reminding us that compatible melody is still important in music and that you don't have to be loud to showcase your talent.

If you know anything about Bill Anderson, you know about his imagination and his creativity dating back to his nineteenth year on this earth when he, on a hot summer's night, moved out on the roof of the Andrew Jackson Hotel in Commerce, Georgia, and wrote "City Lights." He wouldn't cash in on his work until later, but the song is still providing residuals to this one-time Decatur resident who takes unending pleasure in being referred to as a "Damn Good Dawg."

Whisperin' Bill's career has been gilded since that summer night in Commerce. Anybody who receives such high honor as he did in the Big Apple can be justifiably proud. His body of work reflects that he is a man who has respected the work ethic with an emphasis on humility, generosity, and goodwill.

Every day, Whisperin' Bill arises with a smile on his face. Actually, multiple smiles. One for each of the loves of his life. Family. Friends. Music. He gives thanks for the good life he has enjoyed.

There is rampant ingratitude in today's world, but none in Bill's circle. He was at home in New York, performing for an elite group of accomplished men and women in music, but he is just as comfortable at the Waffle House with a guy with no credits, plying his day for minimum wage.

The phone rings and it will be Bill, making my day with that old familiar line, "Did you hear the one about?" It is always a fresh joke. A resonating punch line and an earful of laughter as Bill weaves his story adroitly for my pleasure. This is when I give a thumbs-up to those who still use the phone. You can't text a good joke. A joke requires delivery, pause, and inflection. Bill has the right stuff when it comes to that.

Over the years, I have often been the progenitor of a good story that had Bill reacting from his office in Nashville with such appreciation that I knew it was top-rated when he would say, "I got to call my buddy Jimmy Dean and share that one with him."

While I never met Whisperin' Bill's late friend, I enjoyed being, upon occasion, a "carrier" for a good laugh to Richmond, Virginia, where the sausage king lived out his life.

While everybody has succumbed to electronic messaging, I find it refreshing that Bill will pick up the phone and call his friends and make their day. He is the consummate good neighbor. He is as down-home as they come. His call might be when I am somewhere out in the state, like Tennille or Folkston or Eastanollee. Places he may not have been to but would be happy to go to and sing his latest tune there.

His grandfather, a Methodist minister, had a reminder on his deathbed for Bill: "Son," he said, "Don't ever forget that you can reach more people on this earth in just one of your songs than I could in all the sermons I have ever preached."

Bill won't forget that, just as he won't forget his friends or where he came from. That was keenly obvious here last week in the Big Apple.

PART II

The Sporting Scene and Its Many Side Benefits

While I have pretty much spent my life in the sports arena, which I have enjoyed to the utmost, I have never wanted to treat it as an exclusive genre.

Sports provides an opportunity to broaden your horizons. Meet accomplished men and women in other fields. Unfortunately, all too many sports heroes are myopic. They seldom venture outside the cocoon of the playing field.

I've long maintained that there is no reason that a man couldn't turn the double play ball and not enjoy a night at the opera. I enjoyed an evening at La Scala with the same affection that I had for Yankee Stadium, Fenway Park, the Rose Bowl, and the picnic grounds of Henley-on-Thames.

A person with abiding curiosity is motivated to experience the entire scene, which is why tailgating has become so important in football. While it takes on a different fabric and allure, the picnics during the Henley Regatta evoke a similar passion that you would find at a rival college football game.

Follow a leg of the Tour de France and you are treated to the greatest of social experience in the bars and sidewalk cafés, wherever the Tour takes respite for the night.

Ice fishing on Lake Minnetonka was not accompanied by tailgating, cheerleaders, and referees, but it was a memorable high that I'd be pleased to experience again.

The Super Bowl, the World Series, Wimbledon, Roland Garros, and all the major bowl games are stirring highs and classic venues to remember. Enjoying my own Grand Slam—covering the four major golf tournaments in a single season—was unforgettable. Getting to know and interact with the principals and great champions of all sports is fulfilling and stimulating.

Ty Cobb, Red Grange, Bobby Thompson, Charley Trippi, Frank Sinkwich, Jack Nicklaus, Arnold Palmer, Lee Trevino, Nick Saban, Ted Williams, Satchel Paige, Phil Niekro, Spec Towns, Herschel Walker, Leah Brown, Verne Lundquist, Dan Jenkins, Jim Nance, Billy Payne, Vince Dooley, Keith Jackson, and countless others patiently answered my questions. Most of them allowed me to turn on a tape recorder for in-depth interviews that made my day. I still have most of those recorded interviews but have shared them with the University of Georgia Research Library.

I didn't come looking for controversy. I had no interest in their short-comings—just wanted to talk about their careers and their crafts. A 750-word column is not a definitive biography. Let someone else gloss their warts.

In my world, there was always joy in Mudville.

Aaron Boone
Friend of a Red Sox Aficionado

NEW YORK—Before the Braves moved to Atlanta from Milwaukee in 1966, baseball fans in the Deep South had to adopt a big-league team if they wanted to seriously follow major league action.

The closest team to Atlanta was the Cincinnati Reds, 461 miles away. Without a clear channel radio signal broadcasting Reds games (WCKY programmed non-stop country music, but only carried Reds baseball briefly in the late sixties.) In the Southeast, there wasn't an abundance of Cincinnati fans who recalled Ewell "The Whip" Blackwell and his nasty curve, Johnny Vander Meer's back-to-back no-hitters in 1938, or the "Big Red Machine" of Pete Rose and Johnny Bench in the seventies. Baseball fans in Dixie never heard Waite Hoyt exclaim on the air, "There was the pitch!"

In fact, there were more Cardinal fans around, owing to the clear channel signal of KMOX out of St. Louis, but its signal wasn't that strong in Georgia. Most fans in the Southeast adopted the New York Yankees, who were perennial World Series participants and a team that was the beneficiary of national coverage.

In the World War II era, a big-time star of the Yankees was Spurgeon Chandler, quarterback legend of the 1929 Georgia Bulldogs who defeated Yale 15-0 in the memorable dedicatory game on October 12, 1929. "Spud" would win three World Series rings with the Yankees and become the American League MVP in 1943.

Spud, however, died with a broken heart—he passionately wanted to be inducted into the Baseball Hall of Fame. Through my friendship with Ted Williams' confidante and author, John Underwood, I had dinner one night with Williams in Winter Haven, Florida, in the eighties and asked him about Spud. "Hell of a pitcher," Williams said. "Ought to be in the Hall of Fame." I called Spud and suggested that he might be inducted via the Ole Timers Committee. With that, Spud—the calendar moving forward in his life with alacrity—broke down and cried. "Well they better hurry," he said tearfully. More than a quarter century later, Spud, who still holds the record for the best winning percentage (109-43 for .717) for a player with at least 100 wins—a Yankee record—has still not been elected.

Perhaps because there were several books about the Red Sox in the county library in my hometown of Wrightsville, Georgia, which were the first baseball books I ever read, I became a Red Sox fan and wondered, for years, like everybody in New England, if the "Curse of the Bambino" would be eternal.

I wasn't a "Yankee hater" (it was always a memorable occasion to take the subway out to Yankee Stadium to see the Yankees and the football Giants play), but I never lost my affinity for the Red Sox.

Baseball has always made my day. When I was a senior in high school, my class took a bus trip to Washington and New York. Our high school coach, Red Bullock, one of our chaperones, knew Ellis Clary, who got us tickets to a Senators-Indian game at old Griffith Stadium. We met Clary, a native of Valdosta, after the game. He spent time talking baseball with us, giving us a seasoned four-letter word dissertation that both shocked and delighted us.

When we got to New York, we took the subway out to see an afternoon Yankee game in "The House that Ruth Built," and was thrilled when Mickey Mantle hit a batting practice ball into the right field seats near where we were sitting. Mantle would later spend a lot of time at his place at Lake Oconee. We had a mutual friend, Jimmy Orr, and while I was past the awestruck age, it was fun to hear Mantle talk about his heyday with Roger Maris, Yogi Berra, and those dominant Yankee teams of the fifties.

In that era, you would have bowled me over with a feather if you had suggested I would someday enjoy a friendship with the Yankee manager. Owing to my friendship with Dave O'Brien, Red Sox TV announcer, I first met Aaron Boone when he was working ESPN games with O'Brien. Aaron had a long-standing passion to see a game between the hedges, which came about four years ago.

A descendant of pioneer Daniel Boone and the son of Bob Boone and grandson of Ray Boone, who played in the big leagues, Aaron continued the "Curse of the Bambino" when in 2003, he hit a walk-off home run off Tim Wakefield in the League Championship series in New York. The *New York Daily News* called it the "Curse of the Boonebino."

It surprised many in baseball that Aaron, entrenched as a well-paid baseball analyst with ESPN, would want to take on the high-pressured role of managing the team with the most storied tradition in the game in the toughest media market in baseball. Obviously, he has kept up with baseball and approaches the game as a positive thinker who wants to restore that annual World Series tradition with the Yankees. Naturally, New Yorkers expect that of him. "I could not be more excited," he said in the spring when I visited with him in Tampa at Steinbrenner Field. "To have this opportunity is overwhelming," Boone said.

At this point, the American League East appears to be a classic Yankee-Red Sox pennant race. It has the makings of those fifties and sixties vintage neck-and-neck runs that spur reflections of the past. Yesteryear, the rivalry would have taken place in the original Yankee Stadium (and Fenway Park). DiMaggio was giving way to Mickey; Joe's brother Dominic would have been in the Boston outfield with Ted Williams. There was Yogi, Whitey Ford, Dr. Bobby Brown, and the colorful Casey Stengel managing the team. Mel Allen would have been in the Yankee broadcast booth and Curt Gowdy anchored in the Red Sox booth.

All that history and lore only heightens the experience for Aaron Boone, who is a traditionalist, but keenly aware that expediency is the objective of his current assignment in perhaps the most high-profile job in sports for a non-player. His reputation as a Yankees legend is secure, but he wants more—he wants a World Series ring as a manager.

If my original favorite team becomes matched up in the playoffs against the Aaron Boone-managed Yankees, I'm not sure what my emotions will be. My greatest passion would be for the winner of the American League Championship to face off with the Braves in the World Series. Then I would know who I would have to pull for.

Archie Manning
A Quarterback for all Generations

With J. T. Daniels becoming Georgia's starting quarterback, frequent texts and phone conversations with two sports luminaries have come this way—an all-star twosome of Aaron Boone, manager of the New York Yankees, and Archie Manning, the Ole Miss Great and progenitor of the Manning quarterback clan.

It wasn't difficult to become familiar with J. T.'s sensational freshman year at the University of Southern California. He had such a memorable first year that his name was relatively familiar to collegiate football fans across the country.

Then misfortune struck for the Irvine, California native in the first game of his sophomore season when he suffered a season-ending ACL tear. After rehabbing the knee, he lost his starting job to Kedon Slovis of Scottsdale, Arizona, which led Daniels to transfer to Georgia.

Before there was any mention of his Athens plans, Boone, who fulfilled his desire to see a game between the hedges when he was working with ESPN, sent word that "you guys are about to get one of the outstanding quarterbacks in the country." Boone is still closely connected to USC, where he was a baseball letterman. He knew about Daniels' decision to transfer before it became a headline on the internet.

During the fall, Aaron would send texts asking how J. T. was doing and wondering when he would see game action. "The kid is a special talent," the Yankee manager kept tweeting. I would laugh and reply that Kirby Smart and Todd Monken did not volunteer updates on the status of the Georgia quarterbacks.

After the Mississippi State game, which Boone watched on TV, he sent along a "bout time," text and was excited to see J. T. play so well in his first start.

In a conversation with Manning earlier in the year, he gave J. T. high marks from what he saw in him when the Californian attended the Manning Passing Academy in Thibodaux, Louisiana.

"His father [Steve] came with him but he certainly is not a problem father. He is very supportive of his son. I have had conversations with Steve since J.T. came to our camp, and he has never complained about the way things have played out for his son at Georgia," Archie said.

When Archie asked Steve Daniels if J. T. enjoyed his brief visit to the Southern US for the first time, the father laughed and said, "Yeah, he had a great time. You got him chewing tobacco right away."

The Mannings took note of the fact that J. T. chose to enroll in accelerated classes in high school so he could graduate early, which enabled him to become the starter at USC when he would have normally been a senior in high school. That made him the most precocious QB in college football, confirming that there was unlimited upside in his future.

"That certainly was news to us. We were very impressed with his attitude and his football skills," Manning says. "You could tell that he had a lot of ability and that he fit in well with the other kids who came to Thibodaux. That was an indication that he had very good leadership skills."

Those who remember Archie Manning recall that he was the most mobile of quarterbacks when he played for Johnny Vaught at Ole Miss, 1968–70. Vaught was the mastermind of the sprint draw. He had the perfect talent to run his offense. Archie was 6'3", 212 in college and had excellent speed.

In 1969, his junior season, he had 124 rushing attempts for 502 yards and a 4.0 average, scoring 14 touchdowns. As a passer that year, he completed 154 passes for 1,762 yards and nine touchdowns. Defending him became a nightmare for defensive coordinators. Vaught came with an intermediate route, then a short route with his concept of the sprint draw offense. If the receivers were covered, the last option for Archie was to take off running. He won a lot of games with his feet.

With the New Orleans Saints, he ran the ball as much as 63 times in 14 game seasons, mostly because he played on weak teams and was often running for his life.

While he doesn't expect the pocket passers to disappear from the landscape, he concedes that mobile quarterbacks, Joe Burrow's unfortunate experience at Cincinnati notwithstanding, can really put pressure on defenses. "The offensive coordinators are so clever and can give the defenses so many headaches that it is hard to defend a mobile quarterback today," Archie says. However, he points out "that offensive football goes in cycles."

It may take a while, but the defense will eventually catch up. He doesn't expect the pocket quarterback to go away completely, but holds the view that the current rage of the mobile quarterback will dominate for a while.

Army Football 1958
Hark Back to a Lonesome End
and a Thrilling Season

A good book can take you back to simpler times, allowing one to explore yesteryear, when life was different and much less complicated. *When Saturday Mattered Most* is a treatise about Army's last undefeated football team. A good and well-told story by Mark Beech and brought to you by St. Martin's Press.

To begin with, I have always had a high regard for service academy football, and as a traditionalist, I believe the college game lost something when we reached the point that Army and Navy were rendered inadequate to compete for the National Championship. (Air Force, though having won the Commander-in-Chief's Trophy more than either of the other two military schools, celebrated its first graduating class in 1959. A national title was never in reach for the Falcons.)

The game today is a much more exciting game because we have tweaked it to where speed is acutely accented and the bigger you are, the better you can compete at the highest level. A bluntly honest view spawns this question, however: are we better off with what we have today?

Today's game is not the college game of yesteryear. We compromised standards to accommodate entrance requirements for the best players, but in doing so we took the degree out of the mix. Regrettably. That is a topic for another day—but service academy football could not compete at the highest level with latent rule changes that favored high-scoring offenses.

This was the way it was in 1958. Earl "Red" Blaik, a close friend of General Douglas MacArthur, was the Army coach who enjoyed flag-waving success at West Point. Blaik was reaching the end of his career. In fact, 1958 would be his last season as coach. He stayed on briefly as athletic director.

He had won three national championships during his time by the Hudson River. In addition to MacArthur, his chief advocate, Blaik had an engaging rapport with the established columnists of the day: Arthur Daley, the *New York Times*; Red Smith, who finished his career with the *Times*;

and Stanley Woodward of the *Herald Tribune* were among those who often sang Blaik's praises in print. They were not reluctant to show their patriotism when they punched out their copy about the football heroes at the oldest continuously operated army post in the US.

In that epic season for Blaik and the Cadets, the coach had come up with an idea for a new formation during the off-season. He positioned his flanker out 15 yards, initially calling him the "far flanker." Next the far flanker was referred to as the "lonely end," and ultimately it went down in history as the "Lonesome End."

The first "Lonesome End" was Bill Carpenter, who would earn fame in Vietnam when he and his company, woefully outnumbered, were pinned down by Viet Cong troops. Carpenter radioed a helicopter to drop napalm directly on top of his unit—unthinkable, but it won the day and enabled Carpenter and his men to escape. Gen. MacArthur would have likely suggested that football influenced Carpenter's extraordinary leadership.

Carpenter never huddled with his Army team and communicated with the quarterback with hand signals. At 6'2", 210 with excellent speed, Carpenter was also blessed with good hands, which meant that he could be counted on for big plays to complement Blaik's ground-oriented offensive attack.

What the Army coaches wanted was for the defense to commit to double coverage of the far flanker. When that happened, Army could exploit the defense with its effective running game, which featured Pete Dawkins, who would win the Heisman Trophy that season, and Bob Anderson, an underrated back who could be counted on to come through when a play, drive, or game was on the line, along with clutch play making from the lonesome end.

From this book, there are two vignettes that resonate. One had to do with Col. Blaik's words of encouragement about the game he loved. Coaches are always identifying with catchphrases and slogans; words to motivate. Blaik was given to reminding his players that to succeed in football one had to "pay the price." Anybody familiar with the career of Georgia's Wallace Butts will pick up on the fact that Butts always spoke of the importance of paying the price to achieve excellence on the gridiron.

Which one originated the slogan? Likely, nobody living knows, but since Blaik was born seven years before Butts, it would be natural to assume that he, having begun his career as a coach earlier, is likely to have come up with the slogan. Not sure if the coaches ever compared notes. For all we know, each could have come up with the slogan independently of the other.

Another interesting note about Blaik's career is that the legendary Vince Lombardi was once his offensive line coach. It was at Army that Lombardi was introduced to the sweep, a bread-and-butter play for Blaik.

When Lombardi took over in Green Bay, he installed a sweep, similar to what he had learned under Blaik, which was the key to the Packers' highly successful ground game that enabled the Packers to dominate the NFL.

All this is a reminder, once again, that there is "nothing new under the sun." Except perhaps the lonesome end, once upon a time.

Arnold Palmer
Unparalleled and Warm Memories

AUGUSTA—Every year, a national magazine picks a "Sportsman of the Year," a title Arnold Palmer won like he won everything else but a PGA championship—a man who held such sway with people that we have never known one who could walk with kings and never lose the common touch as well as he was able to do. Those who came along in his era would eagerly vote for him as "Sportsman of Our Lifetime."

If you date back to the sixties and saw his Army form at the Augusta National, then you probably hold the same view that will be trumpeted for the ages. Did you ever see Arnold out of sorts with anybody? Did you ever see him refuse an autograph request? Have you ever known a nicer guy than Arnold?

Everybody has his own Arnold Palmer moment. When Arnold posed for a photo at the FBO hangar at the airport. When you showed up with a pad and pen or tape recorder at an exhibition event—when you, the lowly and smitten reporter—and he, the king of golf, took time to answer your pedestrian questions. When he hit the ball into the rough and you exchanged comments with him. When you were at dinner and he showed up at your table and exchanged pleasantries to everybody. When he paused for a photograph, Anywhere USA.

Both men and women gravitated to his sphere and walked away feeling enriched and special for having been within arm's length of the great champion. Men admired him for being a man's man and women felt they were in the company of a matinee idol. Everybody loved Arnold and Arnold loved everybody—likely the most graphic of mutual admiration societies to exist in sport.

I belong to those who experienced an unforgettable moment with Arnold. There were two times when he was generous enough to let me turn on a tape recorder for thirty minutes. He didn't ask, "How long is this thing going to take?" or make the usual sniff that, "I really don't have time for you and wish you would go away." Arnold never asked a reporter the circulation of his paper or the radioman the power of his station's signal.

While he was never crass or self-serving, the by-product of his universal genuineness was that people could not wait to buy the products he endorsed, play the golf courses he built, and support the charities he supported. Arnold gave of himself to golf fans worldwide, which endured him to legions of people.

Nowhere, outside Latrobe, Pennsylvania, his hometown, was Arnold more appreciated than he was at Augusta. There is a story in this year's *Masters Annual* by his biographer, Jim Dodson, which graphically underscores the passion Arnold had for Augusta.

When the late Bill Lane succeeded Cliff Roberts as chairman, he asked Arnold to host the closing ceremony. On a Sunday when Arnold had missed the cut and was awaiting his final round role, I caught up with him in the clubhouse and recorded his thoughts on a number of topics. Here is part of what I transcribed from that long ago conversation:

> I find that the corner is probably the most exciting series of golf holes that I have ever played—starting with 10, 11, 12, 13, 14 and 15—they might have been the most difficult holes in golf, but they are certainly the most exciting under tournament conditions when the pressure is on and the wind is blowing and all the things that can happen are happening; those holes are going to give you the thrill that you really want or might be looking for in golf or in life.

About the toughest hole at Augusta, he said:

> I suppose even taking in consideration the corner, which are certainly very tough holes, I look at the fourth hole [par-3, 240 yards] as one of the most difficult holes in the world. It is not a hole that you might make a double bogy or a triple bogey on; it is a hole that you just make a lot of bogeys. Number five [par four, 490 yards] is also a difficult hole and I suspect that those two holes, if we ever took an average, we would find more bogeys made there than any other holes on the golf course.

When I went to see him at Bay Hill about five years before he died, I recorded a conversation with him that included the one question I had thought about long before arriving at his office. I wanted to know if he had any idea of how many times he had signed his name. He smiled and said, "Well, I had a secretary who retired a few years ago who estimated in the time she worked for me, that I had signed my name four million times." Consider other times when he was away from the office and that figure might be doubled.

Perhaps it would be safe to say that few athletes, perhaps none, ever signed their name more than Arnold, and the view here is that while countless "kings" mourned his passing, there were far more common people who grieved along with them. That is what made Arnold Palmer so special, and his impact on the sporting world will resonate through the ages.

Bill Stanfill
The Country Boy Who Knew the
Ecstasy of Victory and the Agony of Defeat

ALBANY, Georgia—Bill Stanfill's teammates were a heterogeneous group when they arrived on campus half a century ago, but the sameness that made them champions was reflected in their collective presence at the First United Methodist Church of Albany on November 14, 2016, where they convened to say farewell to one of the truly great football players of our time.

Teammates, especially those who bring about championships, are unalterably connected with bonding that leads to unforgettable moments from which they will never emotionally retreat. Not all who knew Stanfill showed up, although it looked as if they did, as they took up a sizable section of the church.

Among those who came—all imbued with deep and abiding respect—were Billy Payne, whose affiliations make his name household in the game of golf across the globe. Then there were Jerry Varnado, an on-the-field overachiever, who once enjoyed a brush with hell-raisin', but segued, owing to tragedy, into becoming a man of the cloth; Mike Cavan, John Kasay, Charley Whittimore, and Steve Greer, who coached for alma mater; Hugh Nall, local and latent friend, another of the whistle-and-stopwatch society who had to switch loyalties but later moved into business and reaffirmed his unimpeachable commitment to the "G;" Sandy Johnson, whose international business success remains under the radar but who was extraordinarily signature; George Patton, the other tackle who with Stanfill formed an unbeatable tandem, perhaps the best there has ever been at Georgia; a lawyer (Lee Daniel); a doctor (Tommy Lawhorne); a fireman (Tim Crowe); a head hunter, Wayne Ingle, a bear of a man who dabbed his eyes frequently during the service; a career military officer, the pint-sized lineman Anthony Dennard; an egg man (Jack Davis); and a woodsman (Ronnie Jenkins), who lost his teeth to a forearm long ago but is something of a mascot with his blue-collar, down-home vernacular, one who would forever get your ox out of the ditch.

Stanfill's adoring coach Vince Dooley was there, which struck a somber note in that life has no defined order. In a perfect world, the coach lives long and abundantly, advancing into old age before crossing the river of the unknown, to be followed afterwards by his charges from those joyful and celebrated days of yore.

All during the uplifting service there was the reminder that successful teammates truly love each other. In Bill Stanfill's time, there were big guys and little guys, some with special talents, others who got by on energy and heart with priority always on "The team. The team." Say it after me, "The team. The team."

They gave of themselves. They were good at playing the game. They were great at winning. Accomplished and everyday men filled up six pews at the church where a man of the soil, a rurally influenced but gifted athlete, was eulogized in a genial and spiritually elevated atmosphere. There is nothing like football to take a modestly raised country boy—with superior skills—to honor, glory, headlines, titles, championship rings, and fame—only exceeded by the recipient's modesty, deflection of praise, forever-engendering goodwill, and harmony with those who were less successful but were always welcomed in his sphere and in his heart. Any who wore the Red and Black could always sup with Bill. They could always pull up a chair to his table.

This was a man who epitomized the longtime National Football League adage, "You got to play hurt." His inventory of breaks and structural assaults included, but were not limited to: broken left forearm, every finger and thumb on each hand except his ring finger, multiple cracked ribs, two hip replacements, uncountable knee and ankle sprains, and back and neck injuries that led to four vertebrae fusions in three different operations.

A ruptured kidney one Sunday long ago sent him to the hospital for a week. However, he was cleared to play the next weekend. He played half the snaps, bringing about this interesting episode. After undressing to shower, he noticed he still had on his hospital bracelet, which the team doctor refused to cut off, saying, "You probably ought to check back into the hospital tonight." That is yesterday's NFL—no medical personnel who stood up to ownership and ownership that treated even its top players as pieces of meat.

A couple of years ago, Bill and I quail-hunted one sunny January day. It was to be a morning hunt followed by lunch and an afternoon return to the fields. There was hardly anything Stanfill enjoyed more than knocking down a couple of quail on a covey rise, which he did as I watched admiringly. After an hour, he put his .410 shotgun away and said, "I'm done." At lunch, he repaired to his pickup and subsequently took his pain-wracked body to a comforting recliner. That was the after-football life he lived.

On another day, we sat in his office at the Merry Acres Motel in which he had ownership participation with his wife's family and talked about the licks and sprains and bruises. His Outland Trophy was nowhere to be found. There were no All-American certificates on the walls—no artifacts from a Hall of Fame career.

There was an oil painting of him sacking the great John Unitas in the latter's declining years, but the essence of Bill Stanfill—the man and the athlete—was embodied in a mayonnaise jar that contained the original hip joints, that were replaced. He pointed to the jar and said with humility and pride, "If I had it to do over again, I'd do the same thing." No man ever loved the game of football more, even with living his adult life in constant pain.

Everybody ought to have a funeral like Bill's. The reverend Thad Haygood officiated, beginning by "calling the Dawgs," followed by a soloist singing one of Bill's favorite songs by Bobby Bare, "Drop Kick Me Jesus (Through The Goalposts Of Life)." Haygood noted Bill's lengthy list of accomplishments that were hallmarks across the board.

Then the associate pastor, Scott Stanfill, the son of the great football hero, eulogized his father—a most insightful and touching tribute. It was worthy of bronzing.

Scott's message was discerning, cogent, and penetrating, laced with humor—like the time a water moccasin shimmied up Scott's boat paddle, seeking respite in Bill's fishing boat. "That," said his bemused father, "is the only time I ever heard a preacher cuss." Scott spoke with such poignancy, a virtuoso delivery without pause, stumble, or quivering voice. His tribute was the oratorical equal of his dad's performance in his prime, helping the Miami Dolphins to an undefeated season. All who knew Bill Stanfill loved him. Scott made us love him more.

His last words, speaking for his siblings, Kristin, Jake, and Stan, were to convert the acronym DGD, which stands for "Damn Good Dawgs," to "Damn Good Dad."

Fittingly, the organ played "Glory to Ole Georgia" as the church tearfully emptied.

Under my breath, I felt biblical and whispered, "Selah!"

Billy Payne
An Ingenious Visionary,
an Indefatigable Team Builder

PEBBLE BEACH, California—Officials of the World Golf Hall of Fame convened Monday night in this garden spot to induct its latest class, which should have made Billy Payne happy to be where the beauty of the landscape is akin to the Augusta National Golf Club when it comes to extraordinary splendor and raw beauty.

Hall of Fame. That's big-time laurels. However, if you know anything about this remarkable and exceptional visionary, you are likely aware that he has less ego for his luminary status than most mortals who reach legendary status in sport. He has the poise and confidence to comport himself appropriately, engendering respect and modesty. He is uncomfortable in the spotlight, but that is where he has resided since he came up with the notion to bring the 1996 Olympics to Atlanta. There has never been a greater or more effective behind-the-scenes organizer than this 1966 All-SEC defensive end whose enduring respect for his father, Porter, drove him to do his best. He could not fathom the idea that he would ever disappoint his father.

One cannot be chairman of the Augusta National Golf Club without a walk with fame and sometimes controversy. It comes with the position. While Billy was not a blueblood when it came to golf's elite establishment, he set about running the club, founded by Cliff Roberts and Bobby Jones, with a bent on making the club more enjoyable for the membership and to make the hallowed Masters tournament better than Roberts and Jones could have ever imagined.

His innovative grasp and signature thought process set him apart.

If a member needed dressing down, the Chairman was up to the task but with diplomacy and due respect. While he is gracious and affable, he maximizes his time to make monumental things happen. His *modus operandi* is that all goals will be reached.

His ability to keep a firm hand on the tiller, yet effectively delegate and underscore team bonding and his building and development concepts—everything from Berckmans Place, the upscale food emporium, and the classiest media center in all of sports, to the improvement of all facilities and expanding the footprint of the club—is nothing short of sensational.

Buying up land on Washington and Berckmans Road puts the Augusta National in the position to where the club doesn't have any concerns about undesirable neighbors encroaching on the grounds. When Jack Nicklaus was in Athens a year ago for the dedication of the Payne Indoor Center, he noted that only a Billy Payne could get a municipal thoroughfare moved as he did with Berckmans Road.

An advancing calendar is but a reminder that it was a quarter century ago when a thirty-seven-year-old lawyer conceived the idea that Atlanta could host the Summer Olympics. His vision, indefatigability, energy, and consummate leadership skills enabled him to achieve the improbable, if not impossible, dream. He put together a coalition of leaders and financial stalwarts who believed in Billy and Atlanta. He became the "Little Engine That Could." The "ant that moved the rubber tree plant."

I remember meeting with him when the idea of the Olympics was germinating in his mind to ask him for help in fund-raising for Georgia's Butts-Mehre Building. He demurred, noting that he couldn't explain why but he would be unable to join the effort. A few days later, everybody knew as the headlines in the *Atlanta Journal-Constitution* confirmed that Payne had put a budding plan together to bring the ambitious Olympic goal to fruition.

Billy was young, ambitious, believable, and inspiring, with the demeanor of the Energizer Bunny. No successful executive has been more prepared when making a public appearance. He will rehearse his remarks dozens of times, even hundreds, until he is completely satisfied with them, from content to voice inflection and grammar.

While he never wastes a moment, he can relax on the golf course, when he is fly fishing, and when enjoying Georgia football. He gushes, without reservation, when he speaks to the love and loyalty of alma mater. He has a condominium in Five Points to accommodate trips to campus to visit grandchildren who are enrolled, but also to satiate his emotions by connecting with Georgia in his retirement years. To watch football practice, grab a sandwich at ADD Drug Store, visit with old friends and swoon to the ringing of the Chapel Bell. The fundamentals of his leadership principles were learned on the football field when an indoor practice field never crossed anybody's mind. There is one now, named for him and his late father.

Billy Payne's success has brought him recognition, all well-deserved, but the glory that has come his way is nothing that he ever sought. Just one of the attributes that makes him a titan in the Bulldog Valhalla.

The Open Is Extraordinary
with Uplifting Ancillary Benefits

ST. ANDREWS, Scotland—The Open Championship at the Old Course at St. Andrews comes with stirring anticipation. Getting here from London on the Flying Scotsman is a trip to savor—the fields of waving grain, the hedgerows, the meadows, the abundant sheep (if you counted all of Scotland's sheep, you would sleep longer than Rip Van Winkle), and on the golf courses that abound, a solitary figure with his small bag slung over his shoulder, playing alone as the train rushes by.

That is a recurring scene when you travel the Scottish countryside: an obscure golf course with a fairway running parallel to the railroad and one player enjoying the game all Scots adore. Usually there are misting rains and freshening winds, which would send those with a less-than-stellar constitution to the comforts of the clubhouse. Only a Scot would play by himself in elements fit for a polar bear.

It is quicker by air, but the train is more fun. It makes you step back in time. The ride is smooth, and an ample supply of Aberlour puts you in a spirited mood as you recall the thrilling championships of days past. A five-hour journey by train is the best way to begin a week in St. Andrews, the home of golf.

The memories of past Opens rest gentle on your mind. The flashbacks to that first Open make yesteryear a highlight of a lifetime. It was 1978, and the weather was frigid—a new experience for a country boy from the Deep South. Woolen sweaters, thermal underclothing, and windcheaters (British for windbreakers). In July of all times.

A full breakfast—which the Brits call a cooked breakfast as opposed to a continental breakfast—was a daily treat. It was an introduction to sautéed mushrooms, kippers, and English bacon. If permissible, I always went back for seconds.

In those days, bed and breakfast with a family was a memorable experience. The rate then was eight pounds, or something like twelve dollars. How times have changed! The rate in Edinburgh for the Open at an upscale B&B this year is as much as 150 pounds per person per day—roughly $450. At that rate, the championship loses its luster.

Walking the golf course again is an uplifting experience. To see the hillocks on the fairways (tater hills, Andy Bean's caddie and father, Tommy, called them in 1978) and the pot bunkers reminds you that there is no imagination like nature's when it comes to golf course architecture. You can always sense the difference in the Scottish and American ways when it comes to golf. I liked it from that first visit.

Hell bunker, heather, gorse, the Road Hole, and the steeples provided directional sightings for the caddies. "Hit it, sir, to the third steeple on your right," one might say on a particular hole. The double greens and the freshening winds, Swilcan Burn, and haggis. I will order haggis this week, but only once.

That first trip was highlighted with Jack Nicklaus winning for the second time at the Old Course. Seeing the bump and run game for the first time was illuminating and edifying, as the ball seemed to deftly dance about, flummoxing the competitors who faced every shot with trepidation.

Since Nicklaus hoisted the Claret Jug in 1978 there have been return trips to the Open every year but two and an opportunity to play the Old Course a few times. I feel a rush when I recall that first time on the course. My caddie was a man named Sidney Rutherford. The day he caddied for me, he was eighty-two years old. He wore a tie and had played 18 holes that morning.

He knew the course better than Old Tom Morris. It was obvious that he could not see well, but he would say things like, "Sir, you see that gorse bush on the left side of the fairway? If you hit it over that bush, it will bounce right into the fairway where you want to be." Interacting with the caddies at St Andrews is a rich and illuminating experience.

Herbert Warren Wind, the longtime golf writer for the *New Yorker*, once explained what it was like to not engage a caddie in Scotland. Not playing with a caddie, he said, "is to deny oneself the wine of the country."

Charley Trippi
The Iconic Bulldog at Ninety-Nine

Charley Trippi, one of the most celebrated athletes in Georgia history, turned ninety-nine yesterday. The old warhorse was low-key and subdued, advancing age having robbed him of the electric energy and suppleness that once drove him to remarkable athletic achievement.

Yet he was up for blowing out ninety-nine candles on a cake, made by Joyce Philips of Winterville, with his wife, Peggy, egging him on. He rose to the occasion as he often did on the football field and smiled his way through the celebratory moment.

For the first time in his life, he did not spend his birthday outdoors. Well into his nineties, he was usually outside working in his yard most days of the year.

If you had stopped by to see him with the good news that you had hired a yard service for him, he would have refused the perk. Given his clever personality, however, he might have noted that he would take the money but would do the yard work himself.

Trippi was one of the keenest "one-liner" proponents I have ever known. He once said of an associate, who was not known for clever investment decisions, "If he gets in, you get out."

One chilly November day at a Georgia football practice, when Trippi was Georgia's backfield coach, the wind, gusting about, was making it difficult to throw the ball without interference. Quarterback Larry Rakestraw threw a pass on an out route when a sudden burst of wind literally lifted the ball up and caused it to sail over the concrete wall that once surrounded the practice field with a jet-like thrust. Trippi cracked, "Touch 'em all, Rakestraw, that one is outta here."

John Rauch, quarterback for two years of Trippi's salad days in Athens, used to refer to Trippi's caustic and savvy wit as "zingers." That was the refreshing side of this man, whose light-hearted banter characterized his personality.

After he retired from the old Chicago Cardinals in the late fifties, his collegiate coach, Wallace Butts, hired him for the 1958 season as backfield coach, an arrangement where Trippi could enjoy a football connection, raise his family in a college town environment, and pursue real estate interests on the side.

Dealing as a principal, Trippi fared extremely well. Recruiting demands were not anything like today, so there was truly an off-season, which allowed him to make deals and play golf at the Athens Country Club, enjoying the good life—a very different lifestyle from what he experienced growing up.

His Sicilian father had emigrated from the old country and settled in Pittston, Pennsylvania. He lived the hardscrabble life of a coal miner, which his son aspired to avoid. If it had not been for football and Coca-Cola, the coal mines may have been Trippi's future.

In the post-Depression years, Harold Hirsch, an attorney who had graduated from the University of Georgia School of Law, was the legal counsel for the Coca-Cola Company. His feelings for his alma mater were substantial. He kept the Athletic Association afloat in the hardest of times in the thirties. One of his consequential measures was to find summer jobs for Bulldog football players, but before that, many enjoyed a connection with the soft drink company—one of whom was Harold "War Eagle" Ketron of Clarkesville in the North Georgia mountains. Ketron lettered on the 1901–03 teams. He was captain in 1903 but came back to letter in 1906, which was legal in those days. He became the Coke bottler in Wilkes-Barre, Pennsylvania, a mere 7.7 miles from Pittston, Trippi's hometown.

It was Ketron who befriended Trippi when he saw the latter play football for Pittston's high school team. He gave Trippi a Coca-Cola route early on. The enterprising teenager was soon making more money as a high school student than his coal-miner father was making.

Times were nonetheless austere for the family. Trippi's father did not want him to play football. "You'll get your leg broke and I will break the other one," he said to his precocious son. The message was simple. A broken limb would present the family with a medical bill that they could not afford.

Times were so tough that the only way Trippi could compete in football was for his high school coach, Paul Shebby, who later would coach another Bulldog star, Zeke Bratkowski, to gift Trippi with a pair of cleats. Trippi began his career as a punter. In a game when the center snapped the ball over Trippi's head, Shebby saw for the first time Trippi's natural running skills. Trippi retrieved the ball and weaved and juked his way through the defense for a touchdown. He became a backfield fixture immediately and forever.

All the while, Harold Ketron was whispering in Trippi's ear that a scholarship awaited him in Athens, Georgia. Trippi's father was overwhelmed that his son would be able to earn a college education. Later, following a spectacular prep year at LaSalle Academy, he got the attention of colleges everywhere, including Ohio State and Notre Dame.

His old-school father would not allow his head or that of his son's to be turned. Trippi had given Ketron his word that he would enroll at Georgia, and a handshake was as good as any iron-clad contract a seasoned Harvard lawyer could have drafted.

When Trippi arrived in Athens, wearing the Coca-Cola trousers issued by the bottler back home, he set about taking his classwork seriously. He played on the 1941 freshman team, which simulated the opposition's plays for the Orange Bowl-bound Bulldogs, Georgia's first to go bowling. Frank Sinkwich was the big star on that varsity team. Both Sinkwich and Trippi, blessed with different running styles, were mind-boggling great as tailbacks in the single-wing system when Trippi moved up to the Varsity.

With Trippi becoming a sophomore in 1942, backfield coach Bill Hartman recommended to Butts that they move Sinkwich to fullback, bringing about a "Mr. Inside" setup for the Youngtown, Ohio native who played ten games in 1941 with a broken jaw, which, no doubt, helped him win the Heisman Trophy a year later. Trippi, with his remarkable athleticism, was Mr. Outside. Georgia's offense became devastating.

Sinkwich didn't have the greatest top speed. His remarkably quick bursts from a standing start, however, enabled him to make many long-distance runs. He often broke into space before the defense could react. Trippi then became a passer, runner, and receiver. (Today he is still the only member of the National Football League Hall of Fame to have gained a thousand yards in his career running, passing, and receiving.)

Near the end of that memorable '42 season, Sinkwich sprained both ankles, which pretty much sidelined him for the Rose Bowl in which Trippi had a sensational afternoon, gaining 115 yards on 27 carries and setting up the only touchdown of the game. Coach Butts sent a hobbling Sinkwich into the game to score, which caused Trippi to say: "I thought that was the right thing to do. After all, it was Frank who led us to the Rose Bowl."

One of my favorite photos is of the two of them posing together, with Trippi's left arm around Sinkwich's shoulder in that glorious year as World

War II was raging on two fronts—Germany and Japan. Both men served in WWII. Videos of Sinkwich at the Heisman dinner in New York disclosed Frankie accepting the trophy wearing his marine uniform.

When I reflect back on Trippi's days in Athens, I can proudly proclaim that he became a good friend. There are several flashbacks to his time as an NFL great who often entertained coaching friends who were scouting college talent and had known him during his NFL days. He would often invite me to meet them. Sometimes that would include a lunch or dinner. As an enterprising sportswriter, I was able to meet many interesting sports personalities and was overwhelmed to be interviewing well-known players of the past.

When I, with an assist from Mike Fratello, of the Hawks, invited Tommy Lasorda of the Dodgers to speak to the Georgia football team in the late eighties, the colorful L.A. manager wanted to make sure he would be able to visit Trippi, his old friend.

Other flashbacks with the extraordinary Trippi:

His humor endeared him to all. He would recall that Coach J. B. Whitworth used to tell the Bulldog team, "We are taking forty players and Poss." Nobody laughed harder than Robert E. Poss, third-teamer and colorful personality. Poss, later Georgia's concessionaire, used to say about his barbecue and hash, "You eat my product and you think about me all night." That brought a big laugh from Trippi.

Often, Trippi invited me on recruiting/scouting trips to high school games in Atlanta. That meant that I was the beneficiary of a thick steak and a couple of beers after the game. I always took note of his legend, as countless fans at those games would ask for his autograph. The restaurant proprietor always asked to photograph him with staff and customers.

In his day, players did not wear face guards. A mean and underhanded player, John Henry Johnson of the San Francisco 49ers, in preseason 1955, sneaked up on Trippi from the blindside and forearmed Trippi in the face. Trippi's smashed face resulted in a lengthy hospital stay and extensive plastic surgery. While Trippi had no ties with the mafia, a certain visitor showed up at Trippi's hospital room with an offer to make retribution. Trippi said no. Later Johnson, knowing what might have been, said he owed his life to Trippi. He knew the implication of that hospital visit. The mafia loved its Italian sports heroes, principally Joe DiMaggio and Trippi.

Trippi, the ultimate competitor, would scratch your very eyes out for victory on the football field. I once asked him if he ever hunted, thinking he might, like many athletes, have enjoyed wing shooting. He said, with impactful humility, "Oh, no. I could never kill a little bird."

In his senior year in 1946, a year in which he could have turned pro, Trippi led Georgia to the national championship, playing brilliantly in a 20-10 victory over North Carolina in the Sugar Bowl, which included a 67-yard TD pass to Dan Edwards. He then signed a $10,000 dollar bonus contract to play a season of minor league baseball with the Atlanta Crackers. He batted .344. In late summer, his Georgia coach, Wallace Butts, asked Cracker owner Earl Mann to release Trippi so he could play in the College All-Star Game in Chicago. Trippi, playing in this game for a record fourth time (he would make a fifth in that game as an NFL champion), led the all-stars to an upset victory over the defending NFL champion, the Chicago Bears, 16-0. He then joined the crosstown Chicago Cardinals and led them to the NFL championship, which begs the question: has any athlete ever had a better year?

Trippi knew he could hit major league pitching from his experience in the Air Force during WWII. He could have been the first player to play both professional sports. When I asked about that, he said he would not have considered such, since "it would not have been fair to either team." In addition to being one of the greatest athletes who ever lived, Charles Louis Trippi was, above all, a team player.

Charlie Bradshaw
Has Proved That Small-Town Boys
Have the Right Stuff

In sports, there is nothing more fulfilling than to be the best of your time and to be the best that you can be. Furthermore, if one is successful in a high-profile sport, it is incumbent upon him/her to make an impact on society. An athlete's afterlife should include a resume that warrants recognition equal to scoring the game-winning touchdown.

There is no better example of the aforementioned than Charlie Bradshaw, a small-town athletic hero who—from the start—underscored all-around values and epitomized the Ancient Greek view on the significance of having both a sound mind and a sound body.

In high school in Dublin, Georgia, in the mid-fifties, Bradshaw was a member of the Beta Club and was affiliated with countless extracurricular activities; he also excelled at all sports, but particularly as a quarterback in football. He has been called the greatest football player in the history of his high school. Charlie then enrolled at the University of Georgia, where he caught the eye of Bulldog coach Wallace Butts, a taskmaster who took note of the undersized Bradshaw's tenacity, once stopping practice after a sparkling run in a high-intensity scrimmage to point out to his team, "that's the way the option should be run." What got Butts' attention was the fact that the lightweight Bradshaw excelled against bigger and stronger men.

The adjectives that are often commonplace when success is achieved are nothing new but appropriately define the character and worth of a man when it comes to competition. Determination, due diligence, second effort, overachievement, and fair play are among the ingredients that made Bradshaw an Associated Press All-America quarterback at Wofford College (1957); he was also Wofford's MVP that season as excellence in football helped usher him into spectacular achievement as a businessman.

At Georgia, he found a way to compete, but there was the issue of being undersized, which led to a conversation with Bill Hartman, Georgia backfield coach and a member of the College Football Hall of Fame.

Hartman's advice to Bradshaw: "You are going to have a difficult challenge finding playing time on this level, but you would flourish in small college competition."

A pre-season practice field injury impacted Charlie's transfer decision. Charlie chose to enroll at Wofford, and the rest of the story is one of the most inspiring college football resumes one could read.

Charlie's all-around tendencies continued at his new campus. His leadership acumen moved front and center as it had in high school and the University of Georgia. At Wofford, he was a member of the Kappa Alpha Fraternity and Blue Key Honor Society, and president of the student body—one of the most popular students on campus. Charlie was not ego-driven, simply a good guy who was motivated to give of himself.

Postgraduate achievement began soon after graduation when, following a tour of duty with the US Army, Charlie began working for a local Ford dealership. Soon his entrepreneurship inclinations kicked in as he and his teammate, Jerry Richardson (owner of the Carolina Panthers), took over a fledgling Hardee's restaurant. Charlie's business career moved upwards with alacrity.

From 1961 to 1969, he served as president of Spartan Investment Corporation, the forerunner of Spartan Food Systems, Inc. (1969 to 1984). Bradshaw then became senior vice president for Food Services of TransWorld Corporation from 1980 to 1984. He was then promoted to president and COO of TransWorld, which then operated TWA Airlines, Hilton International Hotels, Canteen Corporation, Century 21, and Spartan Food Systems.

His next career move was to return to Spartanburg, where he originated Bradshaw Investments to work with his children and teach them business skills. In 2006, he was inducted into the South Carolina Business Hall of Fame, a heady honor for a man whose playing field credentials were superb.

Additionally, Charlie is a member of the South Carolina Athletic Hall of Fame (1975). He was elected to Wofford's All-Time team, is a member of the school's Athletic Hall of Fame, and each year, the Charles J. Bradshaw Award is presented to "a senior varsity athlete whose academic, leadership and citizenship contributions at Wofford best typify the ideals of the award's namesake." Charlie received an honorary doctorate from Wofford in 1988. In April 2016, he received the "Distinguished American" award from the University of Georgia of the National Football Foundation, the nation's largest chapter.

You would expect a man with the aforementioned credentials and affiliation to be "one who gives back." Charlie has been the events chairman for the March of Dimes, a member of the Spartanburg Boys' Home, and a Multiple Sclerosis United Fund Drive volunteer.

Additionally, he received the Wofford College Distinguished Service Award and the Distinguished Alumnus Award in 1969, and was selected in 2012 as a member of Wofford's Presidential Search Committee.

Charlie, who remains a low handicapper in golf after six decades, is quick to credit the game of football for his substantial success in business:

> The most important thing I learned from football," he says, "is discipline. You cannot succeed in any venture without discipline, and I first learned that by playing football. Discipline in your work regimen and work habits will made a difference in whatever you choose to do in life. I learned more discipline by playing football than any activity in my life. Perhaps I was a better baseball player, but preferred to play football became of its many valuable lessons. I truly love the game. Today, it is a highlight of the fall season for me to watch college football on Saturday. I love the game to the extent that I sometimes sneak off and watch a high school game.
>
> Football teaches you about competition and life is all about competition. Football teaches you about winning, and we all enjoy winning. You can't succeed in business without leadership and competition. I learned that from football, which enabled me to achieve my goals in the business world. There is no greater game with more life lessons than football.

The view of officials from two universities—Wofford College and the University of Georgia—is that no former player is more deserving of College Football Hall of Fame recognition than Charles J. Bradshaw.

A Classic Derby:
Stunning Hats, Thundering Hooves, and All

LOUISVILLE—It was a classic "Run for the Roses," with the favorite American Pharaoh winning with an exclamation point and giving rise to the hopes of many horsemen that he might bring about a Triple Crown to boost interest in thoroughbred racing.

There are concerns throughout sports today. Football and basketball seem to be having the best of times when it comes to talent, fan interest, and limitless resources, but there are troubling issues away from the games. Baseball is worried about the time it takes to play a nine- inning game in this short attention span era. Golf is concerned about growing the sport at the grassroots level. General fan interest in horse racing has been declining for years. Everybody seems to think that a Triple Crown winner would make for elevated interest in the sport.

It is a fact that the Kentucky Derby has such widespread appeal that many sports fans can't wait to throw a party for their friends, socialize, and celebrate the running of the Derby and then forget about horse racing until the next Derby comes around.

Every sport offers a defining moment. A touchdown pass in the last minute of play, a homerun in the bottom of the ninth inning, a birdie putt on the last green—to claim victory. With the Kentucky Derby, it is as the Churchill Downs' slogan suggests, "The Greatest Two Minutes in Sports."

What is different about the Derby is the anticipation. The high you get when the teams come out for the toss of the coin, right on through the kickoff of a Super Bowl, cannot match the pre-race excitement of the Derby. The World Series gives you a lift, but you settle down with the pitcher throwing a pitch that is likely to be a ball or a called strike. NBA tip-offs are exciting; they showcase the best in talent, but the greatest shot of all time still results in no more than three points.

On race day at the Derby, there are thirteen races, the first at 10:30 a.m. The Derby is usually the eleventh race. There is at least an hour and a half between the end of the tenth race and the "Run for the Roses." There is no shortage of food and drink throughout the day. You can read the racing form until you are bleary-eyed and still have time to check a month's worth of emails before the race begins. The routine, however, is not the least bit boring. The festive mood, which begins before lunch, keeps your spirits moving with anticipation all day long, regardless of how you fare at the betting window.

If you have been here before or if you have witnessed it countless times on television, you are nonetheless smitten and overwhelmed with the singing of "My Old Kentucky Home." Its lyrics from another era are powerful on the heartstrings, whether you are a Kentuckian or not. No state's official song gets more widespread attention than Kentucky's—with Churchill Downs playing the tune each year on national television.

The lyrics, however, do not reflect the mood of Derby fans. Stephen Foster, author of "My Old Kentucky Home," wrote of the hard times of the pre-Civil War days. Those at Churchill Downs delightfully singing along are not thinking about 1853, when the "corn top's ripe and the meadow's in bloom, while the birds make music all day, by 'n by hard times come a-knocking at the door," Foster's lyrics proclaimed . They are anxious for their pari-mutuel decision to bring a return that causes their lady to celebrate rather than weep.

If you are positioned on the track where you can see the start and finish of the race, your emotions experience elevated stirrings. Watching the horses mosey up to the starting gate, awaiting the stragglers to join them; then, suddenly, "They're off!" Now comes the pounding of the hooves on the turf. Your heart beats along with the feet of the Derby hopefuls. Hearing the horses thunder by is part of the excitement as you survey the throngs in the infield and the bountiful hats on beautiful women, the sun glistening off the twin spires—all of which confirm that you are on the scene at the Kentucky Derby.

There is more to enjoy than the race, from the tasty mint juleps to the most striking of hats on the most attractive of women; but it's the pounding hooves that give you a sensation, an anticipation, that you don't find in any other competition. "The Greatest Two Minutes in Sports." I'm a Derby aficionado toasting that notion. Last weekend more than 170,000 at Churchill Downs were in agreement.

Vince Dooley
At Home with Touchdown Clubs
and Garden Clubs

Vincent Joseph Dooley, the Depression-born kid of Irish and Italian descent, is much more different in winter than he was in the spring of his life. That makes him as human as the rest of us.

Few have grown as intellectually as this man, who used two fortuitous developments in his life to champion the American dream. He was the beneficiary of a strict Catholic education. It was free and the sisters and brothers at Daughters of Charity and McGill Institute gave of themselves to the kids who came their way. Next, Dooley used athletics—primarily football—to advance his college education at Auburn. Enterprise figured into the next building block of the foundation of his career as he entered manhood and moved forward with the rest of his life's story. He saw the opportunity to advance his education by managing his coaching workload so that he could earn a master's degree.

That would come in handy if coaching, as planned at the outset, was to become the centerpiece of his life and career. There was an endearing sidelight that came with the classroom process—the unadulterated satisfaction that came from the pleasures of research. It was a blissful experience and left him panting for more. He became a regular at the library, which caused quite a stir when he first appeared at the UGA library in the spring of 1964. The grand old gentleman head of the Ilah Dunlap Little Memorial Library, Porter Kellam, was flabbergasted when he learned that the new coach on campus possessed a bent for the library and research. As the newest member of the athletic staff in the summer of '64, I wrote a story about Georgia's thirty-one-year-old-coach spending time at the library. The Associated Press picked up the *Athens Banner-Herald* story and distributed it on their Southeastern wire.

It was a refreshing interlude for the seasoned faculty and curious football fans, but it was not so amusing to the colorful tobacco-chewing Frank Howard at Clemson. Howard told me, "Tell Dooooooley that the library will be a nice, cool place for him to hide when the alumni get after his [anatomy]."

While he has always been introspective, Dooley is now a sage and sagacious elder statesman who maintains a busy schedule—he has never been a front porch rocker aficionado—that keeps him traveling, learning, and satiating his curiosity. The fulfillment of life for him is to stay active. While he is not a Georgia graduate, no sheepskin-possessing Bulldog has identified more with UGA's motto "to teach, to serve, and to inquire into the nature of things."

His credentials as a football coach and administrator are well-documented from games won and championships achieved, all accompanied with the enviable status that comes with an elite coaching career. His resume is chock-full of praiseworthy trappings. He won a national title and was elected to the National Football Foundation Hall of Fame, two of the highest accomplishments of his profession. Plaques for his walls began accumulating after his first season in 1964, a serendipitous one, when his upstart Bulldogs won seven games that included victories over arch-rival Georgia Tech and Texas Tech in the Sun Bowl at El Paso, Texas.

Within five years, he had won two Southeastern Conference titles and had warmed the hearts of all Bulldog partisans by establishing a 5-0 record against Georgia's cross-state rivals, which meant that he never lost to Bobby Dodd, a man whom he greatly admired and appreciated as a coach.

Then came the seventies—the waxing and waning times when the Chapel Bell rang but sometimes did not ring often enough. This was the protest era, the cloud of campus discontent— which often hovered over the campuses of universities throughout the county. The emergence of the black athlete came about in the South. Attitudes changed. Mores were different. Absolute authority went away and so did *in loco parentis*. Universities could no longer act "in place of a parent."

Dooley experienced the best of times ('71, '75, '76, '78), but the rest of the decade was, if not the worst of times, certainly forgettable, highlighted by his only team to post a losing record (5-6 in 1977). Then there was the Jan Kemp debacle when the administration bungled the handling of a faculty dismissal, which ended up in court where it should have never gotten to in the first place. Georgia's constituency has seldom been more frustrated.

Lurking in the finger-pointing gloaming and negative headlines that permeated and became privy throughout college athletics—an embarrassment to a proud university—was an oversized running back with the swiftest of feet just two hours south of Athens. His broad shoulders would bring about an end to all the feuding and carping. Herschel Walker filled seats that caused more seats to be built.

The Bulldog Nation expected four years, but in a prelude to what would soon come to campus, the Bulldogs only got three seasons from Herschel—but what a "Big Three" it was. Three SEC titles and a national championship—just a couple of plays here and there kept it from being three in a row. Losing Herschel to the USFL left Georgia fans with deep and abiding hurt. They felt they had been snookered, but like always, Dooley set about with a "que sera, sera" attitude and finished his coaching years in fine style, although it was difficult with the self-imposed academic restrictions for Georgia to compete with an edge. During this time, Dooley was giving equal time to building a classic all-sports resume that would elevate Georgia in the annual Directors' Cup standings, especially with women's athletics.

Those years segued into an issue about Vince being athletic director *and* head football coach. Joel Eaves, who in retrospect was the beneficiary of clairvoyance when he hired Dooley, noted in particular that his choice of coach "would not panic." The best thing that could have happened for University of Georgia athletics, at the time, was the hiring of Eaves. He ran a tight ship, stressing and underscoring fundamentals for everything, from coaching to strict adherence and expense accounts. He initialed all purchase orders that required the signature of the business manager. "Public relations," he often said, "comes with winning," which is why he literally despised taking members of the Board of Regents and the legislative hierarchy on bowl trips at the expense of the UGA Athletic Association.

What chapped him the most was giving elected officials complimentary tickets. He long functioned under the edict that he said he got from the man who hired him, Dr. O. C. Aderhold, which was that he would not have to "deal with politicians." The art of compromise was as likely as getting him to swallow a sword as part of the halftime show.

It came to a head when a significant appropriation was made by the legislature to the Board of Regents. At a meeting at the Georgia State Capitol that included the chancellor and Fred Davison, UGA president at the time, one of the influential members of the legislature said something like, "If we give you all this money, we will be able to get a few football tickets in Athens, won't we?" Everybody looked at President Davison, who naturally said, "Yes."

Coach Eaves was never directly told, but the Clarke County representative, Chappell Matthews, kept saying, "We are going to get a few tickets for the Tech game and put them in the right hands at the Capitol." This was "Varsity-talk," with which I was privy. Local leaders whose offices were downtown always drank coffee at the old downtown Varsity short-order restaurant.

When I told Coach Eaves what I was hearing, he virtually exploded—which brought about a meeting between him and Fred Davison, who unwittingly submitted to the showdown on the matter in Coach Eaves' office, which sent a curious message to the athletic director. He should have had the meeting on his turf. However, if there was anything that Eaves understood, it was that when a superior makes an ultimatum, subordinates—like it or not—must yield.

After reflecting on those times for many years, I have concluded that while Eaves had a point, it was an unnecessary fight. It didn't do the university any good, and it for sure didn't bode well for the athletic director who endured the behind-the-scenes enmity of the power brokers in the legislature, most of whom were all Red and Black advocates.

The conjecture here is that Davison became convinced that if football was in good shape—and he readily concluded that Vince was a hell of a coach—the main thing with the athletic director was that he was not to be so unyielding and intransigent. Just get along. My take is that it went beyond that. For all his good, and there was plenty to cheer about, Eaves just had to have absolute control. He believed that he should decide who got tickets and it went against his grain to provide complimentary tickets to the legislature.

He was the absolute boss of athletics when he took over, and that included Vince and football. One of the coach's unspoken objectives when he interviewed for the football job at Oklahoma in 1965 and caused the state to go into an uproar was that if he did not take the Sooner job (it was the recommendation of the legendary Bud Wilkinson, who was taken by Vince's management of the flea flicker upset versus Alabama, on opening day 1965, that piqued OU's interest in Dooley), he was going to make all decisions regarding football. Part of the agreement that kept Dooley in Athens was that he become assistant AD. Even back then Dooley was thinking ahead.

As the all-time compromiser, it was Vince who wanted the president to save face and who came up with the plan whereby he would become "Athletic Director for Sports," and Reid Parker, faculty chairman of athletics, would serve as "Athletic Director for Administration." Everybody in the association liked Reid, especially those who drank beer with him, but there was also enduring respect for Vince for his coaching and administrative acumen. It was an awkward situation for everybody.

Years later, when Vince and Michael Adams experienced confrontation, Vince again tried to effect a compromise, but Adams wanted Vince out and to hire his own man over whom he had complete control. Adams told a friend of mine that Adams said, "I've got the hammer and I am going to use it."

None of this is to say that Vince was never at fault, that he never stubbed his toe—while few and far between, I would say he could not have mismanaged his foray into a potential political career when he considered running for the US Senate in 1986; and later for governor when he retired from coaching in 1988.

He did not consort with sitting politicians which made them angry. Some never forgave him, but those who know him fully believe that if he had been elected to high office, he would have served ably and would have been a conscientious and successful politician.

When his days as Georgia's athletic director ended, he took the high road. He was disappointed in the decision but moved on. He delved into gardening and landscaping with the same overt commitment he had as a coach. He kept busy as a speaker, perhaps the only former coach to speak to both touchdown and garden clubs. He wrote books and he turned his home on Milledge Circle into a botanical garden.

Not only did gardening and the outdoors become a fulfilling interest; they have been healthy for him. A Marine with an athletic background, he is one of the most disciplined people you will ever meet. Doesn't matter if he is in a high-rise hotel in Dubai, when he arises in the morning, he will religiously embark on a vigorous routine of calisthenics and related exercises. With parents having passed away in their fifties, he has watched his diet, kept food and drink in moderation, and complemented everything with an emphasis on measured physical activity. Along the way, he has enjoyed a fulfilling life. The Greek principle of "a sound mind in a sound body" is a preachment he read about years ago, and he has practiced its tenets to the fullest. He developed swimming endurance in his youth and often swims as part of his daily exercise routine.

Life in Mobile, Alabama, in his formative years tells you about the making of Vince Dooley. Life was austere for his family. His mother, Nellie, was a housekeeper who stitched and sewed and cooked. His electrician father, William, saw the value in an education when he experienced a man twenty years his junior taking a position over him because he had a college degree. "You got to get some education," the patriarch always reminded Vince and Bill. Vince's parents never got beyond grade school.

Nellie Dooley was proud that his boys were able to enroll in college (Bill played guard for Darrell Royal at Mississippi State), but what concerned Vince's mother most was if there would be a Catholic church at Auburn. She made sure that he had a pair of khaki pants, white shirt, tie, and sports jacket for Mass every week.

From his dad, Vince learned the importance of keeping his word, and often advised that a commitment was a commitment. His mother was fond of saying, "Manners will take you where money won't."

Dooley grew up four blocks from the Mobile River in a house with the first floor ten feet off the ground for protection from any potential flooding. He played football in the streets, good for learning the art of making feints in the open field but more dangerous than any tackler when the opposition became a moving vehicle. He remembers once being hit by a moving car.

He and Bill were enterprisingly adventurous, often catching a freight—teenage hobos if you will—to nearby Pascagoula and Moss Point, Mississippi, which was the home of the Khayat brothers, Eddie (Tulane) and Robert (Ole Miss), with whom they had no relationship. They played in the SEC in the fifties as well. Eddie had long tenure in the NFL as a player and coach and Robert became president of Ole Miss.

Vince and Bill also found their way to an island in Polecat Bay, where their cousin Stevie, who abhorred life in the city, lived in a run-down house with a detached kitchen, where in a case of fire it would not consume the living quarters. There was no running water and no electricity, but the fishing was good. Stevie would often bring fish to the family home. Nellie Dooley was a devout Catholic, and the family, who often had to worry about paying the rent, always ate fish on Friday, adhering to the church-oriented custom.

Stevie rode out at least two hurricanes and survived a couple of floods but would not be moved. He loved his life as a hermit, catching and skinning alligators to sell their hides in New Orleans, taking the three-hour bus ride over and staying just long enough to take care of business.

The two Dooley brothers became inseparable, and as Vince remembers, "fought all the time," even when they came home from college, the elder brother always winning due to being older. But Vince could see that Bill was getting bigger and stronger and suggested that as grown men they should give up that foolishness. Nobody ever accused Vince of not being smart.

One of Vince's best friends was Bobby Duke, who would become a teammate at Auburn. They made deliveries for Sam Joy Laundry, where Duke's dad worked, and it was Duke who perhaps "saved" Vince's football career. Even today, Vince wonders what his life might have become had it not been for Duke coming by his house on the first day of football practice when he was a junior in high school and literally rousting him out of bed to make him show up for practice. With each exhortation from Duke to get out of bed, there was the Dooley disclaimer: "I'm not going to play football. I prefer to play basketball." Duke never gave in until his friend relented and left for football practice.

Taught by nuns for the first eight grades, Vince was first attracted to basketball, his favorite sport. It was Sister Patricia, an Indiana native, who taught Vince the hesitating jump shot by teaching him to jump over a chair and shoot the basketball in the process, making him one of the first basketball players in the South to learn the art of jump shooting.

Since his father had wired Hartwell Field, the home of the Mobile Bears, he was entitled to a pair of complimentary season baseball tickets. Vince seldom missed a game. Sports were a big part of his life early on.

Vince never fails to stiffen his neck with abiding respect when you bring up the name of his high school coach at McGill Institute, which was a Catholic high school. Today it is known as McGill-Toolen, and it features, of all things, the Yellow Jacket as its mascot. Vince learned many of the basic tenets of his coaching career from Coach Dicharry. One particular incident reflects how a coach's guidance can make a difference in a young man's life, something Vince has never forgotten.

The longtime Bulldog head coach will, without hesitation, tell you that he had an intense temper, with the quickest trigger. In a basketball tournament, a team from Selma had won earlier in the day and McGill was struggling in its game. A player from Selma was heckling the McGill team and Vince started up in the stands to confront "Big Mouth." Dicharry literally picked him up and took him to the locker room and later had a talk with his fiery player. When the subsequent counseling session took place, the coach advised Vince that he had to learn to control his temper. The message was, "You need to think before you act." All who know Dooley quickly realize that this lesson was well-learned for the rest of his career. That is when he learned the value that coaches can have on young athletes if they provide the right leadership.

Vince was always getting in trouble in grade school but survived without incident. At McGill, however, he was always eager to seek out confrontation until a priest, Brother Phillips, who had training as a boxer, looked him in the eye one day and said, "You are No. 1 on my hit parade." Vince knew what that meant, and while it did not turn him into a saint, good discipline and restraint were subsequently and permanently ingrained in his makeup.

Both Alabama and Auburn expressed interest in him early on, but the Alabama coaches pressured him to sign, whereas Dick McGowen, who enjoyed praiseworthy accomplishment as a player with the Tigers, was the easygoing opposite. Plus, Vince was influenced by the underdog Tigers upsetting the Tide in 1949, 14-13.

At Auburn, Dooley became a starter in both basketball and football, which led to a defining moment when he learned that there were several football players, some of whom were seeing limited game action, who were getting "fringe benefits." His rationale was that he was in reality "worth two scholarships." He went to a banker, an Auburn alumnus, in Mobile who gave him sound advice: "I understand how you feel, but in the long run, you will be better off if you get what you deserve and what you were promised." Dooley concluded that the advice was all he needed to look ahead.

It is a well-traveled story that he rode over to New Orleans with a friend and his friend's father to the 1947 Sugar Bowl when Georgia defeated North Carolina 20-10. They had tickets and Vince only had a dollar in his pocket. Tickets were being scalped for fifty dollars each. Disconsolate, the fourteen-year-old Dooley sat on a curb outside Tulane stadium and said to a New Orleans cop, "Someday I will get into that game." He would, twenty-two years later, but it turned out to be a forgettable experience with Arkansas upsetting the Bulldogs, 16-2.

There are many vignettes in our association, from the office to fishing in the Cayman Islands and international travel. In Vince's first year, the team went to a movie, a longtime tradition for all teams, but he asked me to walk with him back to the motel. It was in Columbia and he became uncharacteristically effusive, evaluating the South Carolina team and offering philosophical preachments about football. It was insightful and refreshing. I've seen him at his best in one-on-one settings. Conversely, his discomfort came about when there was a group and they asked probing questions.

I have seen him parry with the press before it became the media and realized that he never went into a press conference without being totally prepared for any question.

There were times over the years when I would complain about his lack of interaction and aloofness. He would say, honestly, "A man can't change his personality." However, he did just that. At the outset, his speeches were matter-of-fact, but as he became more comfortable before the mic, whether at a podium or on camera, there was warmth in his candor that confirmed that he was a man who had something to say and could connect with audiences.

In 2011, the Georgia Historical Society named him a trustee, quite a signature honor but deserving for this overachiever who has a passion to learn and keep learning. When the Georgia Center for Continuing Education opened in 1967, the iconoclastic director, Hugh Masters, had a slogan for all printed matter: "Learning has no Age Limit." There was a slash across the word "age." That could have been Vince Dooley's motto.

One of his favorite quotes, which he keeps handy, is that of the genius Michelangelo, who said on his eighty-seventh birthday: "I'm still learning." Vince Dooley turned eighty-seven last week.

Dan Magill
No Greater Proponent of Love of Alma Mater

Dan Magill wasn't a man of wealth, one with deep pockets. If he had been an alumnus with means, however, he would have bestowed generously from his largesse to his beloved alma mater.

Since he couldn't give to the University—the object of his genuine affection from the time he wore knee pants—he did the next best thing. He gave the University of Georgia himself. If you knew him like his friends knew him, you know that there is no way a team of exalted corporate accountants could put a value on THAT gift.

No man ever gave more of himself to his university than Daniel Hamilton Magill Jr., a Damn Good Dawg and a UGA icon who began and concluded every day of his life with Georgia on his mind. He never smote his breast about his love of alma mater; he deflected praise with jocular aplomb and authored self-flagellating humor to remind us that it takes a village to make a university reach its potential and maintain its worth. He was never ego-driven, but no 'Dog (it took him a while to identify with Dawg) ever was more service-oriented.

Magill was a writer extraordinaire. He was prolific and was motivated to "hit the nail on the head." He was not given to lengthy essays, but preferred poignant features that succinctly covered the subject, pocked with revealing facts and clever insights. What we see in *USA TODAY*, the abundant short stories, boxes, dots-and-dashes notes columns, were a staple of Magill's writing, dating back to the forties when he was prep editor for the *Atlanta Journal* and the *Atlanta Constitution*. *USA TODAY* began its approach, in part, because of technology, which has brought on the accommodation of the short attention span of today's restless society.

Magill was an advocate of packing the most information in the smallest amount of space, because he didn't have but a page and a half when he put out his sprightly newsletter, *The Georgia Bulldog*, each week to the Georgia contributors. He wanted to lionize the name of every player who made a contribution—a positive roll call of all, including the unknowns who were worthy of mention and/or praise. It was a Hallelujah chorus to those who wore the Red and Black. An advocate of prize fighting, he loved the Irishman (Dan's ancestry, by the way) Billy Conn and his short jab style of boxing. This is how Magill wrote, peppering us with coffers of stats, insights, stinging quotes, and illuminating humor.

Magill was also a gardener, promoter, and champion tennis coach. It was commonplace for this colorful and unforgettable character to take on more with each passing year. He was typically the jack-of-all-trades, but untypically the master of all.

When it comes to university life, there are doers and talkers. Teachers who love to inspire students. Administrators who are self-serving. There are those who put alma mater first and motivate others to follow in their footsteps. For those who truly contribute, their hallmark is loyalty. Magill, a Marine who personified the tenets of the motto, Semper Fi, set the finest example of loyalty to the University of Georgia when in 1989 he concluded, at age sixty-eight, that his loyal assistant Manuel Diaz was ready to become a head tennis coach. He knew that some school would eventually make Manny an offer he couldn't refuse. Magill still had a lot of years left to coach, but he didn't want Georgia to lose its top assistant.

He stepped aside to allow Diaz to become the head coach at the University of Georgia. That move was as rare as a Keystone typewriter is today. In the history of the NCAA, all sports, I bet there aren't a dozen cases historically of that kind of selfless expression and egoless decision-making. We can always raise a toast to Magill the Magnanimous.

Subordinating oneself to the best interest of alma mater is not very commonplace on a college campus. Was Dan Magill ever the exception when it came to love and loyalty to the University of Georgia!

Dave O'Brien
New England Native "Calls" the End of the Curse

FT. MEYERS, Florida—Last weekend was about as perfect as anyone could expect for spring training baseball, maybe a little on the New England side when it came to the temperatures; but the preferred dress, nonetheless, was shorts and short sleeves.

JetBlue Park, the Florida home of the Boston Red Sox, was teeming with fans accounting for all 9,900 seats at one of the most pristine and cozy ballparks in baseball. This is in contrast to what took place the week before at the new home of the Houston Astros (and Washington Nationals), the Ballpark of The Palm Beaches. It appeared that at least 7,000 of the 7,858 seats in the stadium were unclaimed—a puzzling lack of interest for the defending World Series champions Astros.

The Red Sox spring training facility is a mini version of Fenway Park with a meaningful address: 11500 Fenway South Drive. The dimensions are identical to Fenway Park at 4 Yawkey Way [now, Jersey Street] in Boston: 310 feet down the left field line, 420 feet to dead center, and 302 feet to the right field foul pole. The Green Monster here looks pretty much the same as the one in Boston. Fans sit above the imposing wall—sunsplashed in Ft. Myers, under the stars in Boston. It is a big deal here and there.

In the press box, VIP booths, and cafeteria, vintage photos recall signature moments in Red Sox history. Tributes for Boston pitchers who have thrown no-hitters dominate one section of the wall of fame. The lineup of performers of perfection includes the immortal Cy Young, who pitched for the Sox over a hundred years ago. This brings up an interesting factoid about the big leaguer who won 511 games. In 1902, he coached the Mercer baseball team before his season started. The history of moonlighting has always reflected enterprise.

In the Red Sox television booth, a familiar face and voice, that of Dave O'Brien, calls Boston games. When Dave was a kid, his father, Robert, took Dave and his three brothers to as many Fenway games as a middle-class father could afford. The family suffered through the eighty-six-year drought of not winning a World Series, from 1918 to 2004. Robert's entire life was punctuated by the "Curse of the Bambino," the sobriquet confirming the October futility of the Red Sox for more than eight decades.

When O'Brien finished the postgame show and was walking out of Busch Stadium in St. Louis on that memorable evening when Boston won the World Series in 2004, he linked up with his brothers Mark, Chris, and Paul on his cell phone. They then paid tribute to their late father, regretting that the curse did not end in his lifetime, before rejoicing in the Sox victory.

It was a moment of humility as much as it was a celebration for many Boston fans. Dave has heard story after story about grateful Sox fans who would take artifacts and memorabilia to local cemeteries where a loved one had been laid to rest.

They carefully decorated gravesites in tribute to the ending of the curse not only in Boston, but throughout New England. What made it so special was how it had come about. The Sox were down 3-0 to the Yankees in the League Championship Series but stormed back to win the pennant four games to three, an unimpeachably high moment in Red Sox history itself.

In this rivalry, the most intense in baseball perhaps, the Red Sox had often suffered heart-wrenching defeat at the hands of the Yankees, losing the American League pennant or playoffs on the last day of the season. This time the Sox were not to be denied.

Over dinner with a Sox fan and associate of Boston front-office hierarchy, John Claster, from Naples, the history of the Red Sox was replayed, including the curse—a reminder that the lore and color surrounding baseball make the nostalgia of the game alluring and unforgettable.

O'Brien's family, still keen on the Red Sox, has other rooting interests. Son Michael is a graduate of Alabama. Daughter Samantha, a graduate of the University of Georgia Henry Grady School of Journalism, is following in dad's footsteps. She has a broadcast gig for the Pacific Coast Conference. Who knows—when Dave gets long in the tooth, perhaps "Sammy" might become the first female Fenway TV announcer.

Denis Lalanne
Happy Times with the Most Celebrated
Sportswriter in France

BIARRITZ, France – This holiday paradise, which peaks in summer, has a Georgia connection in that it is the home of former Georgia football master achiever, Richard Tardits, whose remarkable story has never been told enough.

His family is one of two resonating links I have with the enclave known as the land of the "Big Fish."

Biarritz will always be my favorite international home away from home—I glory in the Richard Tardits story, and I am honored to be a friend of Denis Lalanne, one of the most accomplished sportswriters in the history of French journalism.

The narrative dates back. While Richard's story was incubating in Augusta, Georgia, where family friend Edouard Servy had settled (which would impact the life of young Tardits), I was being introduced to Lalanne.

In the late 70s, I became acquainted with the editor of *France Golf*, Dennis Machenaud. We then met at the British Open at Sandwich, England, in 1981. Because I had asked for a credential for the Open for the Athens newspapers, the assumption was that I was from Athens, Greece, which led to my being assigned a seat in the international section—fortuitously beside Machenaud.

Machenaud spoke English fluently. We had a wonderful week of conversation. At the end of the tournament, he told me about his friend, Denis Lalanne. He asked if I could help him become credentialed for the Masters. I was happy to recommend him and pleased to make the effort to assist.

My friends at the Augusta National Golf Club, bent on international hospitality, saw that the leading golf columnist for the French sports daily, *L'Équipe*, was certainly worthy of credentials. Thus began a long and warm relationship that continues today. My friend Denis Lalanne is ninety-one years of age today, but functions as if he were fifty-one, which was about his age when I first met him.

Handsome, gregarious, and clever, Denis was always lovable, introspective, and ready for good wine and conversation. He became an expert in rugby, tennis, and golf, among other sports. He covered the four Grand Slam tennis tournaments—the Australian Open, the French Open, Wimbledon, and the US Open at Flushing Meadow. He added to that foursome the four major golf tournaments—Masters, US Open, British Open, and the PGA.

When he came to the Masters, he stayed in my home. When I went to the British Open, I traveled early to Biarritz and stayed with him and his pretty wife, Collet. The mutual admiration society continues, and I am the better for it.

He is, perhaps, the greatest sports journalist in the history of French journalism. At the French Open at Roland-Garros each summer, they now give the Denis Lalanne Award to the French journalist who writes what is considered the best story on the championship.

My summer schedule for the Open championship at Birkdale a few weeks ago was such that I returned to Biarritz after an absence of a few years. I wanted to see Richard Tardits. I wanted to visit with his parents Criqui and Maurice at their home overlooking the no-holds-barred-Atlantic slamming ashore beneath their lovely cliffside home. If I had a choice of staying at Buckingham Palace or the Tardits' abode in Biarritz, I would choose the latter.

The fury of the Atlantic crashing ashore in Biarritz would make an artist of seasoned travel swoon. A meal with the Tardits is an event. You begin with champagne followed by a Spanish Rosé, followed by a French blanc, Meursault, followed by a Montrachet. How can life be any more robust and rousing?

When Richard Tardits came to Athens, my friendship with Denis Lalanne was beginning. The first summer in Biarritz, Richard's parents and Denis and Collet took me to dinner at Chez Albert down by the sea with Richard and his friend, William Tang.

A Spanish band was playing energetically and came to our table to see if we had a request. I looked at Richard and asked, could they play "Glory, Glory?" Soon, in the most improbable setting—on the shores of France looking west to America—we sang the Georgia fight song with the deepest of respect and affection.

My French connection has resonated in my life, and I will be eternally grateful that the conduit was the serendipitous seating at the British Open press tent and the glory of Georgia football. Selah!

Don Faurot Field

COLUMBIA, Missouri—It is unlikely that the Georgia players—Missouri's too, perhaps—appreciate the impact made on the game of football by the man for whom the playing field at Mizzou is named.

Don Faurot, former football coach and athletic director at Missouri, originated option football and saw his creation become the rage of the college game after World War II. During the war, service football was important to the military. Faurot taught Jim Tatum and Bud Wilkinson the formation at the Iowa pre-flight school.

After the war, Oklahoma hired Tatum, who brought Wilkinson along as his top assistant. When Tatum, who wanted to return as near as possible to his North Carolina roots, left Norman, Oklahoma after one season to take over the Maryland program, the Sooners hired Tatum's popular assistant. Wilkinson would develop one of the most successful football programs in NCAA history.

He would win three national championships and fourteen Big Eight titles. He had a forty-seven-game winning streak during the years 1953–57. His split-T option, which he learned from Faurot, was seldom tested in Big Eight competition. He walked over all competition.

In a conversation with Wilkinson years ago in Oklahoma City, he explained that his success was based on recruiting enough players to have two teams that were near equal in talent. He remarked that "the conference at that time was virtually a wind tunnel. To succeed, you had to run the football."

Nobody agreed more than Barry Switzer, who took over in Norman in the seventies, beginning an era that was similarly dominant to that of Wilkinson's. "If I were starting a football program today, I would run the option," Switzer told me in Norman last year when I visited him during the holidays.

Bobby Bowden, who came to Tallahassee in 1976 from West Virginia to take over at Florida State, said in Athens earlier in the week that the weather can often dictate your philosophy:

When I was at Morgantown, with all that snow and ice, I thought it was best to run the football. Then when I went to FSU and played and practiced in all that sunshine, I was more comfortable throwing the football. In the late eighties, I thought we were ahead of a lot of people when it came to the passing game and that helped us win a lot of championships. It was good for recruiting, too.

On Georgia's two previous trips here, I took time to visit the plaque honoring Faurot, whom I got to know when he came south in the spring to play golf in Florida. Somewhere, there is a videotape of him explaining how he came up with the idea of the option.

Before World War II, most schools ran the single wing. After the war, there was a rush to adopt the "T" formation, which was originated by Clark Shaughnessy in the early forties. Georgia's Wallace Butts was a coach whose offense flourished with the "T," but you could underscore the notion that any offensive formation would have been successful with Charley Trippi in the backfield.

Faurot originally was a basketball coach and developed the option from a simple basketball concept. The guard brings the ball downcourt to the opponent's basket with one of two options. If the defense comes out to confront the ball handler, he can pass the ball to a teammate. If the defense hangs back and gives the ball handler an opening, he takes the ball to the basket.

Faurot felt that the same concept would work in football. The quarterback comes down the line of scrimmage and cuts inside wherever there is an opening: at center, guard, or tackle. If there is no opening, the quarterback pitches to a halfback who takes the ball around end.

Variations of the old split-T option would come about with the passing of time, including the wishbone and the veer, but with so many high schools moving in the direction of pro-style passing attacks, option football has gone into great decline. All the rules favor the passing game.

Kids want to throw the ball today. Score points and keep the defense on its heels. The option has become a dinosaur, although Paul Johnson at Georgia Tech stuck with the scheme his entire career.

At Faurot Field Saturday night, the only reference to the option will be the printed program with Don Faurot's biography.

Farewell to Keith Jackson
Sage of Roopville

PASADENA, California—Late in the afternoon this past Sunday, a colony of the innumerable friends and admirers of ABC's iconic announcer Keith Jackson gathered in the Rose Bowl for a celebration of his time on earth—all convinced that in the afterlife he was looking down with a wink of approval.

The setting was surreal in that the bands were not playing, there were no pre-game warmups, and there was no raised hand in a striped shirt calling for the kickoff, which would have brought about Keith's melodious, folksy verbiage: "Yippee, we're going to play football tonight." You sensed that there was weeping in the surrounding San Gabriel Mountains, which Keith saw daily from his pool and deck in Sherman Oaks, where he lived and raised his family with his closest ally and friend, Turi Ann, whom he called the "Feisty Viking," a reference to her Norwegian ancestry.

Above those mountains, the gods of sport were gathered around a convivial table sipping Stolichnaya or Napa Valley Silver Oak—perhaps a bit of Georgia moonshine, which Keith would have mischievously inserted, as his light-hearted style was prone to cause him to do.

The lineup of eulogizers (in person and via video) included Lynn Swann, Bob Griese, Dan Fouts, Ann Myers Drysdale, Pete Carroll, Verne Lundquist, Al Michaels, Mark Spitz, Peter Ueberroth, Mack Brown, and Kenny Chesney—a "Murderers' Row" of sports royalty, all ushered front and center by Keith's longtime color analyst Tim Brant, who spoke with eloquence and verve, clarity and insightfulness, reminding us that while eulogies should be heartfelt, deliveries should be presented without emotion—family, of course, being an exception. The remarks of the male children, brother-in-law, and grandchildren were touching, but the stage presence of Keith's daughter, Melanie, wife of Tower of Power trumpeter Sal Cracchiolo, was worthy of an Emmy.

Keith's Georgia farm-boy background has always had an umbilical-like connection emotionally with this admirer, from which I proudly cannot disconnect. When you think about the icons in the business, I suspect not one rode a mule named Pearl. Not one of them knew the austerity of outdoor plumbing. Not one of them had to join the Marines to gain a college opportunity to move to a higher station in life.

Few have been as versatile as this Roopville native who was as authentic as he was talented, as humble as he was hell-bent to tell the story without compromise for truth, integrity, and fair play. "My God," he once said of the foibles of college football heroes whose faux pas in competition earned the backhand of some critics, "They are teenagers, they are amateurs. This is a college game."

I loved his sense of humor, I loved his caustic wit, and I was forever warmed by his hospitality and humility. Once I took my son, Kent, his friend Trey Jarrard, and Trey's father, Truett, to Pasadena for a Super Bowl. My son and I stayed an extra day to have dinner with Keith and Turi Ann. When it was time to go our separate ways, Keith reached into a sack and pulled out a can of smoked salmon that came from his place in British Columbia. When he caught a salmon, he looked his quarry in the eye and said, "You are a 'noble' friend." Just as he would have lovingly admired a hamper of field peas or a basket of roasting ears back in Roopville.

He smoked salmon for his friends as much as for himself and his family, a simple act of hospitality akin to that of the salt-of-the-earth folk in Roopville who have less to share but whose hearts are as warm as any he would meet on his life's journey.

When my wife and I asked him for a recipe for a tailgating cookbook, he sent this along:

"We have never had time to do much tailgating since I have been going to the stadiums of the world early for work. Very seldom do we eat in the press box, almost always we bring or order in our own food. There is a certain satisfaction to that, and I guess you have to be in the media business to understand it.

"So-called menu for outdoor dining is basically designed for the back of the boat on fishing days and sometimes for surviving ferry traffic. Start the day with a fried egg sandwich on whole wheat bread—one or two eggs flat fried, one or two pieces of back bacon or thinly sliced ham, mayo, or whatever to taste—and if you want to give it a little pop, add a slice of jalapeno jack cheese.

"Back it up with sliced cantaloupe, sealed in a Ziploc bag. Cantaloupe keeps better than watermelon, but you can do either or both in separate bags. Pepper cheese—we use Boursin with rice crackers—and Norwegian goat cheese on flat bread are great-tasting and filling for snacks.

"And if there is real demand for gusto, then another sandwich of any kind can be added. We like cold, thinly sliced strip sirloin—horseradish and mustard on small slices of a sourdough baguette.

"Top it with some real plain water. Skipper can't drink wine on our boat and it makes him cranky if anybody else does."

Keith had "feeling" for tailgating on his boat, for the games he called, for the people he loved, and for the things he liked. It showed in his work, it showed in his relationships. Many universities—like his home state school, the University of Georgia—are anchored in small towns. He felt at home in Athens, Tuscaloosa, College Station, State College, Lincoln, and most of all, Pullman, where he met his feisty Viking.

During the Christmas holidays, when it appeared that all of his home state was focused on the Rose Bowl—which he gave the stamp, "Grand-daddy of them all" —efforts to contact him reached a dead-end. I learned from a mutual friend that he was hospitalized and had lost a toe to diabetes, all of which confirmed that life's setting sun was sinking low.

I was unable to see him on that trip, as his health was declining precipitously. I could not get his take on the Bulldogs returning to the Rose Bowl, which he had listened to on a battery-powered radio when Georgia defeated UCLA, 9-0, on New Year's Day, 1943. Only the memories were left.

The reminiscing gained momentum as I thought about the times that the game of football brought us together, the gatherings when he represented ABC at a CoSIDA (College Sports Information Directors of America) convention and held court. The experts and the unwashed alike were drawn to his magnetic personality.

There was never a time when he was incompatible with the overtures from a cub reporter or a rookie local announcer who was in awe of the interviewee. This was the same man who could call a football game with Howard Cosell and Don Meredith without irritation. There was room for three voices in that booth, only because of Keith Jackson, a man who was about the game and never let his ego get in the way.

Keith would chuckle about Howard's verbosity and expressed delight in the wit and humor of Meredith. He had grown up with people who were not nuanced or connected with sophistication but were opinionated, nonetheless. After all, in Roopville there were religion, politics, and college football.

As the sun was trending downward at the Rose Bowl and the crowd was interacting and saying goodbye to family, I approached Turi Ann, who is a warm and generous person, to say farewell. The video had continued to warm our hearts in the background with still frames of Keith's life and career. Then a bagpiper's solemn notes began to merge with the shadows from the mountain. She said, touchingly, "Oh, how nice."

Someone has said that "memories are the cushions of life." While Keith Jackson's voice has been stilled, his legacy endures and our spirits are comforted by our warm memories of this big man with a big heart.

Never Doubt the Kid from Nantahala

ATLANTA—It was another octogenarian party for a good friend, and what a time it was. A smattering of superstars showed up, along with some who knew him in adolescence, some from high school and college, some from all walks of life, and the many who accompanied his extraordinary celebrity—from Hollywood to network television to the National Football League.

There were business allies, his closest social friends, and a few who knew him when he was a fundamentalist preacher's kid who was raised with the notion that if he even looked at a neon beer sign, he was committing an unpardonable sin.

Francis Asbury Tarkenton, who grew up in Athens on the other side of the tracks, learned about the cruel and cutthroat business world and the liberal social mores of a fast-moving society that became eager to see him perform on the football field, and just as eager to write big checks to hear him speak. CEOs found him to be just as adroit, creative, enterprising, and engaging in a conference room as he was in the huddle at old Yankee Stadium, where he flourished, even with Giants mediocrity prevailing.

The football world learned early on that he understood the basic principles of playing quarterback. He was in charge, and he loved it. He was the leader. He was the center of attention, and he gloried in that circumstance. It was a given—he *expected* to lead his team to victory. Never doubt the "Kid from Nantahala Ave."

His foundation was built on intense competitive drive. Those of us familiar with his life's story saw his leadership acumen surface in the 1959 Auburn game. Underdog Georgia had taken the lead 7-6 when Tarkenton's rival at quarterback, Charlie Britt, backed into Bobby Walden's punt, literally blocking the kick for Auburn, which turned the miscue into a 13-7 lead. (Auburn insiders have often asked, Why did the Tigers not call for a two-point conversion attempt at that point?)

With the lead and less than three minutes left, all that the visitors had to do on that day was kill enough of the clock to win the game and position themselves to tie for the SEC title by beating arch-rival Alabama. Auburn, in an attempt to move the chains, fumbled on a quarterback roll out and Georgia recovered. The rules of the day—one-platoon football—did not allow for unlimited substitution. For example, players who started a quarter and came out of the game could not reenter until the next quarter. This was why most teams were really two teams.

Tarkenton was on the sideline when the Bulldogs gained possession following the fumble. Coach Wallace Butts, who held contempt for Tarkenton's lack of physical confrontation (his canny quarterback was too smart for that), nonetheless believed Tarkenton was the best quarterback for a crisis moment. Charlie Britt, noted more for his defensive astuteness, came off the field.

The drive began at the Auburn 35-yard line. Tarkenton came with two quick passes to Don Soberdash, fullback out of the backfield over the middle, for 16 and nine yards, which moved the ball just inside the Auburn 10-yard line. This is when drama gripped Sanford Stadium and the record attendance of 54,000.

All of a sudden, it became excruciating. The Bulldogs were faced with a 4th down and 13 (following a three-yard loss on a halfback pass attempt and two incompletions), a winner-take-all moment. Calm, collected, and without a shadow of a doubt, the "Kid from Nantahala" used his forefinger in the grass, drew up a play, and confidently barked out instructions: "I am going to roll to the right, [Bill] Herron you block down for three counts, one thousand and one, one thousand and two, one thousand and three, and then run to the left corner of the end zone."

As you read this, let your mind's eye follow along. The Bulldog quarterback moves under measured control to his right and you see the Auburn defense begin to flow to its left. "Not to worry," was surely the collective thinking of everybody wearing blue, "we will bottle this guy up before he can do any damage." Suddenly the kid from Nantahala pulls up, looks to his left, and throws across his body (uncommon for quarterbacks of that era) to a wide-open Bill Herron who gathers in the soft toss for one of the most celebrated touchdown passes in Georgia history. Following Durward Pennington's kick for the extra point, the Chapel Bell would soon be pealing out victory for the Southeastern Conference champions.

That afternoon has become the centerpiece of Tarkenton's fabled career in which he played eighteen years in the National Football League, the most ever for a Bulldog position player. For years, he held the NFL record for pass attempts (6,467), completions (3,686), total passing yards

(47,003), touchdowns (342), and rushing yards gained by a quarterback (3,674).

Along the way, he cavorted with Hollywood celebrities, vacationed in Acapulco with Tonight Show host Johnny Carson, frequented the executive offices of the major corporations of the country, and learned to appreciate a vintage Chateau Latour. When he played for the Giants, he interacted with the power-broker CEOs of Wall Street, who were Giants fans and enjoyed having him in their company. When Tarkenton, Y. A. Tittle, and Joe Walton were not working on a concept of moving the ball via the short pass, a system that Tarkenton considers the forerunner of the West Coast offense, Tarkenton spent his downtime talking business with the elite CEOs of America.

He has enjoyed exceptional success, motivated by an insatiable curiosity, unrelenting drive, and a thick skin that enabled him to thumb his nose at his critics. He was a little man—as football went in those days—with the loftiest of goals when he became the first mobile quarterback in the NFL. His intelligence and rare instincts set him apart. He invented scrambling but wasn't proud of it.

There has never been a time when he backed away from the fundamental view that the best way to win in football is the long-held notion that you must be fluent at running the football and stopping the run. When the pocket around him collapsed, however, he was not content to take a drive-killing sack. He scrambled for opportunity, and more often than not found one.

Sam Huff, the elite middle linebacker of the New York Giants and later the Redskins, once told me,

> These players today don't know what mobile is. I mean, they ought to get out some of the films and look at Fran Tarkenton. Then they would know what mobile is. I mean nobody ever hit Tarkenton. Everybody wanted to. About the only time you could get a shot at him was when he was sitting down on the bench. Tarkenton set the standard (for a mobile quarterback). He had eyes in the back of his head. He made you play his game. He would wear defensive linemen out. He was a magnificent football player.

Tarkenton's after-football life has had him functioning as an entrepreneur as robust as the French wines he enjoys. He loves and has thrived in the role. He has created multiple companies and found ways to succeed by being what he has always been—a decision-maker who runs the show.

While he likely had the skills to run a major corporation, that would not have fit his personal *modus operandi*. He would not tread lightly if a board of directors stepped on his toes. He would not have been compatible with anyone second-guessing his business game plan. All his life, he has fought to be the leader. He's always had to be No 1. It's in his DNA.

The most fortuitous accident in his life was playing Little League baseball under Jim Whatley, who was also the Georgia baseball coach and football recruiter. Whatley, whose influence was the key to his enrolling at Georgia, saw him creating confidence in his teammates in grade school. If an infielder made an error, it was the "Kid from Nantahala," who went over and consoled the player, helping him to restore confidence and shake it off.

His rapport with what was considered—by the coaches—the second team, enabled the second unit to overachieve because of Tarkenton's defining and audacious leadership abilities. With the game on the line, the coaches knew which quarterback they wanted on the field.

There has been but one thing that has gnawed at him and continues to do so to this day, and that is not winning one of the three Super Bowls in which he played. In the mid-eighties, I took a video crew to his Atlanta office to videotape his career story, from the Athens YMCA days to the NFL. When I asked if it really bothered him that he does not have a Super Bowl ring, striking that raw nerve, he almost leaped out of his chair. I reminded him about the fact that some great players never even played in the Super Bowl, that Ted Williams never won a World Series. "I have heard those who say that I had a great career and that I should be happy...and I wish I could. But I'll tell you I can't. It absolutely bothers me, and I have not been able to live it down," Tarkenton laments.

> The sad part about it is that I don't have a tomorrow. I can't go out there at age forty-six to try to win again. I have thought about that many times. I have had dreams of going back and playing at forty-two, forty-three, and forty-six...in the back of my mind, I still think I could if someone would give me the chance. And that's sick, but that is how much it bothers me. And it will till the day I die. I'll never get over losing those three Super Bowls.

With the good fortune of spending time with the aforementioned Ted Williams on two occasions, it was easy to conclude that while Williams was disappointed that he did not win a ring—losing the '46 World Series to the St. Louis Cardinals in seven games—he believed that it was his body of work that defined his career. He still is considered by many as the greatest hitter who ever lived. Tarkenton has lately begun to embrace the body-of-work stance. He knows how outstanding his records are, and he has focused on his overachievement and his extraordinary success. (By the way, Williams thought Tarkenton got more out of his ability than any football player he ever saw.)

Once, when visiting Sonny Jurgensen in his home in Naples, Florida, we discussed his thoughts about Tarkenton's view. "What the hell does he have to bitch about," said Jurgensen, who never won a Super Bowl ring (he was on crutches when the Redskins lost to the Miami Dolphins in Super Bowl XVII) and has a fine reputation of being one of the greatest—if not the greatest—pure passers in pro football history. "He didn't play defense in those games," Jurgensen said. "How many points did [his defense] give up? How many perfect passes did he throw, that were dropped? I certainly don't look on him, and I think most people would agree, as a loser."

The "Kid from Nantahala" has experienced signature success in life, and he has enjoyed the trappings of his celebrity. An aging Robert Duval sent a video message for his octogenarian evening and so did the NFL commissioner Roger Goodell, Roger Staubach, and Archie Manning. His laconic Vikings coach, Bud Grant, ended his message with, "I love you," which overwhelmed the evening. It was Grant who defined Tarkenton's toughness on the field by saying in a taped interview, "A quarterback's greatest ability is his durability." It was simply a matter of Tarkenton not allowing for a direct hit on the field, but his attitude was as hard-nosed as any quarterback who has played the game of football.

A video clip reminded us that it was Fran who—while a host on the TV show *That's Incredible!*—introduced the world to the phenomenal golfing prodigy, Tiger Woods. *All My Children* star Susan Lucci was there to sing, with Fran's wife, Linda, "Happy Birthday."

Fran's three kids—Angela, Matthew, and Melissa—were prominent in staging his birthday bash, along with Linda, who orchestrated an unforgettable evening.

Now that he is playing the back nine of life, his legion of friends and admirers believe he should forget about any Super Bowls lost. Sonny Jurgensen said it best. "The Kid from Nantahala" has nothing to bitch about.

Greg McGarity
Hometown Boy Who Made Good—at Home

Greg McGarity's career could be likened to that of a caddie advancing into a successful realm that enabled him to buy the country club where he once toted the golf bags of established members; or maybe the kid who bagged groceries at the neighborhood store and grew up to own an entire chain of stores; or perhaps a ballpark Coca-Cola vendor who became the owner of the ballclub.

This fall marks McGarity's tenth anniversary as the Georgia athletic director. Emotionally, it was his dream job, but he never set his sights on becoming the Bulldogs' AD. "In college athletics, dream jobs may never come about," he said over a down-home meal recently as he reflected on his career path. "Because of my love and passion for the University of Georgia, I always thought about how nice it would be to return home for that opportunity, but I really didn't think it would happen."

Growing up in a college town is a blessing to many. Those who do never want to leave. If they leave, they can't wait to find a way back. That idyllic life, centered on the university and its boundless options and opportunities, impacted Greg's life as it has for so many others.

Greg's father, Stuart Sr., had a position in the office of student placement and aid; his mother, Fran, was a member of the staff under Louise McBee, who was the dean of women and later the Vice President of Academic Affairs. Greg's dad managed the football program sales at Sanford Stadium, and one of Greg's early jobs was selling game day programs.

There was an enduring musical bent in the family. Stu put together a local band to play for wedding receptions and other social events. Greg's uncle, Dr. Hugh McGarity, was director of bands at Clemson and wrote the Tigers' alma mater. Another uncle, Lou, spent most of his adult life in New York, where he played trombone in the Arthur Godfrey band, Benny Goodman's Big Band, and Tommy Dorsey's band, among others. He later joined the Skitch Henderson band for the Tonight Show in the early years of Johnny Carson.

Greg grew up on South Milledge Ave., where the McGaritys were neighbors of the Don Basinger family. Greg was friends with Mick Basinger. As youngsters they learned the finer points of tennis from UGA's Dan Magill. Greg was also a playmate of Mick's soon-to-be famous sister, Kim. In fact, Greg was the first to see Kim Basinger topless, but it was not a sensation back then. They were four years old.

Greg had the good fortune to become a protégé of the colorful and extraordinary Magill, Georgia's multi-accomplished icon. Greg's first assignment was that of a ball chaser at the tennis courts. During tennis practice, when a Georgia player connected with a ball with such erratic force that it flew out of the tennis stadium, the Georgia coach would yell, "Ball over, Greg!"

With an eagerness that brought everlasting fulfillment—protégés always want to please their sovereign—the youthful McGarity would dash posthaste into the parking lot and retrieve the ball. After all, no used tennis ball should end its life leaning against a curb in the parking lot, decreed Magill. It should wear out on the courts when it literally falls apart.

From those halcyon days, Greg would lead a consequential life in, of all places, Gainesville, Florida, changing from the red and black of his youth into the orange and blue of the University of Florida. In Gainesville, he became a close friend and confidante with, of all people, Steve Spurrier, one of the Bulldogs' all-time nemeses who had the nauseating habit of deriding McGarity's alma mater any chance he could.

A close relationship with the highly regarded Jeremy Foley, generally considered one of the leading athletic directors in the NCAA in his prime years at Florida, enabled Greg to experience an up-close-and-personal view of athletic administration. He no longer chased errant tennis balls. He sat in on facility development meetings; he often accompanied Foley on high-level hiring missions for prospective Gator coaches. He vacationed with Foley, Spurrier, and Billy Donovan, the Florida basketball coach who won two national championships. He was within arm's reach of the seat of power at a major university. That naturally led to the goal of running his own program someday.

He was learning and growing, eager to take on any assignment that would make his school a big-time player in all sports. After a dozen years, he became the beneficiary of feelers from other schools with regard to running a college athletic program. He and his wife, Sheryl, a native of Moultrie, Georgia, adjusted to Florida living and were very happy. It was a given that when retirement came about, they would have a Sunshine

State address. Greg wasn't going to take just any job, and while he didn't hold out hope that he would be fortunate enough to return to Athens as the chief UGA administrator, he thought about how emotionally rewarding that would be.

His family still lived in Athens. There was a second home on Lake Seed, in the North Georgia mountains where he and Sheryl enjoyed spending time when Florida's summer heat became insufferable. He had maintained multiple friendships in the University community and throughout the state.

When Damon Evans was hired to succeed Vince Dooley in 2004, Greg's name had been frequently mentioned as a possible successor to Dooley, but the stars did not align. Greg pretty much concluded that any possibility of a homecoming was as likely as his buddy Spurrier saying something nice about Georgia.

However, Evans' unexpected departure six years later suddenly opened the door for McGarity again. Serendipity was soon riding shotgun on his career train. This time he became the "most likely to succeed," and was hired by UGA President Michael Adams to run the athletic program that had spawned him.

Support from several corners aided and abetted Greg's candidacy. There was a sentiment for hiring a Georgia man, and he was the best one available. The timing seemed propitious. This time the stars aligned. At 8:00 a.m., August 12, 2010, he got a call from Adams, who asked Greg a simple question. "How would you like to be the next athletic director at the University of Georgia?" Greg's response: "Let's get to work."

Honoring the work ethic is one of McGarity's signature traits. He was ready to roll up his sleeves and have at it. He had experience under two highly successful and esteemed athletic directors: Florida's Foley and Georgia's Dooley. He was well-versed in all facets of college athletic administration. He was ready.

Once aboard, he set about assessing, enhancing, and improving facilities; and strengthening the administrative staff by underscoring communication, teamwork, and morale. You call him, he would call you back. You have a sensitive request, he would listen. He seldom missed a game or a meet. He often supported every Bulldog team by traveling to out-of-town competitions.

McGarity came into an environment where aloofness and heavy-handedness held sway. Harmony and morale were flagging. Greg became engaged with everybody, from the highest-profile coach to the custodians.

He sent hand-written notes of congratulations and encouragement to coaches and athletes.

As we look back on his tenth anniversary on the job, he owns an impressive box score of successes and accomplishments, headlined by football facility enhancements: The Payne indoor facility, the West End Zone expansion at Sanford Stadium, and the more recent expansion (still under construction) of the Butts-Mehre Building.

Regarding football, the chief breadwinner for Georgia athletics, the Bulldogs have won five SEC East championships, one SEC title, and they were runners-up for the 2017 National Championship; Georgia got into the football playoffs by defeating Oklahoma in the Rose Bowl. It should be noted with significance that hiring Kirby Smart was a move that may be McGarity's signature accomplishment.

A high-water mark for the home team.

Hanna Bat Company
Big League in Every Respect

With baseball season about to begin—and news breaking that Hillerich & Bradsby, the bat company, has sold its Louisville Slugger brand to Wilson Sporting Goods—rampant reminiscing has come bounding to the forefront. At least H&B didn't sell to some foreign outfit that is more familiar with sticky wickets than baseball.

No brand has ever been more prominent in sport than the Louisville Slugger. Nobody has ever been able to compete with Louisville Slugger, although the Hanna Manufacturing Company in Athens was a formidable business rival in the fifties. The Hanna Bat Rite model was popular with a number of big-league players.

Dr. Bobby Brown, the old Yankee infielder who attended medical school while he was playing baseball, remembers outfielder Gene Woodling rummaging around an old barrel of bats in an expansive sporting goods store across the street from the team hotel in Detroit. Woodling discovered a bat with the Hanna Bat Rite label. He liked the feel of the bat, paid five dollars for it, and took it to batting practice that afternoon. He hit four or five homeruns in the upper deck. His teammates tried the bat with similar success. Woodling became convinced that the bat had unusual power. "The next day," Brown said, "Our [traveling] secretary was ordering a batch of bats from the Hanna Bat Company in Athens."

It is difficult to recall the career of Brown, who roomed with Yogi Berra, without flashing back to a very humorous incident. The story goes that on a road trip, Brown was deep into a medical textbook while Yogi was passing time with his favorite comic book. When Yogi finished reading his comic book, he looked over at Brown, who was putting away his textbook, and said, "How did yours turm out?"

For years, Hanna made miniature bats, which were given away as souvenirs. Even into the sixties, as declining sales put the company in a precarious financial position, you could go take a tour of the factory and leave with one of the souvenir bats.

Dating back to the thirties, Hanna gave away miniature bats to Georgia students when the Bulldogs hosted LSU in a big game. The Tigers defeated Georgia 13-0 as they powered their way to the SEC championship. This prompted the LSU ROTC Cadet Corps to attempt to tear down the Sanford Stadium goal posts.

The Georgia students, armed with souvenir Hanna bats, took exception. The late Dan Magill was fourteen years old and saw the game. He always enjoyed recalling what he witnessed. "[The Georgia students] came on the field armed with their bats and not only successfully defended their goal posts but chased the cadets all the way to the train station at the end of College Avenue—and I was one of those brandishing my bat."

The game took place in November, a couple of months after the assassination of Senator Huey Long, once the populist governor of Louisiana. When he was governor, Long—an avid supporter of the LSU Tigers—forced the railroad to give the student body cut-rates so they could travel to out-of-town games. It didn't matter that the railroad lost money; accommodating the demands of the governor was expected. Long was a "spread the wealth" politician who championed the underdog.

Long was famous for another shenanigan, which had to do with his passionate support of the LSU football team. Night games had been established as a tradition in those years. However, John Ringling North was bringing his circus to town on a night when LSU had scheduled a home game. Huey demanded that North reschedule the circus. Unaware of Louisiana's tick law, North refused, explaining that the circus schedule had been worked out many months in advance and it would be next to impossible to make all the changes. Long then explained that the state tick law required that every animal coming into the state of Louisiana had to be treated. Long then asked North, "Have you ever dipped a tiger?"

Surely, you know the rest of the story.

Jack Nicklaus at Eighty

With Jack Nicklaus, the Great Champion, turning eighty, I am moved to reflect on his exalted career and also on his extraordinary person. His record of eighteen major championships confirms to most that he is golf's greatest champion. If you need more evidence, consider that he also finished runner-up in majors a total of nineteen times.

The distinguishing characteristic that sets him apart is his exceptional mental acuity and inquiring mind. He acquired the nickname "the Great Carnac" on the tour years ago. You could hardly ask him a question on any subject that he would be unable to answer authoritatively. However, if he had no familiarity with the subject, he was never reluctant to say, "I don't know anything about that."

His routine for years, when preparing for a major, was to spend a few days at the championship venue a few weeks prior to playing the tournament. This meant that he would practice at Augusta in mid to late March. I recall one practice round in which he engaged in conversation with a member of the Augusta National grounds crew, asking detailed questions about insecticides, when to apply and about any side effects if there were any. Go to dinner with him and he may offer an insight into a rare subject, or he may inform you about the feeding habits of the black marlin, one of which is now a trophy mount that hangs in the breezeway from the back of his house to his guest cottage.

He keeps up with the news of the day and has often been a guest of the presidents of the United States, dating back to Dwight D. Eisenhower. He votes republican because he believes that business is more likely to flourish under a republican administration than a democratic one.

Nobody who won the Par 3 Tournament on Wednesday has ever won the Masters; although, it could have happened in 1990 when Ray Floyd, the Par 3 champion, appeared to be the first until he, un-Floyd-like, bogeyed No. 17 to allow Nick Faldo to get into a playoff, and then—as Floyd would say—"gave him the tournament" by hitting his second shot into the pond at No. 11 in a playoff.

Jack never admitted to being superstitious, but it is a fact that he never played the Par 3 until after he retired from the tour. Now he trumpets the ace scored by his grandson, G. T., at the final hole of the little course last spring, his favorite Masters memory—this coming from a man who has won the Masters six times. That shouldn't surprise anyone. Family has always been his priority.

During his prime years on tour, he would often fly home from tournaments to catch his daughter Nan playing volleyball or one of his boys competing in football, basketball, lacrosse, or golf. As his grandchildren aged, his schedule became less intense, but there is plenty of competition among his twenty-two grandchildren to make it a full-time job to catch all their events. He had an almost perfect record in attending his children's sporting events and an impressive record for showing up for the games and matches of his grandchildren. Great-grandchildren are on the horizon, so the beat is likely to go on.

With Nick O'Leary (son of Nan, the Nicklaus' only daughter) playing at Florida State and winning a national championship ring in 2014, Jack made most of Nick's games. When Nan played volleyball at UGA, Jack and Barbara came to Athens to see their daughter compete.

When Nan was graduated from UGA, the Nicklaus' were our house guests. Jack had unending fun meeting and interacting with Nan's friends while we cooked Bubba burgers on the grill. "One of the best meals I have ever had," he said. We knew it was not really "compliments to the chef," but nothing could top an enjoyable evening with his daughter and her friends. Nothing resonates more with a parent than "feel good" times with their children.

Years before, after Nan had enrolled at Georgia and her parents brought her to campus, we took Jack and Barbara to the airport for their departure flight home. My wife spotted Jack wiping abundant tears from his checks as he walked up the ladder into his jet. Just like the other fathers who left their daughters that first time when they went off to college.

One weekend when he was visiting Nan in Athens, we flew over to Augusta where he was managing design work for the 13th hole. His attention to detail was quickly noted. His instructions to the golf course superintendent were succinct and graphic. He has remarkable communication skills.

Once, when I met up with him at Doral for the longtime PGA Tour event in Miami, he said: "I like your shirt, is it one of mine?" Then he reached for my collar, turned it out, and saw that it was not his brand and said, "No it isn't, damnit."

Retirement doesn't mean that he is slowing down. He has the bold and ambitious plan of raising, with Barbara, $100 million dollars for children's hospital charities. There will still be time for corporate golf and fishing for permit in the Bahamas and reading South African author Wilbur Smith's latest novel. Inactivity for Jack Nicklaus would be worse than being diagnosed with a life-threatening disease.

One special memory that will always be treasured: there was a time we visited him at his home in early January in North Palm Beach, Florida, where he hosts a tennis tournament for family and friends. He calls it "Wimbledon East." For years, he EXPECTED to win his own tennis tournament, and he would compete with the hardest edge. (He is still at it, choosing former Georgia tennis player George Bezecny as his partner for doubles matches.)

At the end of a session of his tennis tournament one day, I complimented him on the well-maintained and kempt grass courts in his backyard. "We have these courts here," Jack said. "Across the street we have two seashore paspalum courts." I nodded, but he noticed I was not sure what that meant.

"You do know what 'Seashore Paspalum' is, don't you?" I confessed that I did not. "Well," he chided. "You ought to. It is a grass that can be irrigated with salt water. It was developed by two University of Georgia scientists."

Jim Nantz
Network Voice for all Seasons

AUGUSTA— Not every announcer started out by enrolling in a journalism school and rising up through the intense, competitive ranks into network stardom. Many have, however. Others got their start in a fashion that might have turned Ripley's head, especially Lindsey Nelson, who must have spent time researching the story about Joseph and the coat of many colors from the Old Testament, since he always seemed to have a bent for sartorial splendor.

As a spotter for the Tennessee broadcast, Hall of Fame network announcer Lindsey Nelson had to pinch-hit for the play-by-play announcer who was late getting back to the booth after standing in line to use the bathroom before the start of the third quarter.

Pat Summerall was rooming with Giants quarterback Charley Connerly in the fifties when a CBS producer called to remind Connerly of his scheduled audition. The producer then suggested that Summerall come along and audition, too. You know what transpired after that.

Jim Nantz, who succeeded Summerall as the host of the Masters telecast in 1995, sounds today as if he was born talking into a microphone, his smooth, mellow, and comforting voice making him as much of the sporting scene as the competitors themselves.

Nantz, born in North Carolina, played golf well enough to letter at the University of Houston under its legendary coach, Dave Williams, but couldn't make the top five. (His close friend was teammate Fred Couples.) Williams was winning championships and sending players to the PGA Tour, but Nantz realized he was not headed for the Tour and turned his attention toward the broadcast booth.

One day while watching the Houston Open, Nantz told his buddies that he was going over to the NBC compound to seek out Don Ohlmeyer, the producer, and ask for a job. They were amused but went along to see what might take place. Nantz asked the security guard to see Ohlmeyer, who actually came out to meet whoever was beckoning. When Ohlmeyer asked what kind of job Nantz was seeking, one of his teammates shouted, "He wants to be on the air."

Ohlmeyer laughed but liked Nantz's enterprise and gave him a job driving a golf cart, ferrying the announcers, which included Bob Goalby, John Brodie, and Carol Mann, from the parking lot to the golf course. When Nantz went to thank Ohlmeyer for his opportunity, Ohlmeyer told Nantz, "You showed a lot of gumption seeking me out. If you can find your way to Dallas for the Byron Nelson Classic, I will put you in a tower and find you something to do."

Jim was already freelancing with a Houston radio station, and his career would fast-forward with all sorts of enviable opportunities until he had become a weekend fixture in our homes. NFL football, the Final Four, and the Masters dominate his annual routine. He realizes his good fortune and does not take it for granted. His cup runneth over and he knows it. "To be a storyteller who gets to call sports competition is a dream come true," he says.

"It becomes addictive and you don't want to let go. I'm not a statistician. Being a storyteller is what it is all about. The satisfaction you get when you are a link between the performer to the viewer back home is very rewarding."

By age twenty-three, he had become the play-by-play announcer for the Utah Jazz. In 1985, he auditioned with CBS and his opportunities moved forward with alacrity until he became one of the top network announcers in broadcasting. He feels more at home in Augusta than anywhere else, but understanding the sensitivity of feeling that exists in sports, doesn't forget how important the NFL and NCAA venues in particular are to the fulfillment he has gotten from his career.

With his golfing background, it is easy to conclude that his Augusta connection ranks high with his emotions and his sense of accomplishment. Late this afternoon, you will hear him sign off at the tower at No. 18 when the championship has been determined and the next thing you see on camera is him walking into the studio at Butler Cabin. We are talking about swapping his headset at the tower for a lapel microphone, making sure every hair is in place and that the knot in his tie is in perfect alignment, and collecting his thoughts for the final act of the day: co-hosting the jacket ceremony with Chairman Billy Payne.

Nantz's voice is not only rich and memorable; it resonates. Always composed and flawless, you hear it raised over the din at the Super Bowl and the Final Four, and then those moments at Augusta when he is required to whisper as the drama unfolds.

The consummate storyteller, Nantz is a nice guy with an abundance of friends throughout sports. We witness his composure at high moments, him keeping things in perspective and without ruffle, a perfect fit for his jobs.

What you don't see are the countless hours of preparation that lead to saying the right thing, in golf for example, in three seconds as the ball goes in the hole.

Jim Nantz, after getting a couple of breaks early on—including his audacious connect with Don Ohlmeyer—immediately moved to the head of the class. He knows what it takes to stay on top once you get a break— work hard, prepare ahead of time, and allow understatement to accompany your performance.

J. J. Frazier
Small in Stature, Big in Heart

GLENNVILLE—Friends, family, admirers, and Bulldog aficionados gathered at Tattnall County High School on Tuesday night to pay tribute to J. J. Frazier, Georgia's shooting star who electrified UGA's Coliseum like no other since Dominique Wilkins put his stamp on basketball in Athens.

It was easy for this community to overwhelm with its efforts to show its affection for a local hero, who is a caring and selfless young man who was raised right, acts right, and treats people right. What more could we expect of this young man who overachieves, triumphs, and prevails without ever calling attention to himself?

This factoid you may find interesting: What does J. J. have in common with Martin Luther King, Winston Churchill, Mahatma Gandhi, Napoleon Bonaparte, James Madison, Picasso, Houdini, Ulysses Grant, Lawrence of Arabia, Aristotle, Spike Lee, and Ralph Lauren? J. J. is taller than all of them.

You remember Spud Webb, the 5-7 guard for the Atlanta Hawks? He won an NBA Slam Dunk Contest. Listen up NBA, J. J. has as much on the ball as Spud. You better check out J. J.'s heart.

Driving to Tattnall County from the "classic city" takes you down the backroads, which allows time for reflection. Highway 15 ushers you from Sparta to Sandersville to Wrightsville, then 57 from Kite to Swainsboro, from Metter and Reidsville to Glennville—along the way, you are reminded that folks in small-town Georgia know about J. J. They can close their eyes and hear Scott Howard singing out his name over the airwaves as another three-pointer arches off his left palm, and like rolling down a rainbow with alacrity and aplomb, the ball flows into the net. Another signature moment for the Bulldogs' shooting star. When he is on his game, his work becomes poetic.

From Rabun Gap to Tybee Light, from Tallapoosa to Hahira, Bulldog fans love J. J., the man of the trey! Those without Georgia on their mind, take note, too. One day my phone rang and the voice on the other line said: "I have seen some outstanding athletes in my time, but I have never seen a more exciting player than your little guard. He is amazing, and when he takes over a game, it is a joy to watch. Such charisma, such a competitor. I really enjoyed watching him play." The caller was former Tennessee football coach Johnny Majors.

Left-handers or southpaws are always intriguing. Sandy Koufax, Kenny Stabler. Babe Ruth, Ted Williams, and Ty Cobb. Stan Musial, LeBron James, Gale Sayers, and Reggie Jackson—but not just athletes. What about this blue-ribbon list of portside virtuosos? Alexander the Great was a lefty. Emperor Charlemagne, Michelangelo, Leonardo da Vinci, and Rembrandt. Those of late include presidents George Herbert Walker Bush, Bill Clinton, and Barack Obama. You can add to the list Julius Caesar, Oprah Winfrey, Morgan Freeman, and Richard Pryor.

It was a memorable night. Greg McGarity and Mark Fox were there. Judge John Ellington was eager to drive down from Tarrytown to pay tribute. Matt Sellars, J. J.'s high school coach, came to announce that Faith Baptist Christian Academy had retired J. J.'s jersey, No. 24. Governor Nathan Deal was the keynote speaker. A busy man, the governor was eager to make space on his calendar to participate in the evening.

No organization is more castigated than the NCAA, but it is appropriate that this governing body gets a pat on the back. The only place the banquet could be held was Tattnall County High School. The night of the banquet happened to fall in a "quiet" period, which meant that a wavier had to be granted so Mark Fox could attend.

When Mayor Chris Roessler wrote a sensitive letter to the NCAA, informing the organization that the only place big enough to hold the event other than Tattnall County High would be Savannah, which is an hour way, the NCAA granted the wavier. Let's hear it for J. J. and his hometown, but let's offer a round of applause to the NCAA as well. "J. J. Frazier Day" will forever be memorable for a deserving Bulldog athlete, his family, and his friends.

The affair ended at dusk. You could hear a whip-poor-will in the distance, its mournful sounds signaling that the day had ended. But a new day is beginning for J. J. Frazier, whose life will resonate in some community where his good works will always make someone's day.

Joni Taylor
Teaching the Finer Points of Basketball
and Life Lessons as Well

Sometimes your emotions betray you. You sense that a person has extraordinary qualities, but after plumb bobbing and further review, you find that all the dots, which might be superficial, don't connect.

This leads to the realization that what you see is often not what you get. However, I am happy to aggressively creep out on the limb with confidence that I am secure in submitting to rave review about the Lady Dawg basketball program. It is not premature to sing the praises of the precocious coach, Joni Taylor.

People of distinction, or those moving in that direction, have multiple qualities that reveal a specialness that bodes well for the future. That they know what they are doing becomes obvious—mainly because the results confirm that they are not following a path of self-aggrandizement. In Taylor's case, the evidence is overwhelming that she can recruit and coach.

If you begin with a bio and stat sheet, which are very good places to start, you see the confirmation of accomplishment early on in her career. Taylor is a native of Meridian, Mississippi, which brings front-and-center confirmation that she knows about the cynical world in which we live. Not everyone accepted her; not everybody was willing to appreciate her without reservation. She knows about the second-guessing world we live in, but it only made her strengthen the objective of being the best that she could be and aim to accentuate the positive.

Not everyone gets to enjoy an up-close-and-personal outing with her. If you were to have that experience, you would come away charmed, enlightened, and uplifted. First of all, she has the looks and the personality that puts all at ease. She disarms "Doubting Thomases" with her compelling presence. She has a regal bearing and is imbued with altruistic objectives.

She has a simple philosophy—first and foremost to recruit young girls to help her win basketball games. Life is competitive, and Taylor wants her players to enjoy the rewards of success, but also give back. You give back by developing an affinity for team, alma mater, and community. You honor scholarship and citizenship. When life deals you a lemon, you turn it into lemonade.

In essence, she wants them to be clones of herself. She would never suggest such, however—just too modest. One look at her and you understand why she was homecoming queen at Meridian High. She was Player of the Year in Mississippi, and a resourceful and overachieving forward at Alabama under the accomplished Rick Moody. She was as much about off-the-court conduct as she was on court—three-time SEC Community Service member in college, earning a postgraduate scholarship for the Southeastern Conference for her community service record. Life was good when she was a student-athlete, and she aspires for her players to enjoy the same experience.

She had such a good time on campus that early on she made the decision to become a coach. She knows the influence that a coach can have on the lives of young people. "There is more," she says, "than winning games when you are a student-athlete."

If you probe who she is, you quickly learn that she is all about family. Her parents, Dr. Hargie and Jonas Crenshaw, are structurally involved in her life, mainly because her high-profile job as a coach means that she has to have help with her daughter, Jacie Elise. You see them sitting behind the Georgia bench as often as they can get to town from Meridian. While Darius, her husband, pitches in, he has a professional commitment, too. He is an assistant coach with the WNBA Atlanta Dream.

The dream team objective at home with the Taylors is that everybody is having fun, everybody pitches in, and through it all, family has priority. Her players get to see Jacie Elise when she comes to practice and when they go to the Taylors' for socials.

In her first season, Joni led the Lady Dawgs to the NCAA tournament. She won the Maggie Dixon Coach of the Year Award, an honor that goes to the best rookie coach in the nation.

She now has her team ranked No. 18 in the country with a 20-3 record. She has an old-shoe fit with those who are important in Georgia basketball. She is giving and forgiving. Dale Carnegie would love and respect her just like the countless big-time women's basketball coaches across the country do. However, they are understandably envious.

They know the Georgia boss has the right stuff.

Kirby: Familiarity Engenders Respect

Iconic coaches traditionally were referred to as Coach Butts and Coach Dooley at Georgia, Coach Bryant at Alabama, Coach Dodd at Georgia Tech, and Coach (last name) throughout the profession. Players were known by their last names, primarily. Trippi and Sinkwich, for example. Sapp, Tarkenton, and Dye. Even Catfish Smith, who would be known today as "Catfish," was referred to by both his surname and his given name. Then along came Herschel. And now we have Kirby. The returns are early, but it appears that the Georgia head coach will be one of those "first name" icons who will be a revered first-name personality. Some of that is because of today's informal world. Nobody, other than colleagues and close friends, would have referred to Georgia's exalted statesman, Sen. Richard B. Russell, as "Dick." However, during their time in the US Senate, Saxby Chambliss, and Johnny Isakson were called by their first names by staff members. When I was with them in their offices in their prime years, it was amusing to hear "Saxby" and "Johnny" used to address the two senators. This latent informality is in no way a lack of respect, but rather a singularity that reflects high regard.

When Kirby Smart was hired to coach the Georgia football team, any skeptic who would have forecasted failure in his future, would have been be summarily castigated as someone without merit or credentials. When it comes to clairvoyance, there are no reigning palm readers with a perfect box score, especially when it involves football.

Even Nostradamus, with his canny infallibility, never ventured into the college football forecasting arena. If he had, that would have likely brought blemish to his record. If you look through history, who out there was a wizard and had a successor who became the headline equal of his predecessor? Successful coaches seldom beget successful coaches.

Let's start with Vince Lombardi. None of his assistants brought about any litany of titles. Gene Stallings was the only Bear Bryant disciple to make any noise, and he was fired a couple of times along the way. From Bear Bryant to Nick Saban there was one highlight era when Gene

Stallings won a national title in Tuscaloosa in 1992. It took three hires at UGA to bring about a championship after Dooley retired.

The classic exception was Bob Devaney and Tom Osborne at Nebraska. After winning two national championships in a row, Devaney, who had planned to retire, backtracked with the objective of winning three consecutive national titles. He asked Osborne to wait one more year. The Cornhuskers were unable to pull off a three-peat and Osborne took over. It appeared for a while that Osborne would not be able to win a championship—it took him twenty-one years to win a national title. He ultimately won three, but in Lincoln, the railbirds were in un-retreating doubt for the longest time.

I got to know both Devaney and Osborne well and am keenly aware that Devaney worked unceasingly to help Osborne. There was no rivalry between the two men. Ofttimes, the successor to the successful coach—the icon—doesn't have the right stuff. Then there are those cases when the iconic coach's shadow becomes a problem for the successor, especially if he remains on campus.

Except for Jimbo Fisher, who won the national championship at Florida State in 2013, there are not an abundance of Nick Saban protégés out there making waves. Then there was Glenn Edward "Bo" Schembechler of Michigan, who would be described as "great" in many Big Ten circles. Bo was the head coach in Ann Arbor for 21 seasons and won 234 games. In 16 seasons his teams finished in the top ten, winning or sharing 13 conference championships.

Schembechler, who had difficulty winning the Rose Bowl (2-8 record all-time), never won a national championship. That doesn't mean that he wasn't among the elite coaches of all time. Nick Saban is obviously the most accomplished coach with his noteworthy success, but that doesn't necessarily make him a fundamentally better coach than Schembechler. If you are a fan, however, do you want the most fundamentally sound coach or the coach who wins championships? The answer becomes obvious.

You often hear about the "It" Factor. Bear Bryant had it, Saban has it, and Georgia partisans believe that Kirby has it. If the 2017 season is any barometer, then there is reason to believe he does.

There was disarray when he arrived. This is not to find fault, but to identify the problem. There was disharmony with Mark Richt's last staff. Jeremy Pruitt, a coach who gets high marks in the trade, saw the potential at Georgia and influenced Richt to consider some elements that rubbed some of the staff the wrong way. Even so, the Bulldogs were winning games, much of it because of Pruitt's effective defenses.

Nonetheless, when Kirby arrived, a lot of things needed fixing. He began with attitude. To be a winner you have to think like a winner. You must develop confidence that you can compete with anybody. Winning means that work ethic must be underscored constantly. You must work hard to gain the edge.

However, in the transition season of 2016, there were "Doubting Thomases" in abundance. It was not an easy ride for the alumnus head coach. The players did not buy into his preachments right off, and the situation was exacerbated by having to bus out to practice every day to a temporary practice field on South Milledge Ave., near the community of Whitehall. That alone was a negative of profound influence. A hot and sweaty twenty-minute ride on a bus at the end of the day was a negative highlight among a number of negatives. However, the good news was that the temporary quarters brought on by the building of the new indoor athletic facility (which became the "House of Payne," named for William Porter Payne, letterman under Dooley, and William's late father Porter Otis Payne, letterman under Butts) would move Georgia to the head of the class when it comes to indoor facilities.

As soon as Kirby's wife Mary Beth began house hunting, Kirby was preaching to one and all about, Georgia's woefully inadequate facilities. He told a group of potential donors in Atlanta that "We [staff] may be able to outcoach a few teams, but we sure can't 'out-facility' people." Even when the "House of Payne" and the West End Zone projects were in place, he was asking for more.

He was not like a *nouveau riche* wife embarking on constant spending sprees to confirm her wealthy status. The better the facilities, the better you recruit; and if you want to create a foundation for success, you have to compete with the best. Kirby had confirmed after the 2018 playoffs that Georgia was in a "good place so far," but there was more to get done.

"Kirby" won't be satisfied until the chapel bell rings following the last playoff game in January.

Dr. Leah Brown
Athlete, Patriot, Doctor, and Humanitarian

In Phoenix, a desert town where the temperatures can be overtly compromising in the summer but segue into an oasis in the winter, there is a Georgia connection with Dr. Leah Brown, an accomplished orthopedic surgeon who was an All-America gymnast at the University of Georgia with head-turning credentials that bring warm smiles from all who know her.

If we still had town criers, they would be breathless by the time they shouted out the good news about Leah's life and work. However, her story is not complete—there is a life yet to be lived—but anyone would find her past compelling. You discover that her goals, accomplishments, and agenda are extraordinarily exceptional.

Leah's medical credentials continue to gather momentum. Where she has been and what she has accomplished bring rave review but leave one keenly aware that the best is yet to come. In your mind's eye, you see her brilliant performances for the University of Georgia gymnastics team (a fourteen-time event All-American), and you reflect on her resume that speaks to medical excellence, altruism, character, and service above self.

Her mother integrated the Charlotte, North Carolina school system. She knows the thrill of victory; she knows the agony of deceit—all of which have given her perspective and balance. However, the cruel world out there has met its match when confronted by this remarkable and versatile UGA graduate.

Leah volunteered for two tours of duty in the Middle East. Let it be known that she didn't have to go. She doctored the wounded and dying—not just the victims, which often included many of her friends—but the perpetrators as well. She wasn't opposed to such a humanitarian act, but it was nonetheless perplexing and explicitly convincing that war makes no sense at all. Her presence alone made Afghan women experience empowerment firsthand, Leah quietly making a difference, which has always been her *modus operandi*. A doctor makes lives better, children are comforted and healed—and a woman makes it happen. That sends a powerful message, but in parts of the Middle East, it is often like a soft rain shower in the spring—evaporating almost as quickly as it brings about its blessing.

With an introspective personality that connects with others, Leah has always had a bent for altruism, love of people, and a giving of self. She is about loyalty among other feel-good attributes. She will, on a moment's notice, fly across the country to Athens when her alma mater calls. "We are family," she defines her commitment to UGA. "I love the University of Georgia." She was a showcase student-athlete, and she is now a showcase alumnus.

When you visit her resume, respect hurtles upwards. Encores of hosannas ensue. In conversation, she is often characterized by understatement, as if what she is doing with her life can be done by others easily and that is no big deal if you refuse to "hide your talents under a bushel." She is only doing what she expects of herself and what she was taught growing up.

At UGA, she helped her team win two gymnastics conference titles and laid the foundation for all those forthcoming national championships. She was the first gymnast in NCAA history to score a 10.0 in her initial collegiate meet, and was the first Georgia freshman to win the SEC all-around title, which came about in 1994. She graduated in 1998 with a degree in genetics. She gained her medical credentials at Ohio State and the Cleveland Clinic Foundation.

When she officially became Dr. Leah Brown, she then signed up for two tours of duty in Afghanistan as an orthopedic surgeon with the US Navy. She was awarded the Bronze Star for her humanitarian efforts of treating women and children in Afghanistan. Wherever Leah Brown goes, honor is sure to follow. Makes you wonder why she wasn't the first Navy SEAL.

"It was a privilege to take care of them and to provide medical care to those deployed to Afghanistan," she says. "The military is an incredible entity. It is an experience that I think everyone should have because of the camaraderie and teamwork. I grew up in a family where a commitment to your community, your country, a commitment of service was always stressed. I always thought serving my country would be a pretty cool thing."

Mark Richt
A Popular Coach Segues into a Broadcast Studio

MIAMI—Mark Richt still has that boyish look—that genial countenance that has always characterized him. No man has ever had a more inoffensive mien than this Nebraska-born, Florida-raised football coach with a missionary zeal and do-right-by-others lifestyle.

It was good to be in his company again as we met for breakfast at the Green Street Café in Coconut Grove, which reflects a tropical look. Abundant palms, aging oaks, and "smiling" bougainvillea dominate Miami's oldest neighborhood. Coconut Grove has a rich heritage. It is where Richt and his lovely wife Katharyn have lately found solace and peace, even in the high-strung, controversial environment of football.

He smiled a lot, reminiscing about Athens, reflecting on being a grandfather and "having nothing to do for the first time in forty years." As he was settling in for bacon and eggs at a popular restaurant with a collegiate feel, a diner came over to speak to him. "Coach, I have always appreciated you," said Erik Compton, a Miami native who earned a golf scholarship to the University of Georgia after having had a heart transplant. People feel good around Mark Richt. They enjoy being in his company.

He was the perfect host following a hospitable meal, showing his guests his living quarters across the street from the restaurant. The Richt address is spacious and smart. There is a becoming deck, framed by verdant greenery off the top floor. Excess vegetation blocks the view of the Miami skyline, but cozy chase lounges, bright sunshine, and ambient breezes reflect that this spot has become his comfort zone.

The family-oriented Richts have never been heavy into social outings—but they do socialize because they enjoy entertaining their many friends. They can grill out and watch SportsCenter in the best of rooftop environment. A Miami Hurricane aficionado introduced the coach to high-end Cuban cigars. If this clean-living man has ever had a vice, we do not know about it. An occasional stogie on the deck, with the moon over Miami, should not bring about any rebuke from any corner.

I did not bring a pad and pen. No tape recorder and no football questions. I simply wanted to enjoy a relaxed breakfast with him and Katharyn and our friends, Matt and Jenny Brinkley, who joined us. With so many relatives back in Georgia, I was curious if he might reset roots somewhere in the state. Didn't ask, however. This was a renewing-of-friendship outing. It would have been in bad form to interview a man who has answered enough questions. He has earned his privacy, and I chose not to intrude.

However, I did privately reflect on his Georgia past, which at one time bordered on golden. The measured view is that he won a lot of games and a couple of championships at a time when the money was trending toward over-the-top. While he was never motivated to become a rich man, financial success does make for easy living in the sundown years. His retirement is favorably fixed. A coach today is like a .240 hitter in baseball—hang around long enough and the bottom line smiles on you.

Richt has "done some" television, which makes one wonder if he and the camera might form a partnership. He has a pleasant voice, a winsome smile, and a smooth delivery.

When Richt arrived in Athens, UGA had gone through two coaching changes following Vince Dooley's retirement. The teeth of longtime alumni were being set on edge with championship shortcomings becoming an annual episode. When Richt's 2002 team defeated Arkansas in the old Georgia Dome to break the drought, it appeared that Georgia's program had few limitations. He would claim another championship in 2005. 10-win seasons became expected. Time often runs out on all coaches, however. In today's world, you have to win big. Then you have to top yourself, which is hard to do. When Richt departed Athens, there were many devout Dawgs who hated to see him go—even when challenged with the clamoring that change might make a difference.

I'm not sure what his self-appraisal would be, but Richt's resume reflects impressive highlights. He was the offensive mastermind during Florida State's high-profile run under Bobby Bowden. FSU was among the first to employ the hurry-up, no-huddle offense. "During Mark's time," Bowden once said, "we had some great athletes on offense, but he was very creative with the hurry-up offense which gave us a big advantage." His offenses set records in Athens, and he became Georgia's second winningest coach of all time.

I have always been happy to note that Mark Richt never embarrassed the University of Georgia. His resume is replete with big games to remember along with two SEC titles to toast.

I have always been glad he came Georgia's way.

The Masters Finds Another Star

AUGUSTA—It was a classic Masters, made so in part by a young Texan with class, manners, etiquette, a sense of place, a soft-spoken style, and a boyish smile, all of which will make him a popular champion who will never have to worry about making his Visa card payments.

Jordan Spieth looked good and played well in winning the 2015 Masters. His peers had been thinking about their final year in college. Fraternity parties, that last football season of their campus days before finding a job. Fun and games were still very much a part of their lives.

What's on Spieth's agenda? Primarily the US Open at Chambers Bay in June, the British Open at St. Andrews in July, the PGA at Whistling Straits in August, and what he will order for the Champions Dinner, which he will host at Augusta a year from now. It was a fellow Texan, Ben Hogan, who originated the Masters Championship Club, and you are probably guessing—as am I— that there will be barbecue on the menu when Spieth picks up the tab at the Augusta National a year from now.

Life is different when you are an especial talent. Before his first prom, Spieth was playing in the Byron Nelson Classic in Dallas. Sage observers were predicting back then that the golfing world should keep an eye on him. *Sunup Monday, he was the toast of the golfing world.*

With the pressure to perform and meet all the demands in his life, his patience will now be tested. The irritation factor will accelerate, but I see him as a champion in the mold of Arnold Palmer and Jack Nicklaus, with an ability to control his emotions and not allow people and circumstances to get under his skin. He will conduct his life with an emphasis on avoiding controversy. He won't be short with the media. He won't throw a club in anger, which is something that some champions have not been able to get out of their systems.

Then again, we should remember that the world and its demands make life a challenge to manage. It takes a certain amount of competitive arrogance to compete at the highest level. Some say you don't exceed without it. The exceptions come from those select champions, like the aforementioned Palmer and Nicklaus, who were always under control.

I remember the scene when Ken Venturi dramatically won the US Open at Congressional in 1964, playing the final 36 holes gallantly in the face of a heatstroke. At the end of the round, Venturi was taking respite under a shaded tree, weak and dehydrated, when slipping into view of the television camera was Arnold Palmer to offer congratulations. Venturi did not like Palmer, who with his remarkable play kept Venturi from winning the Masters on two occasions. Something tells me that Spieth will be an Arnold Palmer, but his life is about to change. Here's to precociousness segueing into seasoning and a life well-lived.

In Dallas, Spieth has a laid-back, humble reputation that would suggest that he has his feet firmly in place for the forthcoming public onslaught. The Tonight Show will be calling. Friends will be calling. Teachers at Jesuit High in Dallas will be calling. Charities will be knocking on his door. Corporations will be ringing him up for endorsements. His agent will be overwhelmed. Life will never be the same, but the forecast from those who know him is that he will be able to handle it all, just as he managed himself around the Augusta National Golf Club this week with aplomb.

Not overpowering off-the-tee, his short game with the deft touch is what sets him apart. His driver was sometimes wayward, but he has plenty of assets: golf course management, stiffening composure in the face of pressure, a champion's demeanor, and an ability to connect with the fans who follow him. There is no chip on his shoulder, but there is a grand opportunity to win multiple majors.

A fellow Texan, Jim Nantz, said late Sunday that Spieth represents the next generation of golfing greats. He just might lead the US to dominate world golf again. The Masters champion has a modest bent—how nice!

Ransom Jackson Made
Playing Games Look Easy

Yesterycar always stimulates nostalgic reminiscing and often makes us pine for our good old days—when we were young and our heroes were young; when the world was uncomplicated, when traditions were not messed with, and when we took fulfilling pleasure in making do.

For those Southwest Conference aficionados who have deep ties to the past, there is nothing like the times when Texas and Arkansas fought it out annually for the Southwest Conference Championship and to become the host team in the Cotton Bowl.

The last year of the old Southwest Conference was 1996. Anybody born that year would now be a college senior and almost old enough to buy a beer legally. For those in that age group to remember the glory days of the old SWC, a bent for history would be required. Even the many who pursue a degree in journalism would have to google the names of players like Sammy Baugh, Davey O'Brien, Bobby Lane, Tom Landry, and John David Crowe to learn about those heroes of the past.

Those with seasoned memories of those days would also likely have to engage the internet to learn about a player who owns one of the most distinguished factoids in Cotton Bowl history. Ransom Jackson's singular record might even stump historian and Southwest Conference aficionado Dan Jenkins. It is a unique circumstance that is surely a favorite of trivia advocates. Jackson's record is not likely to be broken, although one could assume that it is possible, but certainly not under existing eligibility rules. What Jackson did was play in back-to-back Cotton Bowl games with two different teams. In addition, he had the rare privilege of playing for two Hall of Fame coaches: Dutch Meyer at TCU and Dana X. Bible at Texas.

Owing to World War II and a father who was fascinated by airplanes, Jackson, a native of Little Rock, Arkansas, signed up for the V-12 program while a freshman at the University of Arkansas. (There were no similar Air Force programs that he would have preferred, given his boyhood study of US German and Japanese aircraft, influenced by his father who had a deep and abiding affection for aviation.) Jackson immediately began making $50.00 monthly and "had money to spend" after the government took out $18.75 for a war bond.

Almost overnight, the navy sent him to Texas Christian University in Ft. Worth to fulfill his V-12 obligation. The only issue was that he had to wear bell-bottom trousers. "That was worse than having to take calculus and physics," Jackson laughs.

TCU, he remembers, was very small. "My guess," he says, "was that there was only about 1,500 students and half of those were navy guys. I remember that there was no more than about five buildings on campus." Dutch Meyer, the innovative football coach, recruited Jackson for football based on need. "We need you to come out for football," he told Jackson in plainspoken language. "Coach Meyer was a small man, but he had a deep, authoritative voice. It was like a command, so I went out for football," Jackson recalls.

Meyer put him at halfback and soon learned that his newest player had exceptional punting skills. "I didn't play high school football, so the first game I ever played in my life was at Kansas. I punted six times out of bounds inside the ten-yard line and had one punt that rolled dead at the one-yard-line," Jackson remembers.

At a pep rally at the administration building the next week, the President of TCU was the emcee and suddenly called to Jackson to join him on the steps of the building whereupon he lauded Jackson as the key player in the victory over Kansas. Jackson was flabbergasted. It was the beginning of his walk to fame as an athlete.

Years later when he reminisced about his days with Meyer at TCU, he recalled that the Horned Frogs had less than twenty players out for football: "No more than sixteen or seventeen," Jackson says. He agrees with the notion that Meyer came up with the spread formation in response to there being so few players in the lineup. "He spread players everywhere," Jackson recalls. "We ran everything from the single wing to the double wing to the spread. We finished with a 7-2-1 record and got to the Cotton Bowl because we were able to beat both Texas and Rice in the rain. This band of brothers were overachievers who won the Southwest Conference Championship.

The insufficient numbers, personnel-wise, caught up with TCU in the Cotton Bowl, where the Frogs were overmatched by Oklahoma A&M. The Aggies, as they were known then, shut out TCU 34-0.

Little did Jackson know that soon afterwards he would be moving on to another campus, this time to Austin and the University of Texas. "The navy," he says, "shut down the V-12 program at TCU and moved the operation to Austin."

It wasn't long before another recruiting pitch came Jackson's way. This time it was from Dana X. Bible, the Longhorn coach who, like Meyer, was another smallish man with a deep voice. He called Jackson into his austere office and began another one of those dissertations based on need.

"No sir," Jackson rebutted as soon as Bible's football invitation was extended. "I am in the navy, the classwork is quite challenging, and I get up at 5:30 in the morning. I don't have time for football." Bible, sounding like Dutch Meyer, said, "I saw you play last year; we have a new quarterback and I think we can win the conference."

At that juncture, Jackson broke in with, "I have done that." Bible stared at him and then repeated, "We need you to win the conference." With that, Jackson got up, said, "Yes sir," and headed to see the equipment manager.

Texas, as Bible had told Jackson, was good enough to win the conference championship, posting a 9-1 overall record. The Longhorns hosted Missouri in the 1946 Cotton Bowl, winning 40-27. Ransom "Randy" Jackson, the reluctant football star, became a member of two conference championship teams by playing football in his spare time. He also played baseball. More about that momentarily.

At Texas, the quarterback Dana X. Bible had referred to was none other than Bobby Layne. Layne had been allowed, because of wartime rules, to play as a freshman. Bible, however, was taking no chances, realizing that Jackson's experience and his effectual punting ability made him a valued team member.

"Bobby Layne was a special athlete," Jackson remembers.

> He was a terrific football player. He was a passionate competitor and a fine baseball player, too. He was a pitcher who had a truly great overhand curve ball. He had an uncanny ability to break the pitch off into the dirt, often in front of the plate. Everybody would take a wild swing at Lane's curve, striking out most of the time. Not sure if that would have worked in the major leagues, but a lot of people thought he was a good enough player to play in the majors. He certainly was the kind of competitor who might have found a way if he had chosen baseball for a career. As it turned out, he didn't do too bad in the National Football League. Years later it was fun following Layne's career with Detroit and Pittsburgh. When I

heard about his late-night carousing as an NFL quarterback, it made me think back to his days at Texas. He was the only player who broke training rules.

Ransom laughs.

For most of the players, playing in a bowl, it was just playing in another game. It meant more time on the practice field and there was little reward, although it resonated emotionally to play in front of 37,500 in the '45 Cotton Bowl and 46,000 a year later. Jackson remembers receiving a bowl watch at each game. "That was nice, and I appreciated them as a keepsake. Playing professional baseball all those years, there were so many moves that they were misplaced and eventually lost," Ransom says.

As a baseball player in college, Ransom led the Southwest Conference in hitting all three seasons. The Cubs, with whom he signed, were among several big-league clubs who took note of his baseball ability.

When he got to the majors, he would stay for ten seasons, playing in two all-star games (1954, 1955). He hit 103 home runs with 415 RBIs and a batting average of .261. He is a member of the University of Texas and Brooklyn Dodger halls of fame.

Jackson, who adopted Athens, Georgia, as his home after retiring from major league baseball, was a gifted athlete whose natural abilities were such that he competed so effortlessly that he developed a reputation for underachieving. His laid-back style camouflaged the competitive embers in the fire in his belly. While his career is not storybook, it is one that includes milestone achievements and celebrated affiliations that countless athletes would kill for.

In addition to his SWC back-to-back Cotton Bowl resume, Ransom was the infielder who the Brooklyn Dodgers chose to replace the dynamic but aging Jackie Robinson, whose considerable skills were in retreat.

While he does not have Cooperstown credentials, Ransom's major league career in the fifties is noteworthy. It linked him with some of the most memorable names and times in a decade when baseball was arguably at its best. If he had played a couple of decades later, he might have enjoyed, like many other big leaguers, opportunity to sup with Midas. As it is, he is enjoying life as a nonagenarian.

Like Bob Hope, Ransom is thankful for the memories, and most appreciative of Marvin Miller's handiwork with the Major League Baseball Players Association. He enjoys the distinction of having cashed a World Series check, but grins sheepishly when he confirms that he was one of the

Dodgers who could not muster a hit off Don Larsen when he pitched the only no-hitter in world series history in 1956.

In addition to his record of being the only player to play in back-to-back Cotton Bowls with two different teams, Ransom is the first major leaguer to be given credit for a free pass for an intentional walk. Before that day in April 1955, hitters were docked for an at bat when they were walked intentionally. That milestone gained him recognition at the Baseball Hall of Fame at Cooperstown. He is the last Brooklyn Dodger to have hit a home run. As an athlete, Ransom Jackson was "the dog that could hunt." If he had joined the PGA Tour, he would have likely been a very successful professional golfer.

Today, he enjoys his rocking chair and the golden years. He has written a book that recalls his life and times. It's interesting, and it is good. Unfortunately, it won't make the New York Times Best Seller list, but Randy is given to insightful reminiscing. Published by Rowman & Littlefield, this autobiography, *Handsome Ransom Jackson: Accidental Big Leaguer*, is well worth the purchase price.

The book's title comes from his early nickname, "Handsome Ransom." If you hung out in the sports pages in the fifties, you would enjoy Ransom's narration of his life's story, which he tells with Gaylon White, whose research accents and illuminates the author's recollections.

To have spent the better part of your youth at Texas Christian University, the University of Texas, Wrigley Field, and Brooklyn when the Dodgers were the toast of the National League, must have been an eventful and joyful ride. To live through Ransom vicariously as you peruse the pages of his book allows you to recall the days when the war was over and sports arguably had never had greater love and passion. There's love and passion today, but it is mostly all about the money.

Sports teams have cult followings now, which can be a good thing, but can you imagine the era when Cub fans knew that every home game would be played as baseball was meant to be played—in the afternoon sun? Can you not bleed emotionally along with all those Brooklyn fans who felt that they were losing their birthright when the Dodgers lit out for California?

Handsome Ransom Jackson is not only about a man's life and experience, but it is also about an era that we perhaps won't see again. Hank Williams, Frank Sinatra, Bing Crosby, John Wayne, Marilyn and Joe, Truman and Ike, "I've Got a Secret," the Grand Ole Opry with Martha

White and no crossover stars. Helping hands all around, a chicken in every pot, and a time when a man's word was his bond.

The country was growing and life was better for most of those who had emerged from World War II with "The Greatest Generation." Hope sprang eternal every spring with the crack of the bat. Life, for the most part, was good, and baseball, including the plethora of minor league teams, was central to the good times.

Those times were Handsome Ransom's times. From the Cotton Bowl to Jackie, the Duke, Willie and Mickey, Stan the Man, and others, you can enjoy slow dancing and soft rock 'n roll scenes of yesteryear, which are comforting if you remember the fifties as Ransom remembers them.

It was a treasured highlight for him when the University of Texas honored him by inducting him into the Longhorn Hall of Fame. It gave him an updraft emotional updraft that two athletes he has always admired—Tom Kite and Ben Crenshaw—were in attendance.

Jackson's parting shot: "I have a lot more appreciation for the Cotton Bowl than I did when I was at TCU and Texas. You just think differently when you are young. Now I know what a big deal it was to play in the Cotton Bowl."

Today, he is especially appreciative that two of the greatest coaches in the history of college football needed him.

Remembering Spec Towns
From the Georgia Campus to Berlin's Olympic Stadium

Today, eighty-four years ago, Nazi Germany was peaking with its war production and would soon shock the world with its senseless aggression and heinous brutality, but was at parade rest when Berlin hosted the 1936 Summer Olympics.

Taking a boat across the ocean in the company of Herman J. Stegeman, UGA athletic director, and his wife, Dorothea, was a freckle-faced collegian from Augusta, Forrest Grady Towns—better known as "Spec," a dual sport star for the University of Georgia. Towns would compete for an Olympic gold medal in the 110-metre hurdles. The race, in US competition, measures 120 yards, but the distance between the hurdles is the same as with 110 meters.

Towns was implacable and unrelenting when it came to training for his specialty. With a lanky build and long legs, he could straddle a high hurdle flat-footed. I saw him do that often when I ran the mile for him when he was coaching the Bulldog track team in the late fifties.

The trip over to Germany was not a problem. He was never seasick, but as a small-town boy who was a vegetable advocate, the menu was not always to his liking. He admitted that he enjoyed wiener schnitzel, however. His body adjusted to all nuances of international travel; he was fit and in peak form for the race of his life.

Spec was truly a great champion. His story was that of a small-town boy reaching the pinnacle in sports. One day his father and uncle placed a cane fishing pole on the top of their heads, and Spec, a raw teenager, leaped over the fishing pole. Serendipity immediately reared an opportunistic head. The Towns' next-door neighbor wrote sports for the *Augusta Chronicle*. He witnessed this feat from his kitchen window and immediately contacted the Georgia Athletic Association.

As soon as Spec submitted to a workout in Athens, the football coaches claimed rights to his participation, which was fine with the future Olympian who was happy to compete in football for a scholarship in return. He played end and played it well, but the track coach, Weems Baskin, saw a remarkable high-hurdles "diamond in the rough."

Spec trained on wooden hurdles that appeared to the naked eye to be an Inverted "T." You hit one, and you were going to pay. (Late in Baskin's life, he told me that if the "L" shaped aluminum hurdle had been around in Town's day, Spec would have likely set records that might have never been broken.) When a hurdler hit the old-style hurdle and crashed onto the cinder track, the resulting language would make a boatswain's mate blush. Spec also employed a training technique whereby he would balance a book of matches on each hurdle, knocking them over without hitting the hurdle. No hurdler of his time had better form, which is why Spec never lost a big race.

Spec had embarked on the transatlantic voyage the best high hurdler in the country—actually the best of all time. Now he was poised to become a world champion. Reflecting on Spec's remarkable success, his career is confirmation that he was among the greatest of champions. He hurdled for his country's honor. There was no pot of gold at the end of his competitive rainbow.

For him, it was a short window, which heightens his greatness. Track and field superstars today enjoy substantial wealth. Still, their window closes fast. They are not like golfers who can play forever right into a champion's tour largesse. As long as a tennis player's legs hold out, he or she can compete and earn big bucks.

The career of a track athlete is like a thundershower in late summer. It comes with a rush and exits the same, which is why the best ones today, especially the superstars, turn professional after high school. Spec, who led Georgia to the SEC track championship as an underclassman, won 60 consecutive races between 1935–37.

At Berlin, winning the gold, Spec set a world record with a time of 14.1. His name as an Olympic champion is etched in the façade of the stadium today. Adolf Hitler was on hand to recognize the German gold medal winners and Spec remembered seeing him for selected events at Olympiastadion, a showcase facility built for the Olympic games.

As a gold medalist, Spec received from Adolf Hitler a sapling from Germany's Black Forest, to which Dorothea Stegman gave tender loving care on the trip back home, putting it in the hands of the University gardener, who was of German descent. The gardener nurtured it into maturity after planting it behind the original stands on the north side of

Sanford Stadium. Spec remembers seeing many of his American team-mates toss those potted saplings overboard once the ocean liner got under-way.

The Towns' tree flourished in its Sanford Stadium location, but when the stands were decked for the 1967 football season, the decision was made to transplant the tree to the Coliseum. The story is that the hole which was dug for the tree was too small. With no sensitive and informed super-vision, the workmen cut off the roots to make the tree fit the inadequately dug hole. It was late in the afternoon and the crew was ready to go home. Another case of ignorance that ruined somebody's day.

The tree unfortunately died, but the late dean of men, William Tate, contacted the German consulate in Atlanta and a replacement sapling from the Black Forest was procured and planted in the same spot. It too failed to survive. However, a commemorative bench honoring Georgia's Olympic hero sits on a hillside between the current UGA track and Pine-crest Street. There is an honorary oak just beyond the bench.

From Berlin, Spec went on a tour that had been arranged by the US Olympic committee, but he was not the least bit in agreement. He was ready to return home, not once thinking that he would soon be back in Europe for a different reason—trying to help the Allies win World War II.

As the war was winding down, Spec was in charge of a prisoner-of-war detail. He became good friends with three German POWs. I got to meet all three, one in Amsterdam, one in Meinz, Germany, and one who had settled in Australia. I was fascinated by the POW story. One of them found his way to Athens. We hosted them—Spec and his wife, Martha—for breakfast. As they were headed out to their car, Spec wheeled around and said discretely: "Don't make me look too sentimental. They are still a bunch of [expletive] Germans." You see, Spec's brother, Preston, died at Bastogne during the Battle of the Bulge. That was an unforgettable mo-ment for Spec, albeit a negative one.

When the Olympic exhibition tour reached Bislett Stadium in Oslo, Norway, Spec was fit to be tied. He would be running the familiar 120-yard distance in his race there, but he had had enough of Europe. He wanted to go home. Three weeks after the Olympics and in perfect con-dition, he astonished the track and field world when he posted the sensa-tional time of 13.7 in that high hurdles race at Oslo. Meet officials could not believe their stopwatches. It was a world record that would stand for fourteen years, one of the greatest hurdles races of all time.

Spec then received a cablegram from his football coach, the clever Harry Mehre, who did not congratulate him on his electrifying record-setting race. Instead, the telegram read:

"Minor sports are over. It is time to come home. Football practice has begun."

Sad to Saye

Losing a best friend is like losing a family member. Death is so abrupt and leaves one with such emptiness. You reflect on the happy times when there was never any resignation that there would be an eternal separation. You were always aware that finality eventually comes about, but when you thought about the end time, you likened it to a violent storm. Make it through the night and it will be gone by morning.

Sadly, there are times when the storm does not pass. You are gripped by the pain and you become resigned to the reality that there has to be a regrouping. A new day has come and one must cope. Emotions need rehabbing. Broken hearts need time to mend.

With my friend Bill Saye, I thought of him as immune to the ravages of age. He ate right, he took daily walks. He never bounced around the emotional scale—was never too high and never too low. He was a hard-nosed football player who embraced fair play but expected himself to pay the price to measure up to the taskmaster edicts of his colorful coach, Wallace Butts. Practice field rigor was to be respected. After all, the squarest deal a man could have was to play a college sport and receive a free education in return. Bill never lost sight of that glorious dividend.

There was an endearing benefit that accompanied his time wearing the Red and Black—the camaraderie he enjoyed with his teammates. Lasting friendships were always a reminder that those with whom you shared the locker room experience had the same core values—that there was life after football.

Bill was not a man given to blather and emotion. He was proud to have been a Georgia football letterman, one who never gave less than his best, one who quietly but passionately swooned to the ringing of the Chapel Bell. Even when he became an alumnus.

Bill lived a good life. It just didn't last long enough. Most would agree that eighty-five years is a number many fail to reach on this troubled earth. He outlived many of his friends and many in his family.

There is no exact formula for longevity. There are reprobates who seem to gain momentum with advancing age. Conversely, there are health practitioners who never take shortcuts with diet and exercise, living with an acute emphasis on healthy living, but something befalls them prematurely.

Choosing a healthy diet and walking energetically every day, Bill seemed temperate and conditioned for a longer haul, especially with a helping of good genes. He was in the business of the sale of spirits, but he was an abstainer. He could have written the book on moderate living.

In his sundown years, he took up art. He was never content to accumulate idle time—he was always finding something to do. Functioning with an altruistic bent, Bill became a community volunteer: Bulldog Haven at Oconee Hills Cemetery, Piedmont Regional Hospital, The Wally's Boys Association.

When he retired from General Wholesale in Atlanta, he and his lovely wife Margaret settled in Athens, where life offered lift, learning, and good living. The campus experience had brought them lasting fulfillment and compatibility as undergraduates. They wanted to reconnect in their golden years. It was rapture, a homecoming that stimulated personal hosannas and brought about a stimulating lifestyle in their sundown years.

When he settled in, he stopped by my office one day and I greeted him with, "Congratulations." He replied with, "For what?" The answer was, "You are now treasurer of the Wally's Boys Association." I had assumed the role of managing the association, but felt that a football letterman should be involved. Bill did a masterful job of bringing structure and consistency. When a letterman noted, as lettermen often do, that they didn't have the greatest experience, owing to practice field drudgery, Bill would say: "We can't do anything about that, but come enjoy fellowship with your old teammates." That resonated, and participation was soon on the upswing.

We put together a newsletter, and obituaries of fallen teammates became a staple of the publication's function. It fell to my lot to write about the passing of our friends. The next issue will offer the best possible tribute to our fallen leader. It won't make my day.

Sanford Stadium at Ninety
Thanks for The Memories

Ninety years ago today, the Roaring Twenties were about to come to an end. The next decade would be a contrast and would suffer a fissure that would not go away until V-J day on September 2, 1945, when the unconditional surrender of Japan took place.

The Great Depression of those times brought long suffering and consequential financial loss to our great nation. Bankruptcy, financial collapse, and ruin—even hunger—overwhelmed the United States. The fallout was felt worldwide.

October 12, however, was a high time in Athens, Georgia in 1929, as the Bulldogs of Yale came south from New Haven, Connecticut, to help the Georgia Bulldogs dedicate their brand-spanking new stadium, which hovered inauspiciously over an undistinguished creek that ran the length of the field. Little kids played in the creek underneath what is now "Dooley Field," and big kids played on the field above the creek, bringing fame, glory, and preeminence to the nation's oldest state-chartered university. For years, it was rumored that gold was panned in Tanyard Creek, but that bit of lore has been patently debunked—by the UGA geology department.

However, the largesse that comes from football competition in the fall at Sanford Stadium brings a profit that would equal what a gold rush might generate if someone struck the mother lode.

College football has become big business, and the University of Georgia can compete with the best today; but consider the circumstances of the coming of Sanford Stadium and the ensuing opportunities that would be enhanced by a signature moment in UGA history nearly a century ago.

To fully appreciate how it all came about, we hark back to December 3, 1927. The athletic director was H. J. Stegman and the coach was George Woodruff. The man of the hour, however, was UGA President Dr. Steadman V. Sanford. With the Georgia team undefeated and visions of Pasadena dancing in alumni heads, the atmosphere in Athens was saturated with high hopes and anticipation.

At the time, Georgia's football field was the baseball field at the foot of Lumpkin Street. Old photos reveal a football field marked off in front of the wooden grandstand, which seated only 6,000 fans.

In 1902 the Bulldogs began playing Tech annually at Grant Field for the larger gate. The seating capacity at Grant Field by 1910 was 18,000. Imagine, however, giving up home-field advantage to your main rival every season. The Bulldogs played at a disadvantage but posted a 7-10-2 record during those trying times.

When the Bulldogs met up with Tech in '27, the team featured small but very fast backs. Heavy rains fell during the week. However, according to Bulldog icon and historian, Dan Magill, Tech was taking no chances and watered down the field on the eve of the game, making the playing surface a quagmire. Tech upset the Bulldogs 12-0 and knocked Georgia out of the Rose Bowl. (Georgia would get revenge seventeen years later when Tech arrived in Athens with a Rose Bowl invitation on the line. The winner would be invited to Pasadena. Georgia, led by Frank Sinkwich and Charley Trippi, destroyed the Jackets 34-0.)

After the disappointment in Atlanta in 1927, Dr. Sanford was so incensed that he, according to another devout UGA historian, John Stegeman, vowed to build the biggest and best stadium in the South. Not only did he meet his own ambitious expectations; he also brought about the building of the prettiest stadium. The stadium cost roughly $300,000 dollars to construct and represented a landmark fund-raising effort by the University, perhaps the best of all time.

Dr. Sanford went about the state, coaxing 300 fans and supporters to sign banknotes of $1,000 dollars each to pay for the cost of construction for the stadium that would bear his name. The cogency of Dr. Sanford's brilliant brainchild is confirmed when you become aware that seventeen days after the dedication of the stadium, with the 15-0 victory over Yale, the stock market crash—Black Tuesday—took place, and not a single one of those banknotes was called.

There is another impactful message inherent in the building of Sanford Stadium. When Georgia people unite with enlightened and selfless leadership, there is no limit to what can be accomplished.

Sanford Stadium was built on two natural hillsides that give it extraordinary beauty, especially with the privet hedges surrounding the field. The planting of the hedges was the idea of a former Georgia business manager of athletics, Charlie Martin, who had gone to the Rose Bowl with his counterpart at Alabama in 1926. Martin had marveled at the beautiful roses that circled the playing field at Pasadena. He wanted Georgia's new stadium to reflect the same look that he saw at the Rose Bowl.

However, he learned that roses would not flourish in the Athens climate, which is why the decision was made to install English privet hedges. They were about three feet tall when Georgia hosted Yale in the dedicatory game.

Georgia won the Southern Intercollegiate Athletic Association Championship in 1920, but the first hint of coming glory that the little community of Athens so desperately aspired to experience began to gain traction when Wallace Butts became the head coach in 1939. His aggressive recruitment of players north of the Mason-Dixon Line brought campus legends-to-be such as Frank Sinkwich, Charley Trippi, John Rauch, and others. Had it not been for World War II, there is no telling the powerhouse that Georgia football might have become.

Butts won three Southeastern Conference championships in the forties and national championships in 1942 and 1946, but the fifties would not be good to him.

With increased interest in the Bulldog program following World War II, Sanford Stadium needed expanding. Wooden bleachers were added to the side of the original concrete stands but were not often filled, except when Tech or Alabama came to town. They became rickety, unsightly, and—not to be overlooked—unsafe.

To enhance the gate, lights were added to the perimeter of the stadium, nestled in the hedges. While the hedges retained their evergreen beauty, the light poles were ill-favored, an eyesore until Joel Eaves had them removed when he became athletic director in 1963 and hired Vince Dooley. The success of Dooley's early teams would cause an ever-advancing enlargement of Sanford Stadium. Initially, Sanford Stadium seated 30,000. Several enhancements and upgrades have followed:

- 1949   6,000 seats added to the south stands (total capacity 36,000)
- 1964   7,621 seats added to the end zone (43,621)
- 1967   19,640 seats added by decking both sides of the stadium (59,000)
- 1981   19,000 seats added by enclosing the east end zone (82,122)
- 1991   4,205 seats added to the west end zone
- 1994   30 Sky Suites (683) seats added (86,117)
- 2000   20 Sky Suites added (86,520)
- 2003   5,500 seats added to upper north deck (92,058)
- 2004   688 seats added to north side suites (92,746)

The pure beauty of Sanford Stadium in 1929 would bring about issues in the future. With any and all expansions, the attractiveness of the facility and the unobstructed views have always made it special, but access, bathroom lines, and concession stands conflict with pedestrian traffic on the Southside of the stadium. The only way to alleviate the problem would be to tunnel underneath Field Street, but at a near-prohibitive cost.

Expansions have, nonetheless, increased the size of the facility to where it is the nineth largest on-campus stadium in the country, with a capacity of 92,746. There is the view by insiders that Georgia does not need any more seats in Sanford Stadium, but there *is* a pressing need for more premium seats. That would be possible by connecting the Sky Suites of the north and south stands with an expansion around top of the horseshoe at the east end of the field.

All expansions have been tastefully done, and the beauty of the stadium has never been compromised. The man whose teams were largely responsible for the major expansions is Vince Dooley. His name has now been added to the stadium's playing surface, which brought considerable harmony among the Bulldog constituency.

Once again, expansive alumni support coupled with positive leadership has always been one of the University of Georgia's most valuable assets. Sanford Stadium will always be confirmation of that salient fact.

The genius and legend of Dr. Sanford should always be lionized and forever remembered with the warmest of respect and affection. There were likely many in 1927 who considered his new stadium concept as unlikely, and perhaps as foolhardy, as tunneling under Field Street.

Satchel Paige
The Life and Times of One of America's Most Colorful Legends

The early weeks of baseball season are a reminder that perhaps the game does not hold sway over the country as it once did. However, baseball remains a grassroots game that continues to fight off greed and substance abuse, and somehow or other remains compatible with the changing times.

We still love that first sound of the crack of the bat in March. A July 4th double-header is not what it once was—too many distractions to hold our attention for eighteen innings of baseball—but the lore and traditions keep taking us out to the ballgame for peanuts, popcorn, and crackerjack. That theme song, with the most pedestrian of lyrics, still strikes uplifting chords in our lives.

Things are decidedly different in this "let me have it now" world. Few players play their career with the same team, like Chipper Jones did with the Braves. With thirty teams, a lot of players come and go, even playing for a decade and seldom making a dent in our consciousness.

Seasoned fans usually have a historical bent. They remember the celebrated players of yesteryear, from Cobb and Ruth to Aaron and Mays. And, of course, the ageless and colorful Leroy Robert "Satchel" Paige, who warned us about fried foods before any health food soothsayer published a book about such cooking.

I often hark back to 1968 when Atlanta Braves owner Bill Bartholomay learned that Satchel Paige could earn a major league pension with a contract of less than a year—he only needed 158 days. Atlanta signed Satchel as a trainer, but the team also allowed him to pitch in an exhibition game at the ripe old age of 62 in April of 1969. According to Lee Walburn, a former Braves public relations executive, Satchel retired, in order: Junior Gilliam, Wayne Causey, Ken Boyer, Gil Garrido, Don Drysdale, and Hank Aaron—striking out Dodgers pitcher Don Drysdale. "If they wouldn't bunt on me, I could pitch nine against them guys," Satchel said.

Bill Veek, the iconoclastic owner of the Cleveland Indians, signed Paige to a major league contract in 1948 when Satchel was forty-two years old, making him the oldest rookie ever in the big leagues.

I got to know Satchel through a chance lunch with the Cardinals' Stan Musial and a well-known minor league owner, A. Ray Smith, at Musial's restaurant in St. Louis in the early eighties. Smith, then owner of the Springfield, Illinois Redbirds, was fond of Satchel and hired him to "hang around the clubhouse." He wanted the players to become exposed to Satchel's sage advice. Smith named Satchel "Vice President" and had business cards printed.

Smith arranged for me to spend a day with Satchel, who pontificated on everything from the day fans stormed the gates when he pitched in Chicago—and subsequently tore off all his clothes for souvenirs before he could find respite in the clubhouse—to the days in the Negro Leagues, when he would make his infielders sit down on the grass while he struck out the side. Satchel was ever the showman, which is a reminder that some of his legend includes self-authored embellishment—yet it was harmless and colorful, making him the most unforgettable of unforgettable characters.

Ray Smith said that Branch Rickey of the Brooklyn Dodgers considered Satchel as a player to break the color line in baseball but preferred Jackie Robinson because, among other things, Robinson had a college degree.

Durability was perhaps Satchel's greatest ability. He often pitched nine innings four or five days a week. Playing for Bismarck, North Dakota, when his team won the National Baseball Congress tournament in seven straight games, Satchel won four of the games and pitched in relief in a fifth game, striking out sixty batters.

On the day of our conversation, more than three decades ago, I turned on a tape recorder and Satchel immediately went into overdrive, never pausing for any reason. When we finished and the recording was transcribed, there were twenty-one double-spaced typed pages.

Satchel was in a good mood that day, but he had reached the point where his bones ached and he had serious stomach issues. He was nonetheless as colorful as his widespread image, which had gotten unrelenting traction. He spoke with a seasoned softness. His vernacular was entertaining and insightful. He made a lot of sense, owing to his worldly exposure.

He had grown up in Mobile, Alabama, and had seen every corner of the country with an introduction to people of all walks of life. He was not formally educated, but when it came to life and its mutability, he was an expert. He had been around, and his street sense was honed and insightful. His conversation was laced with the dialect of his native tongue from the segregated times that shaped his early life.

A few months after our time in Springfield, I was in Kansas City, where he lived out his life. I called his home number and asked his wife, Lahoma, if I could come by to see him where he lived at 2626 East 28th Street. I knew he was bedridden and suffering from emphysema and congestive heart failure. I was not surprised when Lahoma met me at the door and said, "Satchel is just not up for a visit." Satchel died a few days later.

Most of us have Hall of Fame memories when it comes to our exposures in sports. Satchel is prominent in mine, and I often recall that day with him in Springfield, Illinois, where Abraham Lincoln rests in peace.

Satchel's view on staying young:

Avoid fried foods, they angry up the blood.

If your stomach disputes you, lie down and pacify it with cool thoughts.

Keep the juices flowing by jangling around gently as you move.

Go very light on the vices, such as carrying on in society. The social ramble ain't restful.

Avoid running at all times.

Don't look back. Something might be gaining on you.

Tommy Lawhorne
Doctor of Goodwill

COLUMBUS—Tommy Lawhorne's considerable credentials are impressive, multi-faceted, and not without enterprise. As a teenager, he wrote a letter to the President of the United States. John Fitzgerald Kennedy wrote him back.

That says something about both individuals. Who but a Tommy Lawhorne would have the temerity, before he had earned his driver's license, to write the most powerful man in the world? Who was as PR-savvy as our 35th president who subsequently reached out to a teenager?

In high school at Sylvester, Lawhorne was as well-rounded as anyone who ever grew up in Worth County. No question he was a diamond in the rough as a student-athlete. He took overachievement to laudatory excess. He played whatever sport was in season but knew that his ticket to a free education, his foremost objective, was football.

Timing can make an extraordinary difference in life. Tommy was good enough to excel in a team sport, but was not of superstar ilk. Those time-honored clichés were insightfully applicable when his abilities were surveyed: discipline, second effort, coach-on-the-field, heart for the game, love of competition with an advocacy for sportsmanship and fair play.

There is an emotional and altruistic side to Lawhorne that is inextricably tied to passion, benevolence, and goodwill. No former player has done more to embrace concern for his fellow lettermen—especially when in need. He calls to extend comfort and encouragement when they are sick and ailing. The family of a fallen teammate can expect Lawhorne to show up for the final service.

The Georgia football letterman's directory is on the same shelf as his medical books and the Bible. He will thumb through the directory of former teammates and call out of the blue to say hello to an old friend. When his former roommate Ronnie Jenkins lay dangerously ill for days, Tommy reached out to Ronnie and his family every day, sometimes twice or more.

The most curious vignette is the latent and abiding friendship that took place in his postgraduate years with his Jewish teammate, the late

Paul Handmacher, who grew up in Montgomery, Alabama. Handmacher, after playing for the Dawgs, returned to live out his life in his hometown, which is a little more than an hour from Columbus. Handmacher would often drive from Montgomery to Columbus to have lunch with his former teammate. As incongruous as it may seem to some that a Baptist from South Georgia and a Jewish man from Alabama would become the best of friends, it suggests something that should resonate with all—two good men with good hearts took the high road in life and let their friendship flourish, forever underscoring brotherly love. Neither would ever castigate the religion of the other.

Lawhorne passionately lobbied for his old coach, Vince Dooley, to be honored by having Dooley's name associated with Sanford Stadium. Tommy researched other schools in the conference and around the country that had made such a naming move. He concluded that his old coach, who, like Tommy, underscored scholarship as much as competition, had a record that was as good, and in some cases better, than those who had been given title to the primary football facilities on their respective campuses. "It was the right thing to do," Tommy says.

In a recent fortnight, I came Lawhorne's way for a visit with him and his wife, Susan. They, after living in the country in nearby Hamilton for years, elected to move into downtown Columbus to the Eagle and Phoenix Mills Condominiums on Front Street. Their charming spot overlooks the busy waters of the Chattahoochee, as picturesque of a setting as a couple could possibly want in their sunset years. It offers refreshing views that would turn an accomplished artist's head.

Dinner at Epic Restaurant, walking distance to Columbus' finest dining venue, was for reminiscing about Tommy's Georgia years and to remind a visitor that Susan was a contributing member of the brain trust that revitalized downtown Columbus, making it one of our state's most vibrant cities. The Lawhornes patronize the institutions that have given them solace and fulfillment, especially their community, their church, and their alma mater.

Underscoring scholarship, citizenship, stewardship, and fellowship, valedictorian and overachieving varsity letterman Tommy Lawhorne has lived by the golden rule as exemplarily as any man that I know.

Verne and Emmy
Certainly Not an Odd Couple

Last spring in America's most exciting city, official validation of Verne Lundquist's career came when he won an Emmy for lifetime achievement amid toasts and slaps on the back that had him in a postgame party setting throughout the evening.

The Lincoln Center, which hosted the National Academy of Television Arts & Sciences annual Sports Emmy Awards for the 37th time, was abuzz, starting at 5:00 p.m. when New Yorkers were fighting never-ending traffic as they headed home at the end of the workday.

The Lincoln Center soon reached capacity for the event with the spotlight of the evening routinely focused on Lundquist. Presenters and honorees kept giving him shout-outs as the Academy honored producers, directors, technicians, editors, studio hosts, and Uncle Verne, who is perhaps the most beloved announcer in sports.

His professional associates paid tribute; his colleagues raised enduring and heartfelt toasts; and speaking to the character of the man, friends and family were invited to come along for the ride. The industry's finest—from Jim Nantz to his on-air partners such as Bill Raftery and Gary Danielson—spoke about Verne for being the good guy as much for his remarkable talent. Somewhere Leo Durocher was chagrinned that a nice guy finished first.

At a CBS-hosted party at Bella's, an Italian restaurant near Central Park, Verne was in his element. His industry friends were there. His brother Dan and Dan's wife Herbie Kay joined him and so did friends. Michael Irvin showed up and so did Calvin Hill, the headline-making Cowboys of yesteryear. Sean McManus, the CBS executive, offered generous and sensitive remarks. It would not have been tacky in the least if those who had gathered in the southwest corner of this classy restaurant had jumped to their feet and sang, "For He's a Jolly Good Fellow."

That is what Verne Lundquist has always been. It seems to have intensified since he became the face and voice of Southeastern Conference football for a network troubled by not having any college football coverage in its portfolio, gambling on making the centerpiece of its fall Saturday sports coverage SEC football. Seldom has there been a mutual admiration society in sports like this one. A league with a national network? How over-the-top is that?

The network *could* have found an accomplished announcer. It could have found a competent play-by-play voice, but it could not have found greater ambassadors for the network than Verne and his wife, Nancy, who is always by his side. They are social and they are likeable, having made friends with the Big Eye network for years. There is good reason for this. Verne has time for the little guy. He does not let the passionate fans around the SEC get in his hair. He embraces them, yet keeps them at arm's length when it comes time to do his work.

Laughable, lovable, and honorable, Verne has always been a professional who enjoys his work and goes to the various venues to do a sterling performance in the booth; but when the final gun sounds, he is ready to belly up to the bar.

A delightful and accomplished raconteur, he never minds if the joke is on him, like the time he was honored as the Texas Sportscaster of the Year. The emcee, in rehearsal at Salisbury, North Carolina, had difficulty with his name, first asking, "Is it Vin Lindquist?" Verne replied, "No, it is Verne Lundquist." As they were positioning the honorees for the ceremony, the emcee approached him again, this time asking, "Is it Van Londquist?" Verne again, "No, it's Verne Lundquist." Finally, the big moment came, and the nervous emcee announced that the Texas Sportscaster of the Year was "Verne Ludicrous."

The Emmy Awards Committee showcased Verne's signature calls, including his famous Masters calls: "Yes sir" on Jack Nicklaus's birdie putt at No. 17 when the Golden Bear won in 1986, and Tiger Woods' chip-in at No. 16 in 2005: "Here it comes, oh my goodness…oh, wow. In your life, have you seen anything like that?" And his first stirring football call when the Cowboys' Jackie Smith dropped a touchdown pass in the Super Bowl, Jan 21, 1979: "Bless his heart, he's got to be the sickest man in America."

The best line of the evening, however, came when his buddy Raftery noted, "The only call Verne never liked was 'Last Call.'"

Georgia-Yale 1929
A Dedicatory Game with Historical Implications

The principal subject on the collective minds of Georgia's athletic officials these days is the raising of funds to develop a state-of-the-art indoor athletic facility that will primarily be used by the football team.

While I am not sure by the way each team—Alabama and Georgia—played last Saturday that an indoor practice building would have made any difference in the outcome of the game, being able to practice indoors should significantly impact the UGA football program. Everything is connected to recruiting these days. Not to have an indoor facility when everybody else does puts the Bulldogs at a disadvantage.

After Auburn lost to LSU and Mississippi State recently (and could have lost to Jacksonville State), a very substantial Auburn alumnus said blatantly of the team's negative results, "We just don't understand. We have put tens of millions of dollars into that program which gives us great facilities. This [the game results] is unacceptable."

As I listened, I realized that the arms race in college football confirms that facilities can make a difference, but are not necessarily THE difference. In Georgia's case the need is dramatic, but no more significant than it was in 1927 when Georgia was undefeated and headed to the Rose Bowl, where the Bulldogs were upset by Georgia Tech at Grant Field.

To apply a poignant perspective, Georgia athletic officials back then agreed to play Tech every year at Grant Field for the larger gate. A mere one thousand dollars was significant in the budget and athletic associations not only scrimped; they also sought every avenue possible to break even. Even so, can you imagine never having home-field advantage against your main rival? From 1900 through 1928, Georgia posted a 7-10-1 record playing Tech on the road. (Due to a feud, the two teams did not play for eight years, 1917–1924.)

In 1927, Georgia had an undefeated team and was headed to the Rose Bowl when Tech, according to legend, watered down the field to slow the Bulldogs' fast but small backs and upset the Red and Black, 12-0. That is when President Steadman V. Sanford became incensed and decided that Georgia would build the classiest stadium in the Southland and play its home games in Athens.

He would go to the people to make it happen. The stadium would cost $300,000. (For comparison, nowadays there will probably be at least a dozen contributors to commit at least a million dollars each to the new indoor facility.) Dr. Sanford traveled the state and secured a commitment from over 275 Bulldog supporters to sign banknotes for $1,000 each (some chose to participate at the $500 level). They were known as guarantors.

Sanford Stadium was dedicated on Oct. 12, 1929, a monumental day in Georgia athletic history. A packed house saw Georgia upset mighty Yale, 15-0. Even the youngest fan today with any brush with Bulldog history knows that score. They probably know, too, that Vernon "Catfish" Smith scored all the points, which led to his making All-America. One New York newspaper featured a headline that yelled, "Catfish, 15, Yale 0."

Less than two weeks later, the stock market crashed on Oct. 24th, remembered in history as the beginning of the ten-year Depression that devastated the United States and crippled economies throughout the Western world.

This factoid is quite revealing—none of the guarantors defaulted on their banknotes. Dr. Sanford may not have been clairvoyant about the Great Depression, but accurately sensed that the Georgia people would always give generously to their state university. Dan Magill always reminded one and all that "Georgia is the majority party in this state." He was right. With harmony and forthright leadership, Georgia can move mountains. Only infighting has caused the institution to stumble.

Georgia will soon have its plush state-of-the-art indoor athletic facility. It will be a gift of the people—like the Butts-Mehre building and the incomparable Sanford Stadium.

PART III

Travel: From Hitchhiking to St. Simons Island to Crossing Oceans

One of my first exposures to travel was hitchhiking, which likely makes you appreciate why I was nonetheless blatantly flummoxed on my first trip to Ireland, when I discovered that the fresh-faced Irish girls were given to moving about by thumb.

This would have been in the eighties, a time before the custom apparently went away. On my last trip to the Emerald Isle, I didn't notice young maidens on the roadsides awaiting pick-up anymore.

It was a nice experience, stopping to offer a lift to a smiling red-haired teenager and engage her in conversation. They all happily admitted that they had cousins in New York or Boston. It was every Irish girl's dream to visit America.

You likely have heard it noted that travel is educational. I would say, "Amen," to that.

A sojourn to Ireland revealed that the Irish love of country music is deep and abiding. When I went to hear Big Tom McBride, the Kenny Rogers of Ireland, perform it made me feel very much at home.

You can read all the books you like, and that is good, but nothing is more connecting to the customs and local way of life than to "get amongst the people." Years ago, I learned that the first thing to do when you arrive in London, Paris, or Rome; Copenhagen, Budapest, or Prague is to take the city tour. Experience the highlights and history of the metropolis, then and now; then go back to selected addresses and attractions to delve deeper.

English-speaking guides are everywhere, even in Moscow and Beijing.

The bed-and-breakfast routine is a godsend for those who want to accumulate local knowledge. England, Scotland, and Ireland—B&B signs blanket the landscape, offering the warmest of hospitality. You sleep well and are treated to a "cooked" breakfast in the morning. A "cooked" breakfast is one of the grandest travelling indulgences I have ever experienced.

You can connect with a "local" almost everywhere you go. Just a little enterprise goes a long way. An informative tour guide from the daytime might join you for dinner or invite you to his/her home for a drink.

While there are con artists, street thieves, and charlatans across the globe, I have never been victimized, forever taking a good-sense approach and never venturing into unsafe zones.

Exploring landscapes, shrines, gardens, and historical buildings and monuments can be accompanied by drives through the countryside where you see how the rest of the world goes about earning its daily bread.

Pasta with the proprietor's wine from his own vineyard in Italy; the exquisite experience of a white-tablecloth dinner in Bordeaux; running with the bulls at Pamplona; feeling the soft mist that envelopes you at Victoria Falls; skiing the Alps, even in summer; fishing with a guy named Munson in the Orkney Islands; spending a couple of nights with a farm family in New Zealand, watching their border collie manage the sheep; marveling at the Opera House in Sydney, perhaps the most beautiful city in the world; touring the capitals of Europe, including Eastern Europe; playing the Old Course at St. Andrews—and other resonating experiences were all brought about, for the most part, by side trips from summer sojourns to annually cover the British Open.

I will always be appreciative of the friendships made from international travel, and am now saddened as so many of them are leaving this world.

The memories will, nonetheless, light up my life until I join them someday.

Big Ben
London's Iconic Landmark

LONDON—Time spent in London through the years has always been an experience to savor with memories to keep. It was once colorfully described by Roger Miller in his 1965 song that came about after he had visited the city for a performance at a country music concert.

> England swings like a pendulum do,
> Bobbies on bicycles two by two,
> Westminster Abbey, the tower of Big Ben,
> The rosy-red cheeks of the little children.

Ole Roger had a clever and gifted way with words and music. His ode to the land of the forebears of many Americans left not only country music aficionados amused but those who are not country fans.

The city, where pavement paint at intersections reminds you to "Look Left," has always been one of excitement and hospitality. The "bobbies" without handguns have always been an endearing sight—even today when you remember the people who want to kill innocent people in the name of religion.

With the passing of time, I feel that I have done it all in London, from riding the double decker busses and the underground tube to the charming taxis and embarking to Edinburgh on the Flying Scotsman from Kings Cross Station. The museums, St. Paul's, Tower Bridge, Piccadilly Circus, and Trafalgar Square. The British Museum, Parliament, No. 10 Downing Street, the River Thames, and the Churchill War Room.

I can remember being smitten by the British accent on that first trip, along with the charm and dress of an international population—the comingling of peoples, cultures, and languages. There are over three hundred languages spoken in London.

Now when I walk the streets of London, I wrestle with emotional discomfort. Could there be a gun underneath one of those robes? I have to fight off stereotyping when I take my seat on a flight or board the Eurostar to race underneath the English Channel to Paris.

Even with apprehension invading my thoughts, I nonetheless enjoy moving about London and marveling at the scenes that reflect so many traditions. I am always moved to pause in reverence when I hear Big Ben sounding forth. There are small bells that chime on the quarter-hour, but on the hour, the Great Bell's 118 decibels are louder than a jet taking off.

Fascination with Big Ben brought about a search of facts, which you can easily find on the internet. Big Ben was commissioned by Parliament in 1854. Parliament wanted it to be the "biggest, most powerful chiming clock in the world," according to the internet. Anyone hearing Big Ben would readily assume that the government got its wishes.

Big Ben dates back to Victorian times and went through World War II unscathed, and that was remarkable since the Germans did their best to level the city.

The magnitude of Big Ben is overwhelming. The bell weighs fourteen tons. It is accurate to within two seconds every week. Its copper minute hands are fourteen feet tall—as tall as a double decker bus.

Londoners tell time by looking up at the clock, which is one of the classic symbols of the city. Any movie set in London usually has a scene with Big Ben prominently featured.

London is the most visited city in the world when measured by international arrivals. All European capitals have redeeming features—from Paris and Rome to Brussels and Amsterdam—but London will always be a favorite. The language alone gives it a redeeming flavor.

We fought the British for independence, and they burned down the White House in the War of 1812, but since that latter skirmish it has been the best of times. If only our British cousins would learn to drive on the right side of the road.

The Hub, Beantown, the Cradle of Liberty
Boston, a Great City by Any Name

BOSTON—Appreciating that when we travel, we place paramount emphasis on the sights and sounds that make our day and avoid any and all seedy geography, you can find unremitting joy from a sojourn to the heartbeats of our nation's cities, weather permitting.

Can't think of a city that has recently left me wanting less, and I am a down-home proponent. Atlanta, for example, has more to offer than locals sometime realize. A favorite for this sojourner is Denver with its 16th Street Mall and sensible light rail, making you want to take on the role of town crier and ask why the rest of the world can't fall in step with that concept.

Anywhere in downtown America, you can find a Brooks Brothers suit; if you look hard enough, more than likely you will find an institutional greasy spoon that will leave you filled and fulfilled, like the South Street Diner, located not far from the Tremont Courtyard Marriott in Boston. In Athens, my hometown, our downtown breakfast oasis is the Mayflower Restaurant on Broad. If eggs, bacon, grits, and toast in a congenial atmosphere don't make your day, Lynn and Lisa will at the Mayflower.

It does heighten compatibility with any city when you are connected to local flavor, as in friends. Owing primarily to the University of Georgia, anywhere I go there seems to always be a Bulldog in the midst. Wear a cap with a "G" on it and people will come up to you in the street and initiate conversation.

In Boston last weekend, perhaps the best-known voice in the city, Dave O'Brien of the Boston Red Sox, and his wife, Debbie, hosted a dinner that could have been the scene of an alumni gathering. It included John Parker, Bo Rutledge, and Malcolm Mitchell, who owns a Super Bowl ring from the New England Patriots. You may know O'Brien's connection to UGA in that he has an ongoing streak of making tuition payments to the University of Georgia. You can't beat an afternoon at Fenway Park, followed by dinner that was apropos of breaking into "Hail, Hail, the Dawgs Are All Here."

Breakfast Sunday morning was an extension of the night before when Anne Noland, a University of Georgia alumnus by way of the Henry Grady College of Journalism, met up with a friend named Jonnet Holladay for breakfast. Jonnet's late husband, Howard, had been indoctrinated with all things Southern growing up in Augusta, a dynamic later garnished by his relationship with close friend Sonny Seiler, who never met a Bulldog, human or canine, he didn't like.

When Howard passed away Jonnet stayed put, a California girl and Stanford graduate who remains enamored with the history, charm, and verve of Boston, where she mixes with the proper Bostonians and the expats alike. It is her town now. She wants you to know she is proud of that.

Jonnet knows who to call to reserve you a seat at the John F. Kennedy booth at the Union Oyster House and point out where Daniel Webster sat when he came for lunch most days, enjoying a dozen raw oysters and a tankard of brandy. Whether you take your seat in the Old North Church, where Paul Revere organized the lanterns, or Fenway Park, Jonnet can update you on the history of each. "I love Boston and its history," she says with a grin and twinkling eyes. "I've seen it grow as it still honors its past."

Furthermore, she can take you over to Harvard and serve as your tour guide—crossing the Charles River and pointing out where Howard docked his boat, the *Southern Drawl*. That Bulldog dinghy has found its way to the uppermost ports of Maine, and even made it to Savannah for the '96 Olympics.

You might come to Boston when the tall ships are in port. Any day you show up, you can spend time at the *USS Constitution*, still the oldest commissioned active vessel in the US Navy.

There is overwhelming energy in Boston. Holidays, most poignantly July 4th, are especial. Whatever you choose from what Boston offers, do include the Isabella Stewart Gardner Museum, where a brazen robbery occurred nearly three decades ago, with thieves cutting from its frame Rembrandt's "Storm," among other works of art, a $500 million dollar haul that reminds you that evil often triumphs in our world.

What can you and I do about it? Nothing; except that if the world cries out long enough and loud enough, maybe someday somebody in the underworld will notice our tears.

Early Morning Walk over Brooklyn Bridge Makes One's Day

BROOKLYN, New York—Witnessing sunrise is one of life's glorious treasures. More often than not, ole Sol comes up over a body of water, enriching your life and cleansing your soul. It is invigorating to see the sun lift upwards over the vineyards of Bordeaux or the Rockies or the cornfields of Iowa. St. Simons and the Outer Banks. Kennebunkport. The Golden Gate Bridge.

I had the privilege of seeing the sun rise and set the same day on Nantucket, which made my book more arresting, the drinks more inviting, and dinner so fulfilling that the best night of sleep followed—long and deep, sweet dreams and restful reverberations.

Seeing the sun make its presence known in a city is different. Not as inspiring as when nature's blissful outdoor environment kisses you good morning, but nonetheless an uplifting experience. It takes longer, but witnessing the sun make its way over the apartment buildings of Brooklyn, once the garden spot of New York's boroughs, is a reminder that the amalgamation of the peoples of the world confirms that we all are different, yet very much alike.

Up in the morning, out on the job, and working like the devil for our pay. Walking around and sensing the beauty of the world, even in a big city; jogging and biking, bent on invoking good health. A tourist and a new experience. Cab drivers with a running back mentality—out of the way or you will be run over. Automobiles of all descriptions, polluting the air while racing its hosts to work.

Following sunrise here in Brooklyn recently, I turned west and began a 1.1 mile walk over the Brooklyn Bridge. At the outset, there were flashbacks to the days when Brooklyn was blessed with an idyllic environment. The Dodgers had not taken flight to Los Angeles, and it was not necessary for residents to triple-lock their doors.

Ahead of you as you walk the bridge is the Manhattan skyline with all its imposing majesty—the Chrysler Building, the Empire State Building, and the 1,776-foot One World Trade Center, an in-your-face response to the terrorists who caused so much grief with their dastardly, cowardly act of 9/11 in the year 2001.

Even with the exhilarating early morning trek over the bridge, where joggers, cyclists, and pedestrians move forward at varying paces—often with stone faces—you think about how wonderful America is, but how despised we are in certain distant ports.

The Brooklyn Bridge was completed in 1883, connecting the boroughs of Manhattan and Brooklyn. It became a designated National Historic Landmark in 1964 and brought about a book, written by David McCullough, who was given to walking the bridge year-round.

On each side of the pedestrian thoroughfare, traffic's cacophonous sounds become monotonous with the sounds of a motorcycle's muffler rising above the din, bringing about a constant reminder that we should enact legislation with regard to motorcycle mufflers. There has never been a greater invasion of one's privacy than the unspeakable muffler-enhanced motorcycle.

A guy with a saxophone is jazzing up the atmosphere at one point on the bridge—creating welcomed sounds to appreciate. There were multiple cameras and a man with a clipboard, gesticulating vigorously and shouting, which suggested that he was a director of a photoshoot for some publication. Look north and there are other bridges spanning the East River. To the south, you can see the docks and cargo ships. You can spot the Statue of Liberty, making you feel good again. Every time I see it, I am proud.

With any public structure, you can expect graffiti. The Brooklyn Bridge has not been spared. Most are love messages. "Nika and Telly, 9-2-15." "Chrissy, I miss you." All along the way there are love locks attached to the bridge like the Pont des Arts over the Seine in Paris. Those Parisian love locks had to be removed in the interest of safety, however. The love locks on the Brooklyn Bridge don't seem to be a threat yet as was the case with the Pont des Arts.

If I were to add a love lock to the Brooklyn Bridge, it would be a message about how magnificent America is. The Brooklyn Bridge is just one piece of our great land. I don't have a "bucket list," but walking the Brooklyn Bridge has always had priority on the "to-do" list. Now, I am resolved to walk it again.

Budapest
Sad History on the Banks of
a Magnificent River

BUDAPEST, Hungary—The rivers of the world are fascinating and bring about enlightenment as well as adventure. The Ocmulgee and Oconee rivers form Georgia's Altamaha, a river to explore and appreciate. If the Altamaha is not pristine, it remains pretty much like it was when the Creek Indians made do with its currents and contents.

The mighty Mississippi. Where it begins and where it ends remind you of our nation's greatness and expanse—our heartland, our midsection with different cultures facing the sunrises and the sunsets. The Missouri River! It is like the Mississippi, mighty with impressions to savor, a tributary that enraptured Lewis and Clark (and Sacagawea). Real men plied the Missouri to conquer the unknown.

If you float the Nile, you can't help but search the banks for the bulrushes, imagining a baby and a princess, and remembering that their biblical story became a centerpiece of ancient history. The scenes along the Elbe River—the picturesque German towns—reflecting the postcard image, take your breath away. The Rhine, the Thames, the Loire, and the Seine. Never crossed a river I didn't like. And the Danube. It begins in the Black Forest and empties into the Black Sea. Such grasping history is found along the Danube. A river defines life; life defines a river.

In a brief stay here, I have walked across the Danube daily, pausing to enjoy its enriching beauty. The Danube separates the cities of Buda and Pest. During the day, you are mindful of tourism and commerce on the river. At night: romance and levity, the fulfillment of life. Today there is hope and laughter in Budapest, but few cities have endured more suffering—the Nazis during World War II and the Communists afterwards.

None of that kept me from enjoying a nice respite in a vibrant city. Mainly because Szandra Szántó, a pretty Hungarian actress, is my guide. She is the cousin of Christopher Lakos of the University of Georgia sports information staff. After a tour of Budapest, a city of endless bridges, which bring about memories of Pittsburgh, we enjoyed dinner at an outdoor restaurant overlooking the Danube. Szandra not only introduced me to historical landmarks like the Chain Bridge, Heroes Square, and St. Stephen's Basilica; she outlined Budapest's history and provided an insight into the past that was the highlight of my brief stay.

Before we said goodbye, she took me to the Shoes on the Danube Bank memorial. It is another reminder of the sad plight of history—in reality, not so long ago. Shoes, made of iron, are anchored into the walk along the Danube. These shoes of men, women, and children represent the Jews who were Holocaust victims a little more than a half-century ago. The beautiful Danube has a connection with atrocity.

This is where the Nazis heartlessly lined up their victims, told them to take off their shoes, and shot them, letting their lifeless bodies fall into the river. Those who didn't die along the banks of Danube were sent to Auschwitz. Christopher Lakos' grandmother (Szandra's step-grandmother) died at Auschwitz, the family has determined.

Christopher, a friend and colleague for many years—a very competent professional—has a link to the Nazi terror that I never knew until making the trip to Budapest. Christopher's father Alfred and an aunt were hidden during the war by a Hungarian lady who despised the Nazis.

If you google Maria Madi, you will learn about her diary, which is now in the Holocaust Museum in Washington. After the war, Alfred became a freedom fighter against the Russians who in 1956 squashed the uprising in Budapest. Subsequently, Alfred found his way into Austria and on to Italy where there were relatives. He then emigrated to Canada and ultimately ended up in the US.

These tragic reminders of history always lead to this question:

How could a society that gave us Brahms, Beethoven, Bach, Strauss, Mendelssohn, Handel, and Goethe, give us Hitler and the Nazis?

Bushmills
Visiting the World's Oldest Active Distillery

BUSHMILLS, Northern Ireland—This village on the north coast of Northern Ireland is where the oldest licensed distillery in the world is located. The population of Bushmills is 1,319, leading one to suspect that there are that many bottles of the famous Bushmills Irish Whiskey produced here every day.

This part of the world is a very pretty and becoming place. There are fields and streams, sheep and cattle, a jagged coastline, and a nearby golf course by the name of Portrush, which as you likely know, hosted the British Open in July. Rave reviews ensued, just as it was when Queen Victoria, who after one sip of Bushmills was given to adding a "wee dram of Bushmills in her morning cup of tea." No wonder she became regarded as one of England's greatest monarchs.

In the area, there are redeeming attractions such as the Dunluce Castle—which was built in 1300 by Richard de Burg, the Red Earl of Ulster, for whatever that is worth—and the Giant's Causeway, a spectacular rock formation that resulted from an eruption of a volcano some sixty million years ago.

Locals have suggested that the Giant's Causeway is the ninth wonder of the world. Bushmills' historians like to say that if that is the case, then the distillery two miles away is the tenth.

Bushmills hasn't been making whiskey for sixty million years, but the aging process is well-established in a picturesque setting that gives rise to the notion that the Irish who brought us Bushmills are artists.

It is the setting that causes one's emotions to elevate with alacrity. The distillery stands near the Bush River, which yields nice-sized salmon. I don't have a bucket list, but it would be something memorable to return some day, cast a fly into the waters of the Bush, hook up with an Atlantic salmon, organize dinner, and pair the bounty with a Bushmills or two or more.

The setting is old-world, along with the Bush River and its tributary that provide the water for the fabled Bushmills whiskey. To make whiskey, the leading ingredient you need is water, and Ireland has plenty of that. Although alcohol, according to a beautiful coffee-table book about Bushmills (written by one Peter Mulryan) is a "corruption of the Arabic word 'al-khul," nobody to anyone's knowledge has ever distilled whiskey in the desert.

There is an inside story that came about on a tour hosted by my friend Mike Cheek, a passionate UGA graduate, and his Irish friends, Colum Egan and David Gosnell. Joining the tour were friends Matt Borman and John Parker of Athens, Dawgs nonpareil. I had made a deal with them. I would arrange the tour and they would host dinner. I felt like singing "Glory, Glory."

The inside story has to do with the fact that while Scotch whiskey sales have become dominant, there was a time when scotch was so second-fiddle to Irish whiskey that it would have caused Old Tom Morris to 3-putt from three feet.

Originally, Irish (and all other) whiskey was made from pot stills, which is a long and "messy business." Along came someone with a better mousetrap. In 1839, Aeneas Coffey, a born-and-bred Irishman no less, came up with a still to which he gave his name. The "Coffey Still" compromised the taste, just a wee bit, but it could produce far more whiskey than the venerable pot stills.

Coffey got stonewalled in Ireland, but entrepreneurs do what entrepreneurs do. He crossed the Irish Sea and sold his creation to the Scots, whose inventiveness segued into overtaking Irish whiskey in the marketplace. Scotch became dominant.

Bushmills may have stumbled along the way, but it never was in danger of going out of business as many Irish distilleries did. Bushmills is a prestige whiskey. I have always enjoyed Scotch whiskey, but only drank Irish whiskey on occasion.

Moonshine, that classic drink of the South, has a link with Irish whiskey. As far back as Victoria and her daily wee dram, whiskey has always attracted the tax collector. The Irish, like their Appalachian descendants, didn't take too kindly to being taxed on their home brew that they called poitin, which became known as poteen.

One visit to the Bushmills distillery on the banks of the Bush River has persuaded me to switch my drink of choice. Going forward it will be Bushmills single malt.

I am not exactly a newcomer to what the Irish can do when it comes to distilling. The eighth wonder of the world might just be the guy who created the recipe for Bailey's Irish Cream. If I were president, I'd give him the Medal of Freedom.

Deer Slayer
A Whitetail Twenty-nine Point Story

KIRBYVLLE, Texas—A few miles from here you will find Rock Creek Ranch, where trophy deer abound, attracting hunters from all over the country with a mission to take home a nice rack for their "man cave," along with enough venison to throw a party for everyone on the block and then some.

A friendship with a longtime Georgia fan, Billy Sage, led to an introduction to a salt-of-the-earth family with a consummate love of the outdoors and an abiding affinity for the study, research, and cultivation of white-tailed deer. "White-tailed deer are my passion," Richard Burch said recently as he drove his Ranger Polaris deep into the woods in East Texas that has been the family home for generations.

Richard and his twin brother A. J. operate the ranch in association with their parents, Jerry and Daphnne. Jerry is a seasoned hunter and an astute businessman who learned about the woods and wildlife from his late father Tommy, a member of the Texas Forestry Hall of Fame.

When Richard and A. J. decided they wanted to offer prized whitetail trophy hunting to passionate hunters, they went to their grandfather with their plan. The patriarch of the family—an avid deer hunter all his life—was excited but didn't want to show it.

Wanting to make sure that his grandsons were good businessmen, he told them they would have to invest their own money into the grand scheme and uphold wildlife conservation practices, and also that it was necessary that they be good neighbors. "He believed in us; he liked our concepts. He just wanted to make sure we were committed," Richard said.

Tommy Burch was a logger and a very successful one. *Timber Harvesting Magazine* named his company, B & W Logging Contractors, Inc., the 2002 Logging Business of the Year. His memory is recalled by that distinction, which proudly hangs on the wall by the fireplace in the lodge at Rock Creek.

One trip here and you quickly realize that the grandsons would have made the grandfather proud. In addition to being successful businessmen, they have made it a family affair—which was very important to the grandfather. Their mother Daphnne is exceptional in the kitchen, occasionally getting an assist from A. J.'s girlfriend Sayde, which often causes hunters to say that a meal with Daphnne's touch "makes" the Rock Creek experience.

Deer hunting takes place in early morning and late afternoon, which offers plenty of time for conversation in the blinds. Blinds at Rock Creek Ranch are all of stand-alone construction and ground-level. The Burches refuse to build blinds the most traditional way—attaching platforms to trees. Beyond the legal implications, Richard and A. J., compassionate young men, could not cope emotionally with an accident to a hunter. If any family ever lived by the golden rule, it would be the Burch family.

Richard and A. J. enjoy deer talk with an accent on familial traditions and excursions. They are avid Houston Astros fans and often make the three-hour trip to Houston to take in games. Getting to the World Series this year put the entire family on a high, especially paternal grandmother Velma who never misses an Astro game on TV—unless she happens to be in attendance at Minute Maid Park.

They are now college football fans with an Astro-like affection for the Georgia Bulldogs. That of course came about when Richard married Kalee, Billy and Mitzi Sage's daughter. It didn't take long for the Burch family to make plans to travel to Athens to see a game between the hedges.

"We believe in hard work," Richard said one early morning, "but we also believe in enjoying life. We love the outdoors, and it has been such a wonderful experience to meet so many people, many who come from faraway places, who enjoy white-tailed deer hunting like we do."

Native to North America, more white-tailed deer exist in Texas than any state or province in Canada—an estimated four million. That is why deer hunters flock to Texas every year. You may recall that Braves Hall of Fame third baseman Chipper Jones developed his 10,000-acre white-tailed ranch on the other side of the state at Carrizo Springs.

If you are interested in an unparalleled outdoor experience and are keen on white-tailed deer hunting, you would do well to come this way. The hunting is superb (even a novice like the author of this piece has a 29-point buck ready for mounting) and the hospitality is unequaled. I made friends with Daphnne right away. I'll soon be shopping for a bigger belt.

Doc Holliday
Consumption Sent Him West and to Gunslinger Fame

GLENWOOD SPRINGS, Colorado—Doc Holliday, the notorious gunslinger, gambler, and dentist—not in any particular order—was born in Griffin, Georgia, grew up in Valdosta, and died here from consumption at the age of thirty-six.

Tuberculosis was a common cause of death in that era, and since a person literally wasted away, TB was often referred to as consumption. Reference to consumption dates back to the days of Hippocrates. It was fatal until modern times. Doc Holliday succumbed to the disease here when he was a young man, but if you google him, you find that his life and career consume nineteen pages of search results. He gained an extraordinary amount of fame, owing mostly to his role in the Gunfight at the O.K. Corral in Tombstone, Arizona. He died a pauper.

As a result of his low standing at the time of his death, Doc was buried in the potter's field of Linwood Cemetery on a nearby mountain. There are signs indicating the trail that leads up the mountain to the cemetery. Signs warn visitors that the half-mile climb is steep and that it is a good idea to take plenty of water up the mountain. I made it without complication, but am not sure I would advise any senior citizen to take the hike.

When you get to the top of the mountain, you easily find the monument that memorializes Doc Holliday. Nobody knows for sure where he was actually buried, but it was most likely in the potter's field, which many communities have had over the years to bury the unknown, the pariahs, and the indigent. According to the internet, the tradition of the potter's field dates back to the New Testament, when the dishonored Judas Iscariot was buried in a potter's field.

Not sure how fascinated I would be with Doc Holliday's story if he wasn't a native Georgian—but the Old West and the legend it spawned keeps your curiosity buzzing. You wonder how much of it is true, but I am emotionally spellbound when I read about Doc's friends: Wyatt Berry Stapp Earp and his brothers, Bat Masterson, and Big Nose Kate. You flash back to all those Western movies where gunslingers were heroes. The guys in the white hats only shot the bad guys. They were the image of the guy who walks softly but carries a big stick. If you came to town looking for trouble, they were going to put you in your rightful place, which sometimes could be six feet under.

Today in Tombstone, Arizona, there is a daily reenactment of the Gunfight at the O.K. Corral. It may be embellished, but whether or not it is authentic doesn't matter to me. I went there believing the legend and was keen on watching a Georgia native shoot it out with the toughest hombres in the Wild West. It makes you feel proud that Doc and the Earps were disposing of the Clanton gang, good guys triumphing over the bad guys. Whether the Clantons were truly bad guys, I'm not sure, but I have always been seduced by the popular accounts of the gunfight at O.K. Corral.

Doc's family moved him to Valdosta in 1866 when he was fifteen years old. When he was nineteen, he left home for Philadelphia, where he entered dental school, graduating after five months. He began practice in Atlanta, according to one account. His cousin by marriage was Margaret Mitchell, the author. A family cousin, the noted physician Crawford Long, once performed surgery on Doc. Or so some say.

There is limited documentation of the accounts of his colorful life, but we do know that he moved West to a drier climate with hopes that he could enjoy a better life. Apparently, he gave up the practice of dentistry and became a gambler. He learned to play cards, gaining a reputation not only for his gambling instincts but his quick reaction to anyone in the game who could not play by the rules. He had a knife and a pistol that he had no reluctance to use if the situation warranted such.

After Tombstone, he moved around the West before settling in at Glenwood Springs. By that point, his life was wasting away. He no longer needed his knife or his gun. I am not sure if I would call him a hero. All I know is that I enjoyed learning about his legend and wonder why there is not an impressive museum in his honor in Griffin or Valdosta. For sure, he is one of the most famous of Georgians.

Fenway Park
Venue in Hubtown

BOSTON—Before the Braves left Milwaukee—which had been as eager to embrace them when they arrived from Boston as Atlanta would be thirteen years later—Southerners, with a bent for baseball, had to adopt a big-league team.

In the fifties, many chose the Yankees, the perennial World Series champions. Cincinnati was the closest team to the Deep South. The Reds drew some interest, but I don't recall a groundswell of affection except in Tennessee and Kentucky. There was great attachment to the St. Louis Cardinals, especially for those who lived in the Mississippi Valley and could pick up KMOX's Clear Channel signal out of St. Louis.

Radio linked fans of those years to the big leagues. It fired our imaginations and made us loyal to our adopted teams. I chose the Red Sox because Boston was the first team I read about in our county library.

Beantown was another world to a country boy like me, who developed a passion for the Red Sox as soon as I learned to read. Saturday afternoons when my parents—who functioned austerely on a cotton patch, corn, and an expansive garden—went to town to grocery shop for the week, I lit out for the library to read for several hours until somebody came and fetched me for the return trip to the farm, always with a bundle of books to read the ensuing week.

It was at the library that I learned owner Harry Frazee sold Babe Ruth to the Yankees. I considered Frazee a mean man, likening him to a troll whose image kept me awake at night after my grandmother told scary tales to us when we gathered around her fireplace in wintertime.

My love of the Red Sox never subsided. I suffered through the Curse of the Bambino. I read every book I could find about the Red Sox. Even when I began to travel, it would be some time before I would set foot in Fenway Park. Now I try to find my way there at least once a season.

When I was there a few days ago, I found myself sitting in the Red Sox dugout during batting practice next to Will Middlebrooks, who has relatives in the North Georgia counties of Jackson and Hall. He wanted to talk football. I wanted to talk baseball. It occurred to me that I was sitting where Babe Ruth once sat. Ted Williams gazed out to the big Citgo sign beyond the left fence from where I was reminiscing. I was overcome with emotion and tried to imagine what they were like when they were the boys of summer.

Fenway Park is baseball's antiquity. It is the oldest park in the big leagues, two years older than the Cubs' Wrigley Field. The third-oldest park is now Dodger Stadium. The classic parks of yesteryear have all given way to the wrecking ball, which is about to happen to Atlanta's Turner Field, a mere nineteen years old. Fenway, over a hundred years old, was built in 1912. Then, Boston's baseball team was known as the Pilgrims. Fenway Park is an antique, a treasure, and one of Boston's countless addresses where ancientness holds sway. I come here and I am overjoyed. I feel fulfilled and my spirits are renewed.

Fenway's irregular architecture makes it unique. It was crammed into a small acreage at Lansdowne and Jersey streets. Its fabled 37-foot-high wall in left field is only 310 feet from home plate. It would come to be known as the Green Monster, where a wind-blown pop fly might become a dramatic homerun—a routine out in most other ballparks.

Now that I am here again, enjoying encore after encore with the passing years, I recall the days down on the farm when I loathed Frazee's decision to sell Babe.

Today, I find one of the most fulfilling things in life to be a Broadway musical, and can't help but play the "what if" game. What if Frazee had made a bundle before *No, No Nanette* and kept Babe in Boston?

Grabbing a Taste of the Real West

SAN ANTONIO, Texas—If you are fascinated by the Old West, San Antonio is a mighty fine place to explore. They've got a good number of old Spanish missions here that includes the Alamo, a remarkable place to hang out.

I did stroll the delightful downtown river walk and eagerly sampled the Mexican cuisine. The locals will tell you that Mexican fare is better here than anywhere, except perhaps Mexico. They say that the Mexican food is more authentic than what you find at restaurants elsewhere. Sort of like some well-known places east of here that proclaim that their barbecue deserves the slogan "best barbecue anywhere."

When it comes to missions, after the Alamo, there is none better to tour than the San Jose mission, which was among those founded and developed by the Franciscan friars who came here as representatives of both the cross and the crown. Their objective was to Christianize the local Native Americans, mostly gathering bands who appreciated walled protection from the aggressive Apaches.

Native Americans were expected to render allegiance to the Spanish throne and to convert to Christianity, a classic example of how the world and government have always been influenced by religion. If you purport to represent God, government knows no bounds.

You can't come here without experiencing the Alamo, where Santa Ana won a battle but would eventually lose the war as a young America began to push out the Spanish south of the Rio Grande and take over lands from Texas and New Mexico to Arizona and California. In determining and defining our borders we were far from magnanimous, but what nation is when it comes to gaining possession of land?

A favorite stop here is the Buckhorn Museum, an animal mounts-unlimited venue, accompanied by the Texas Ranger Museum. The history of the Texas Rangers is quite intriguing, as the museum's curator, Hillary Gimbel, explains. She notes what it took the Rangers to maintain order on their frontier when you could literally get away with murder. The Rangers always got their man—their man and their woman, in the case of

Bonnie and Clyde, who were killed in a shootout in Gibsland, Louisiana. The Rangers cross any border to bring criminals to justice.

The museum displays an authentic jail cell, discovered in Kansas via eBay, but I was most intrigued by the gunslinger lore, such as reflected in this epitaph: "Here Lies Lester Moore, Four Slugs From A 44, No Les, No More."

On one floor of the Buckhorn Museum, there is a lineup of busts of the most accomplished gunslingers. Bat Masterson killed more than twenty men. Doc Holliday, the one-time dentist from Valdosta, killed thirty-four. A man I never heard of, Ben Thompson, killed more than forty. I remember that the tombstones of the accomplished gunslingers buried in Boothill Cemetery in Tombstone, Arizona all had R.I.P etched on them, which stimulates runaway thoughts.

You kill forty men and you rest in peace. You kill a man over an inconsequential insult and you rest in peace. You kill a man just to see him die and you rest in peace!

Then you reflect on those named Adolf, Joseph, and Mao. These Western gunslingers were but mere bush-leaguers when it comes to murder.

Monuments to War,
Monuments to Stupidity

GOUTRENS, France—Goutrens is a typical French village that I know little about—not even sure if the internet would reveal very much—but there is a universal reminder here that reflects the sad plight of history.

In World War I, this small village gave up sixty—yes, sixty—of its sons to France's cause, mainly to reclaim the Alsace-Lorraine lands taken by the Germans in the Franco-Prussian War of 1870–1871. World War I was largely comprised of trench warfare, resulting in the mass murder of young men in the prime of their youth. Stand fast no matter the cost.

Historically, we are reminded that military commanders have often been fixated on claiming and reclaiming certain hills and passes, whatever the cost in human life. At Verdun, the French lost 400,000 men in one battle. Great Britain and its Commonwealth nations lost 310,000 at a place called Passchendaele in a three-month effort to capture a hill in Belgium that became synonymous with war's enduring futility.

At a square in Goutrens, you move closer to read the listing of names etched on four sides of a small monument and notice that two families gave up four sons each. Four brothers in a family died, probably before they could start families of their own.

There are similar World War I monuments throughout France. As you drive into a charming village, ushered refreshingly through fields of waving grain, vineyards, and buildings made of stone that was cut and anchored centuries ago, warm feelings ensue. You never tire of this scene. The villages beckon and offer fulfillment to those who get off the beaten path, even though Europe has motorways and toll roads as modern as they come. It is just that I prefer to make my way through the small villages, where the simplicity of life seduces any enterprising traveler, making you want to return again and again. Come back and photograph that steeple once more. Return for a lunch with all the French culinary delights and wine to be savored at a table near a window overlooking a romantic stream. That is what France (and England, Italy, and the rest of Western Europe) offers to those who take the time to immerse themselves in the country-side.

Then you walk by one of those death-of-your-youth monuments, and emotional indigestion overwhelms. Although I am resolved to enjoy my trip by absorbing the charm of the countryside, I cannot help but reflect that the world has so much to offer but that history is characterized by governments and leaders who never recant.

They drag us into war and sap our youth. And forever and ever, it is not the sons (and now daughters) of the decision-makers whose names show up on the obelisks of the world's villages, but the poor villagers' sons, the farmers' sons, the working man's sons. It is happening in Iraq today.

An election year is coming up soon. Some candidate will say, "Hey, vote for me. I believe in a strong military. I want to keep America safe." They might as well add, "And if there is a dirty little hill in some faraway country, don't blame me if I have to have your son killed trying to take that hill. War is hell, you know."

Fortunately, after my stop at Goutrens, I found time to experience the best of the French countryside, including a visit to La Couvertoirade, the walled city of the Knights Templar, and Roquefort, the only town where Roquefort cheese is made. It is like Vidalia onions being commercially produced from only the twenty or so counties in South Georgia.

At Roquefort, ewes are bred to give the milk that gives Roquefort cheese its distinctive flavor, a flavor that caused the smitten emperor Charlemagne to procure two mule-loads of the cheese at Christmas every year. On a tour of the caves where the cheese is seasoned and stored, I tried to escape history's downside, but soon another reflection was to invade my conscience.

It is evening, and I am sitting in the Abbey Church of Sainte-Foy in Conques, a mountain village of 130 residents. I am the guest of Francois Pelou, a retired French journalist who spent considerable time in his life trying to make sense out of the conflicts in Korea and Vietnam.

At Sainte-Foy, columns reaching up to the roof of the cathedral provoked the revisiting of a question that has haunted me for years. How did they, mostly with their hands and their backs, build these towering monuments?

And another nagging question. The cost of human lives and the taxing of the resources of the peasants who provided the construction of labor—is that really what God wanted? "Somehow," my friend Francois remarked, "I think He would have been more pleased if they had built hospitals. We don't know about that, but what we do know is that the church became rich, often at the expense of the poor people."

Francois' family home in the Conques was constructed by his ancestors in 1758. It was built on two levels on a hillside. The furnishings would bowl over any American antique aficionado. The hearth beside the kitchen looks the way it surely looked in 1800 when it was built. There is a cooking apparatus that swings over the fire. On each side, there are small alcoves where family members and neighbors probably sat and warmed themselves while exchanging gossip and small talk.

The streets are made of stone. Tourists flock here to learn about a young Christian girl named Foy who refused to make a sacrifice to pagan gods and was put to death on orders of a local governor. Pilgrims making their way from Le Puy to Galicia—a trek akin to enthusiasts who traverse the Appalachian Trail—stop here for a respite to visit the church and soak up the warm hospitality of Conques.

With a flat in Paris and a home in Conques, Francois has the best of both worlds: the cultural options of France's capital city, and the peaceful and laid-back pace of the Conques and its inspirational solitude. Cell phones abound here, but you still step back in time when you visit.

Our evenings were spent in conversation accompanied by local Marcillac wines. Two in particular stand out: one from his friend Jean-Luc Matha that carries the vintner's name; the other, Le Sourire de Ste. Foy (The Smile of Ste. Foy), made from the grapes of the vines that form an arbor leading from Francois' patio down to the gate at the end of his property.

His friend Jean sells his wine to a few outlets in the San Francisco area, but if you want to sample Le Sourire de Ste. Foy, you must be the beneficiary of an invitation to Conques from Francois Pelou. Count me among the very few with that good fortune.

We had grocery shopped for our stay in nearby Saint-Cyprien by browsing through the street market, choosing fresh vegetables, fruits, and meats. No grocery chain could offer better.

On a Sunday, Francois and his friend Bernadette roasted chicken on the grill. Vegetables and salads were enhanced with herbs from his garden, everything fresh and nutritious. We were humbled by cathedral bells ringing inspirationally in the background, leaving you feeling uplifted and grateful. I am not a soldier—never the warrior type—but I think I would be willing to give my life if the world could live as harmoniously as Francois Pelou's friends live in Conques.

Lunch was followed by a nap under a light blanket. You could hear the waters of the Dourdou River in the valley below you as you drifted off to sleep.

For most people this is not the real world, but it should be.

Homer Harding, Vintage Plainsman

PIERRE, South Dakota—It makes my year to come to South Dakota during pheasant hunting season. Historically, vehicle tags have billed this state as one of "Great Faces" and "Great Places." I have a suggestion. If they want an eager aficionado's opinion, state officials should add "Great People" to their license plates.

South Dakota is not such a big place, with the total population standing at just over 853,000. There are about a dozen US cities that are bigger, in terms of population, than South Dakota—a place where the governor seldom wears a tie. My favorite governor out here, the late George Mickelson, often wore cowboy boots and a string tie to the office.

More pickup trucks dominate the parking lots than any other type of vehicle—that should be no surprise. I never remember seeing a Lexus in Pierre, the capital city. There *must* be, but in just a few short weeks, a Lexus won't get you to the grocery store in a snowstorm without debilitating complications.

Folks here identify with the work ethic. Farmers and ranchers in South Dakota live hard and work hard. They are hearty with a rawhide appreciation for life on the plains. Their days end with a trek out for dinner where they order the hard stuff and a big steak.

I've been coming here for years, dating back to the early eighties when an introduction to the aforementioned Gov. Mickelson resulted in an invitation to join him for pheasant hunting. After his tragic death in a private plane crash, Homer Harding, the state treasurer of that era, keeps inviting me back.

Homer is remarkable. He loves his home state, where he flourished in business. Owner of a Ford dealership, Homer also made his way in banking, in politics, and with the wise investing of his money. Along the way, he found time to identify with the most impassioned avocation in the state—pheasant hunting. A man with deep affection for the flag, Homer is a retired brigadier general in the Army Reserve, having served in the Philippines in World War II.

For years, Homer worked as a hunting guide for groups that came from out of state to enjoy the unmatched thrill of shooting the cock pheasant in the corn and grain fields of South Dakota. He can remember when the daily limit was seven—four roosters and three hens. "My mother, Rose, was an excellent shot," Homer recalls. "She would cook and can pheasant to put up for the winter."

Over dinner with Homer and his wife, Pat, and Homer's hunting and fishing pal for years, Dick Schoessler, and his wife Jean, all conversations are spiced with hunting and fishing stories. All the time, in my mind, there are flashbacks to those times when I enjoyed memorable days hunting with their friends Darrell and Brad Reinke and Jay Etzhorn.

You recall the trips in which you shot your limit every day. Other days less favorable are forgotten. You remember the shots that brought compliments from the South Dakotans, and are forever reminded of those shots when you walk through your study and see their mounts prominently on your wall. You remember the fellowship and the good feeling of walking through the fields and seeing a rooster rise, with a cacophonous cackle, and your aim bringing down the most beautiful of game birds.

Riding home from the fields after a successful hunt, there is much to savor. The sense of fulfillment is enduring. Hunting in a bottom by the Missouri with Homer one day, I came to an immediate halt. Lewis and Clark and Sacagawea floated by on that consequential river, on whose banks I now stood. There are still cowboys in South Dakota. The buffalo continue to roam, and genuine people are as prevalent as the cock pheasant.

As the trip was coming to a close, we were out in the fields with a yellow lab named Dakota. We were walking our last food plot when suddenly a rooster thundered up. With the greatest of aplomb, the wiry and gentlemanly Homer Harding, ninety years young, raised his black Benelli as he has done for years. Suddenly a robust pheasant crashed into the corn rows. Dakota retrieved him with composure worthy of an oil painting.

I've said it before, and I'll say it again. I want to be like Homer when I grow up.

Ireland
The Emerald Isle and Its Epic Struggle

DUBLIN, Ireland—I returned here from a 186-mile sojourn to Tralee, which is home to the famous Rose Festival. It was emotionally reverberating to tour EPIC The Irish Emigration Museum, a museum that came about, for the most part, by Neville Isdell, the one-time Coca-Cola chairman, and Mervyn Greene, his brother.

That experience led to an introduction to a charming lady by the name of Fiona O'Mahony, who enjoys helping those of Irish descent find out about their ancestry, which is the goal of University of Georgia alumnus Ted McMullan and his father, John. They came here knowing that the "original" John McMullan emigrated to Virginia around 1760, but wanted to know more about their family. The conclusion is that they have come to the right place—the EPIC museum.

Fiona told us about an associate with the same given name, Fiona Fitzsimmons, who was able to trace the ancestry of the actor Tom Cruise back to 1825. If you are Irish and want to know whether you are a Norman or a Viking descendant, for example, you might be able to find out if you visit the EPIC museum and connect with its affiliate research organizations, such as Findmypast, and associates like Fiona O'Mahony. I've never been overwhelmed by genealogy, but I've been told that my forebears were Scots-Irish. Someday I want to return to the EPIC museum and visit with the Fionas to see if I might be related to Maureen O'Hara, my favorite Irishwoman—the flaming redhead with knee-buckling beauty. She and John Wayne, whose ancestry was English and Scots-Irish, performing in a vibrant Western always left you on an unsurpassed emotional high.

If you want to delve deep in the Irish influence on the US—actually the world—you get a stunning glimpse from the EPIC museum that confirms that it would be difficult to find a people who have influenced the world more than the Irish, who were about as abused as the Native Americans. Under the long-term domination of the English, the Irish, who were mostly Catholic, could not own land for example, just one of the many penal laws that make one wonder how a dominant society can direct such inhumane treatment on others.

I remember a dinner here one evening years ago, with a writer, David Guiney, who was wont to espouse the continuing regret of the heinous English rule. The eternal curse of the Irish, he noted, was to "put bandy legs on the Queen."

Considering the Civil War and its aftermath, you become aware that it was always a source of emotional pride to castigate those who were born or lived above the Mason-Dixon line. "Forget, Hell!" the colorful Confederate cartoon, does not reflect the deep sensitivities that the Irish have had for the English for years.

Those deep-rooted discriminations, however, led to an Irish exodus that had a positive influence on the world, albeit tragic in that conditions were so bad in Ireland that emigration was the best option. Yet many of those who left their homeland only transferred their plight at home to a similar one abroad.

At least in the New World they were free to worship as they pleased and could own land and property, provided they could afford it. Out of those troubles and strife grew a legion of accomplished men and women, who helped America, among other nations, become truly great. Times were not great in their courageous venture, but they were not starving and faced no unconscionable penal laws.

Of course, most everyone is familiar with the mass exodus brought about by the potato famine, owing principally to a blight, in 1845. Ireland over a period of time lost about half of its population. The Irish diaspora had an influence on culture worldwide— especially food, music, and literature. Just as the potato blight left its mark on Ireland, the Irish have left their mark on the world.

There's crooner Bing Crosby; actress Grace Kelly; George Cohan, the Broadway icon. John Fitzgerald Kennedy; Robert Fulton, the inventor; and James Hoban, who designed the White House. George Bernard Shaw, the only person to win both a Nobel Prize and an Academy Award. Mike "King" Kelly, baseball's first superstar, and Jack Norworth, who wrote, "Take Me Out to the Ball Game." The writer, James Joyce. Physician Sir Hans Sloane, whose extensive collections led to the founding of the British Museum and whose recipe led to the origination of chocolate. And whoever it was that invented soda bread.

Boxers, singers, dancers, poets, actors, and writers. Then there were also Billy the Kid and Catherine O'Leary. You know the impact Catherine and her cow had on Chicago.

And of course, what could be more fun than the Irish tradition of Saint Patrick's day? Here's to the Irish and emigration, as sad as it was for so many.

The EPIC museum is an epic experience.

Joanna Troutman
Georgia Lady Who Sewed the Lone Star Flag

AUSTIN, Texas—There is a native Georgian buried among statesman, soldiers, judges—prominent men and women—along with "Father of Texas" Stephen F. Austin and author James Michener at the Texas State Cemetery. Not many Georgians know about Joanna Troutman, including those in the small Crawford County community of Knoxville, and why Texas became so proud of her.

Joanna Troutman was the creator of the first Texas flag, which allowed for her to be buried where well-known governors like John Connolly and Ann Richards are interred. Football coaches Darrell Royal and Tom Landry are memorialized here, too.

The Texas State Cemetery is a well-kept place with rolling hills that offer final resting places for those who qualify for burial here. There is a state highway, route 165, only a few feet wide, that runs through the cemetery. It is not well-traveled and there is no traffic to disrupt the serenity of the cemetery. Hardwood trees abound. At least one stately magnolia, with its penetrating fragrance, adds to the dignity of the cemetery.

My acquaintance with the legend of Joanna Troutman came about when I became familiar with Knoxville, Georgia, which is twenty-five miles southwest of Macon. Although its municipal charter was dissolved in 1996, owing to a state law that abolished city governments that were defunct or minimally defunct, Knoxville remains the county seat of Crawford County. It was the home of Joanna Troutman. Born in Milledgeville, she married Solomon L. Pope in 1839 and moved to Elmwood, a plantation that is near Knoxville.

When her husband died, she married a Georgia state legislator, named W. G. Vinson. She died in 1879 and was buried next to her first husband. You would assume that to be her final resting place, but in 1913, Texas Governor Oscar B. Colquitt "secured permission" to remove her remains to the Texas State Cemetery. Her connection to Texas, as mentioned previously, had to do with her sewing the first official Texas flag.

In 1835, when Texas sent out a call for help for its cause, a Georgia brigade led by Col. William Ward, Joanna Troutman responded. She designed and made a flag of white silk, bearing a blue five-pointed star, a 'lone star.' The flag was unfurled at Velasco, Texas, above the American Hotel and was carried to Goliad where one James W. Fannin Jr. "raised it as the national flag when he heard of the Texas Declaration of Independence," according to historical documents. The inscription on the monument honoring Joanna Troutman's memory reads in part:

"When Texas was struggling to establish her rights as a state in
the Mexican Republic, she sent forth an appeal for help. Georgia
responded by raising a battalion of volunteers, and Miss Joanna
Troutman then 18 years of age, fired with love of liberty and the zeal
of the volunteer, with her own hands made a beautiful lone star and
presented it to the Georgia Battalion and they landed in Texas with it
in December, 1835.
The flag was symbolic of the lone star struggle Texas was making. This
flag was raised as a National Flag on the walls of Goliad when he
(Fannin) heard of the Declaration of
Texas Independence on March 8, 1836.
It was constructed of white silk with an azure star of five points, on one
side was the motto:
'Where liberty dwells, there is my country.' The tattered shred of
this flag silently witnessed the murder of Fannin and his men at
Golliad, Sunday, March 27th, following. Gentle pure, patriotic, the
hands of Joanna Troutman wrought her love of liberty into
the beautiful star flag which witnessed the sacrifice of the men who
brought it to Texas as the emblem of Independence.

Over the years, I have discovered Georgia connections everywhere. They always make me proud.

Key West
There Is More than the Sunset at Mallory Square

KEY WEST, Florida—On trips here in the past, there was that anticipation of a discovery excursion as you drove down through the Keys from Miami, but it is different when Delta brings you to the Conch Republic and you later begin a trek north up US 1 with the thoughts of someday staying the course until the road ends at Ft. Kent, Maine on the Canadian border.

There is a certain fantasy about where the road would take you. Miami, Ft. Lauderdale, Palm Beach, Daytona, Jacksonville, Waycross, Wadley, Augusta, Cheraw, Rockingham, Raleigh, Petersburgh, Richmond, Fredericksburg, Washington, Baltimore, Philadelphia, Trenton, Newark, New York, Norwalk, New Haven, Boston, Portsmouth, Portland, Brunswick—ending up in the north woods with a bull moose staring at you with a maple leaf hitching a ride on his hindquarters.

At each end of this fabled route there is legendary fishing and stops along the way where history mixes with the rural and the metropolitan. Whether US 1 begins or ends at Key West might be an interesting debate. Most would agree that it ends here, but it's like the Appalachian Trail—does it begin or end in North Georgia?

If you were to commit to a US 1 sojourn in its entirety, would you initiate your journey at the top in Ft. Kent or work against the grain from the bottom at Key West? It probably makes no difference—you are likely to meet an endless pool of interesting, savory, and unsavory people along the way. Someday, I will reflect on such a journey—not in a three-month gulp, which would be ideal, but in multiple takes as time allows.

Having been here before, I quickly realized, meant nothing. I remember Harry Truman's "Little White House," Ernest Hemingway's home that was long ago turned into a museum (which I suspect would gall the hell out of him), and the sunset at tourist-infested Mallory Square.

What travel does for you can vary, often influenced by your own investment of time and curiosity. Travel connects one with the past. It reminds you that among all the artifacts, lore, and sparkling history, there exist abundant shysters, charlatans, and proponents of ruse and discrimination. Greed and piracy have reared their ugly heads in these parts for centuries. Thankfully, there is latent, consequential concern about the environment and conservation. Pollution is an ever-present enemy.

I have been here more than once, and I am yet to buy a souvenir or a trinket. Let alone succumb to a tattoo inking. Book stores, museums, and restaurants can make your day when you allocate time for any community.

One local sage noted that when you are watching the sunset at Mallory Square, you are a mere ninety miles from Cuba. The nearest Walmart at Homestead is a greater distance than that. In case you have plans to come here and take in the view of ole Sol ending its day in Key West, keep your hands on your purse while you are mesmerized by that glorious sunset.

Key West is an amalgamation of cultures, accents, and flavors. Take the time to know your neighbor and you never know whom you will meet. Like when I stopped by a table at Bo's Fish Wagon, which was occupied by a man whose home is Southern Utah. His name? Not kidding when I tell you Rob Roy. "You are famous," I thought. "They named a drink for you." (Or was it the dude from Glengyle, Scotland?) Rob's take on Key West: "I come here for a month each year. I like the sun and the happy hours." I can confirm, there is plenty of each.

Mel Fisher's Treasures museum is a study in commitment. It took Fisher years to discover the Spanish galleon *Atocha*, which turned out to be akin to the story of the "Little Red Hen." You remember that nobody would help her plant the grain, till it, harvest it, and turn it into bread, but when she sat down to eat, all residents of the barnyard were eager to join her for a meal.

Fisher found the sunken treasure, worth more than $450 million dollars, thirty-five miles from here and offered the governments of Florida and the United States a third of his bounty. Guess what? They informed him that they wanted it all.

Fisher fought his governmental adversaries all the way to the Supreme Court. Guess who won? Mel Fisher in one of the classic times when the underdog had his day.

Anything having to do with the life and times of Harry Truman always stirs my emotions. Truman, a hard-working president who considered the presidency a thankless job, vacationed here. He was broke when he entered the White House and broke when he left. He stole nothing while he was there. No president has ever honored the work ethic and shunned the spotlight more than this plain-speaking Missourian.

He enjoyed a daily shot of bourbon and a brisk morning walk. He played poker for relaxation and never thought of himself as anybody special. Humility was his hallmark. Whatever became of politicians like that?

Luckenbach, Texas
Population of Three with Car Tags
from Everywhere USA

LUCKENBACH, Texas—If you know about this unincorporated town in the Texas Hill Country, you probably are a country music fan who has heard Willie Nelson and Waylon Jennings sing of going back "to Luckenbach, Texas," or "The Basics of Love."

If you are familiar with the history of this part of the country, where German immigrants put down roots before the Civil War, you might expect any social gathering to be accompanied by the polka, but this is a place for country music aficionados—all three of them. That, officially, is the population of Luckenbach. The post office was closed on April 30, 1971, and its zip code, 78647, was retired.

There are two main buildings here—one of which was once the post office. This building also serves as a working saloon and a general store that is mostly a souvenir shop, where business seems to function briskly. The other building is the dance hall where "Waylon, Willie and the Boys" perform. The town's motto (Everybody's Somebody in Luckenbach) is often referenced in the local newspaper, an eight-page monthly known as the "Luckenbach Moon."

Wonderfully, Luckenbach is an alluring piece of Americana. A trip here is worth the effort. Its proximity to Fredericksburg, thirteen miles away, offers considerable options for tourists. Thirty minutes east of here you can visually take in the landscape that greeted Lyndon B. Johnson daily when he was growing up in Johnson City.

This is the heart of the Texas Hill Country, where Spanish and German influences are experienced in food, beer, architecture, and music. And don't forget about the Comanches, who got here first—back when none of their kind staked out claims and they had no need for barbed wire.

They make highly regarded wine here, which is gaining in importance. Tourists can't get enough of the Texas Hill Country. Retirees have a deep and abiding affection for the Hill Country, too. Only Florida attracts more retirees. If you are among the well-to-do in Austin, Houston, or San Antonio—even Dallas—you likely have a ranch in these parts to retreat to when downtime comes about.

Linda Baardseth made an introduction to Leah and Greg Thomas, followed by one to Lorna Bowermaster, assistant manager of the store. Lorna has a niece, Rachel Swartz, who lives in Athens. Greg then hosted a tour of the dance hall, built in 1870, where leading names in country music have performed. It can seat up to five hundred, and many weekends, it is jam-packed. When Willie last performed, in a nearby field, more than 17,000 came for an up-close-and-personal performance. They pick and sing in the general store every day at 1:00 p.m. There are two "house guitars" if you mosey in without one and want to join the fun.

When I am out this way, I often pause and recall Gene Autry singing that endearing and classic Western, "Back in the Saddle Again." You remember? "Out where a friend is a friend / Where the longhorn cattle feed / On the lowly jimson weed." As I was driving into Roger Cameron's spread, there stood a stately longhorn—the kind you have often seen in movies. Made you feel you were in the movie. Only needed some cattle rustlers and six guns popping.

I have driven out of the way to have lunch with Roger and his wife, Rene, to renew a latent friendship, owing to the friendship of a man from the hills of Tennessee, Gene Hartman. There was no agenda with the Camerons—it was purely social. Once you know a gentleman, there is always cause to enforce continued interaction.

Roger's remarkable success was built on recruiting military officers for the business world. He realized that junior military officers could integrate quickly and successfully in business. For over forty-five years, Roger and Rene provided leadership and training that enabled thousands of military officers to flourish as businessmen. Their firm, Cameron-Brooks, became a pacesetter with the concept of recruiting from the military. That should make you feel good about our Armed Forces!

Retirement has enhanced Roger's quail hunting opportunities. His card should read, "Have (shot) gun, will travel." Not even Paladin the gentleman gunslinger could shoot like Roger, whose affection for the sport of quail hunting has him traveling all over the US. His favorite sport often brings him to South Georgia, the quail hunting capital of the world.

You find interesting people—and places—wherever you go, and you don't have to look under a rock to find them. Not even in Luckenbach.

You Don't Have to Be Rich to Enjoy Scenes of the Monterey Peninsula

MONTEREY, California—If you are fortunate enough to book a room by the water at a motel or resort in these parts, you can listen to the surf cascading ashore as you drift off to sleep. When the power of the sea is not threatening, it becomes inspirationally calming as you enjoy a peaceful respite.

The tide comes in with abandon and retreats with harmonious tranquility, which makes your emotions peal with thanksgiving. Nothing like nature to overwhelm. You feel the exhilaration of a rambunctious Pacific slamming against the shore, its path stonewalled, as your emotions let out a sigh of relief that the controlled power of the waves is soulful as you segue into a night of rejuvenating rest.

Monterey is all about Carmel-by-the-Sea, with its upscale shops and restaurants giving off an ambience that brings the well-to-do and the modest traveler to swoon at its classic beauty and intoxicating charm. The beach is figuratively within arm's reach. The beach at Carmel is like a goddess who beckons. You can't wait for the embrace.

You must have deep pockets to live here, but you don't have to be rich to pay Monterey a visit. However, it is pricey, so bring cash and plenty of it. The rationalization in this corner is that there are places where an entrée at dinner may cost seventy-five dollars, and a scotch and water a quarter of that—but the views are on the house and that makes the cost of coming here worth it.

To experience a sunset in this corner of the earth is as uplifting as ringing the Chapel Bell after a Georgia game, experiencing a night when Broadway peaks at its finest, tasting strawberry ice cream pie at the Georgia Center on the University of Georgia campus, walking the Augusta National Golf Club in the spring, and hearing Rosemary Clooney sing "Shine On, Harvest Moon" in October.

If you have a historical bent, you may wonder what this land was like when it was under the Spanish influence and mission padres were hanging out there. Back then, you could have claimed real estate that is now worth millions by driving a stake in the ground.

That is what many did as America moved West. Following the defeat of Spain in the Spanish-American war, the United States gained possession of this alluring landscape, which would eventually allow a real estate agent to "make his or her year" with the sale of a single lot. To the victor go the spoils that enabled the US to take control of Cuba, which had fought for independence from Spain, and also gain possession of Puerto Rico, Guam, and the Philippines. The war lasted three months, three weeks, and two days.

Later, a financially successful Easterner, Samuel Finley Brown Morse, imbued with the pioneering spirit, migrated to the West Coast. Perhaps he was influenced by the Horace Greely preachment in 1865. "Go West and grow up with the country," the New York editor had famously said. Morse was a man of extraordinary vision, a reminder that some have vision and some don't. You can't give Herschel Walker's running ability to another back. Sadly, you also can't give vision to those who don't have it.

Morse foresaw what Pebble Beach is today, but the Monterey Peninsula was not always a place of luxury for the many who flocked here. All you have to do is visit Cannery Row in downtown Monterey, which merges with Pacific Grove. Sardine canneries dominated the waterfront here for years but the fishing industry eventually collapsed. John Steinbeck authored a moving novel about Cannery Row.

Shops and restaurants abound where sardines were once canned. There is an aquarium in downtown Monterey, and simply walking along the waterfront leaves one overwhelmed with affection. You must share the thoroughfare with walkers, joggers, cyclists, and baby carriages pushed leisurely about by young mothers. Everyone has a Chamber of Commerce smile. You suspect that property taxes are outrageous and that the cost of living borders on overwhelming.

The views, however, available to one and all, are priceless. One never spends time on the Monterey Peninsula without being anxious to return.

Nantucket
Go There for a Whale of a Good Time

NANTUCKET, Massachusetts—Life on this cozy island, which was once the whaling capital of the world, is like a sumptuous smorgasbord that leaves you flummoxed with the choices you have. There's difficulty in making up your mind as to what you like best.

Luxury yachts are docked about and so are dinghies. Nantucket is also a sailboat haven. It is fun to walk the docks and observe the diversity of sea-going vessels. It is also enlivening to walk the uneven cobblestone streets, made from the ballast rocks brought over by sailing ships in the old days.

Find a coffee place; enjoy that first cup as you remind yourself that some of those rocks were offloaded more than four hundred years ago. There's no neon, no eyesores in the way of signage. The island is clean and kempt because those who live and play here police up after themselves.

A long weekend here puts you in high spirits. You can come here and do nothing if you like. I've never been good at that, but I think I could succumb with more time on Nantucket. From the cottage where my wife and I were staying, I could go outside and look out to the Atlantic past foliage, steeples, and main-masts to catch the sun peeking over the horizon. Think of those who have that option every day!

Living where trees surround our property is nice, but I have to leave town to witness sunrises and sunsets. When I have the opportunity to see the sun start and end the day, I consider it one of life's grand rewards. Here last week, I got to do both.

At Wauwinet, a place where the environment gets top billing, you can move out back of a restaurant like Topper's and look past the low-lying bushes and water to see the sun slide down past the horizon. Then to get up the next morning and see the sunrise over the Atlantic, that doubling of your pleasure, makes your day.

At Topper's, a waitress, Joy Cran, perked up when she overheard mention of Georgia football. She is from St. Simons and immediately summoned her husband Hieu to talk football with us and our friends Jay and Clare Walker. I have come to believe that you could wander up to an oasis in the Sahara and find a Bulldog.

On Weymouth Street there is a gray shingled cottage, built in 1755, that has a neat sign that reveals that John Greenleaf Whittier wrote *The Exiles* there in 1839.

Downtown there are shops unlimited, restaurants and alluring watering holes, churches with tall steeples, charming cottages, and life unrestrained.

Then there is the whaling museum, billed as one of the places you must see before the end of your days. Many seem to agree as they line up to enjoy the story of the days when Nantucket was the epicenter of the whale trade. It was a risky business, especially when a harpooned whale retaliated with fury and resolve. A quartet of smiling ladies takes turns making presentations about the whaling industry—a mean (danger at sea) and nasty (handling all that blubber) business, but one that brought about excessive wealth for the Quaker-inspired community.

They will tell you about the *Essex*, captained by George Pollard Jr., whose ship met an inglorious fate when a whale attacked and sank the vessel in the South Pacific. Pollard's men set out in small boats, and even with resorting to cannibalism, only eight survivors returned home to Nantucket. The fate of the *Essex* inspired the novel *Moby Dick* by Herman Melville.

The retelling of the tale and a review of the artifacts in the museum are a reminder that doomsayers need to remember the history of Nantucket. For a century, Nantucket prospered because of the work ethic and the whale industry. Industry depended on whale oil to run its machinery. Our forebears lighted their lamps with whale oil. Candles made from the whale were a luxury item.

Then crude oil was discovered in Pennsylvania. Soon we lighted our lamps with the cheaper-to-produce kerosene and the less offensive by-product of whale blubber. Kerosene lamps were prominent in rural homes in the US in the fifties until the Rural Electrification Act brought cheap electricity to the rural masses. Kerosene gave way to the electric light, championed by Thomas Edison. Whaling died away, but Nantucket survived.

First it became a place for artists and later a vacation retreat. Today it is one of the favored summer colonies on the East Coast. All of this is to remind us, once again, that necessity remains the mother of invention.

New Orleans
The Crescent City, the French Quarter, and all that Jazz

NEW ORLEANS—After Atlanta, my home turf, the first major city I got to know well was New Orleans, which has a variety of pronunciations and nicknames. "New Or-leans" is commonplace, or New "Or-lee-uns." Doesn't matter how you say it; a party image comes sauntering to the forefront of your mind when the city is mentioned. "Nawlins, NOLA, the Crescent City," all suggest that the birthplace of jazz is the place to be when you covet a festive occasion.

Just don't come here when it is raining or when it is bitterly cold, if you can help it. New Orleans is a walking city best enjoyed on a sunny day. In 1968, when Georgia played Arkansas in the Sugar Bowl, the weather that week was not much different than what you might expect for Nome, Alaska.

At a party for the two teams the night before the game, Georgia President Fred Davison almost caused Vince Dooley to suffer apoplexy when he jokingly said, "With the temperatures dropping, tomorrow ought to be a good day for a hog killing." Not sure if Vince ever forgave Davison, since Arkansas played a peak game while the Bulldogs were about as lethargic as they had ever been in a bowl game, losing 16-2.

"Way Down Yonder in New Orleans," reminds you of the French Quarter, Satchmo, the Mighty Mississippi, unparalleled dining options, meandering bayous, voodoo practitioners, graves above ground, tugboats, and ocean liners—like the tide—coming in or going out.

I first came here during my college days to participate in a cross-country race, a five mile trek up Canal Street. Whenever the Southeastern Conference held its annual meetings in New Orleans, there was a spike in attendance.

Before learning a smattering of the city's charming history, I would walk the French Quarter and read the street signs. I would say out loud the names, wondering if I had gotten them right: Bienville, Carondelet, Chartres, Dauphine, Dryades, Freret, Iberville, Gravier, Pontchartrain.

Even the aforementioned country boy knew that when it comes to names, Canal Street is as out of place in the foregoing list of names as an evangelist showing up at the Chris Owens Night Club, unless it were to be Jimmy Swaggart doing mission work.

Tourism has long been significant to the city's economy. The latest statistics confirm that nearly eighteen million visitors come to New Orleans annually and spend more than $8.7 billion dollars while they are here.

If you take respite in the Crescent City and enjoy the sights and sounds that are uniquely New Orleans, bring money. New Orleans is not cheap, but is there any place out there that could be considered a traveler's bargain?

Nothing could be more exciting than to spend a week in New Orleans with an unlimited expense account. Everywhere you go, there are white tablecloths, a signature dish, seductive ambience, and a casual pace that reminds you of how the French treat mealtime—an unhurried experience to be savored.

Breakfast at Brennan's is about as good of a way to start your day as there could be. Bloody Marys and milk punches get your heart beating, but it is best not to linger since you have signature mealtime options at noon and sundown.

Locals prefer Galatoire's, which does not take reservations, meaning you may stand in line for a long time, which doesn't seem to bring about any business deterrence—although it would fit Yogi Berra's description of a popular New York restaurant: "Nobody goes there anymore. It's too crowded."

For a while, a good friend, Vernon Brinson, had an apartment virtually next-door to Commander's Palace, owned by the famous Brennan family. There are times during the week when 25-cent martinis heighten the elbow-bending and morning-after regrets.

Potato puffs still resonate with diners at Antoine's Restaurant; "shrimp Arnaud" at Arnaud's—which I leaned about from the late Dan Magill, who knew about Arnaud's from his wife Rosemary, a New Orleans native—would be great for a pre-game meal.

Raw oysters at Felix's Restaurant and Oyster Bar are still in demand. Nothing like bellying up to the oyster bar at Felix's and ordering, along with a dozen oysters, a Dixie beer, which was originated in 1907.

War, hurricanes, jazz, fine cuisine, Tabasco sauce, and Cajun accents have all comingled for years to give New Orleans a mystic flavor that takes one back again and again. I am grateful encores are still taking place.

Orkney Islands
Where You Can See the Northern Lights Most Days in Autumn

KIRKWALL, The Orkney Islands—The Orkney Islands are anchored about as far north as possible in Scotland. The islands are graphically pretty and becoming with a diverse geography and history. The environment is alluring and intoxicating. Upon deplaning at the airport, I immediately knew that I would leave with an inclination to return to this capital city.

When we think of Scotland, we mostly think of golf and single malt whiskey. I raise a hearty toast to that uplifting daily double. Nothing like a good scotch and water in an aging clubhouse, which is older than Bonnie Prince Charlie's baby carriage, following a round of golf with the sun having set and yet broad daylight tricking your senses.

Here in Orkney, the local folk get to see the northern lights most days when summer segues into autumn. If that visual highlight is to come about for one sojourner, another trip has to be scheduled. I'm already thinking about that.

The Orkney Islands are the best place to see the northern lights, having to do with the location of this pristine area, which is devoid of light pollution. Even though it is a common occurrence, residents here look forward to seeing the green, purple, and red lights dance across the sky year after year. Like being in Sanford Stadium between the hedges every October. It never grows old.

There has been exposure from many magazine and travel blogs about the Orkney Islands over the years, which piqued my interest in coming here to enjoy an abbreviated connect with an ancient land that has much to offer to those who journey to the Scottish Highlands.

There are good roads in the Orkneys, but no motorways. The peaceful countryside is not compromised by noise pollution. The Scots have an affection for strong drink—there are two single malt distilleries here—which means there is gaiety and elevated conversation in the abundant bars. Theirs is not a bad routine when you think about it—work hard, live a measured and uncomplicated life, and enjoy toasting the day when it ends.

Flying to Kirkwall on a twin-engine prop from Edinburgh stimulates the notion, as you are flying over ready-for-harvest grain fields dotted by sheep and cattle, that you are headed some place where the living is easy to enjoy a populace with an appreciation for the simple life, grateful that the fast lane does not exist in their neighborhood. There is nothing big about the Orkney Islands, except for the love of the land and environment, the outdoors and hospitality.

A longtime travel-agent friend, Marianne Stackhouse, found a bed and breakfast location, called Heatherlea, up on a ridge that overlooks downtown and the sea. Debbie Low once ran a hotel on the main drag below. She sold out but couldn't get away from the lodging business. "It is fun to extend hospitality to travelers," she said one morning after she had served a "cooked" breakfast. I'd come back just for breakfast alone: cereal, eggs, potatoes, bacon, sausage, tomatoes, and toast.

She arranged for a taxi to tour the island, and we got lucky. Another native, Colin Sinclair, took us to see places like the Italian Chapel, which was erected by Italian POWs who built causeways to keep German U-boats from trespassing into the harbors. They got permission to build a chapel for Catholic services and left Orkney with one of its most popular landmarks.

You are blindsided with awe when you visit Skara Brae, the "best pre-served Neolithic village in Northern Europe," a historical brochure trumpets. Uncovered ruins have given historians an insight into what life was like 4,500 years ago—before the Pyramids of Giza were built in roughly 2500 BC, to give you a perspective of ancient history.

Instant networking brought fulfilling Orkney moments. Debbie has a friend, Malcolm, at the Lynnfield Inn, where you can find the best salmon in the archipelago for dinner. Malcolm has a friend named John Munson who fishes for a living, operating out of the nearby Merkister Hotel. A native of Edinburgh, John came here on holiday and became enraptured with the fishing opportunities and immediately called the movers. You could say he is living happily ever after.

He took me out on Loch of Harray where there are abundant brown trout. I have caught brown trout in the North Georgia mountains, Arkansas, and Colorado, memorable experiences all. Unfortunately, the record still shows that I have caught brown trout in North Georgia, Arkansas, and Colorado. You couldn't be more chagrined than I was when John, his fly rod rigged with four hooks, reeled in a cast with four trout.

The Orkney experience, nonetheless, was unforgettable in that I became a friend of John Munson, who was intrigued by another fishing aficionado, also named Munson, a one-time football announcer who fished on Georgia lakes with the same passion that John does on the lochs of Orkney.

The Orkney experience makes you feel that you might vicariously be the centerpiece of a cover story by *National Geographic*.

South Dakota Pheasant Hunting
Has No Equal

PIERRE, South Dakota—When it comes to the avian world, there are birds so beautiful they leave you in awe when they take flight. The sheer beauty overwhelms. One of the reasons to become a fan of the St. Louis baseball team is the nickname. How could you not pull for a team named the Cardinals? The beautiful redbirds!

Bluebirds would soften any heart when they cavort about a fountain in the spring. The bobwhite quail is beautiful and so is the mallard, the splendorous greenhead duck. If you google the ten prettiest birds, you might click away with disappointment. The northern cardinal is included and so is the peacock, but others are fine-feathered friends you may have never heard of: the hoopoe, the quetzal, the Atlantic puffin, and the Bali bird-of-paradise. What a boggle your mind endures when you learn that the creator of this list ranked the California condor as one of the prettiest birds in the world. Since when did vultures become ranked for their beauty?

How could any listing of beautiful birds not include the ring-necked pheasant? This bird, which came to us by way of China, is without question the prettiest game bird there is. There is nothing like hunting pheasant in South Dakota, which attracts hunters each fall by the thousands, at least sixty thousand or more. The pheasant is the state bird of South Dakota. Residents take pride in hosting hunters annually. You simply cannot enjoy a greater experience than hunting pheasant in the "Mount Rushmore state."

If you visit the internet, you learn that in 1881, a judge, one Owen Nickerson Denny, brought thirty pheasants from China across the Pacific to Oregon, with twenty-six of them surviving. The pheasants flourished immediately and eventually spread to thirty-nine states in the US and seven provinces in Canada.

In 1908, a group of South Dakota farmers purchased a pair of pheasants from an Oregon farm. The pheasants thrived on the prairie. South Dakota kept purchasing more pheasant, and by 1919, the state had enough pheasant to stage a one-day season. Today, you can hunt pheasant from mid-October to early January. Pheasant hunting is a $219 million-dollar industry in South Dakota. I'm always happy to do my part to contribute to the state's economy.

For years, I have been hunting pheasant with a friend, Homer Harding, who is as hearty as the pheasant. He is still hunting at age ninety-four. Over the years Homer has spent a lot of time in the fields. He knows farmers and landowners who are keen on hunting pheasant, like Darrel and Brad Reinke, who own 560 acres of farmland not far from Pierre. Brad is a financial advisor, operating Reinke Gray, a wealth management firm.

Theirs is not a commercial operation. They host pheasant hunts for friends and business associates. They also host hunting outings for non-profits. "You are going to see pheasant hunting like it used to be," Homer had said. "Brad does it like it was done in the old days." There are stocked birds in the commercial operations but not with the Reinkes. The Reinkes bought their acreage, which only had one tree, in 2003. They have since added fourteen thousand trees. Their property is ideal for pheasant hunting. Corn and grain, rolling hills—which brings about pheasant galore.

Pheasant can fly up to forty-eight miles per hour. Normally, pheasant lift up slowly, rising like a helicopter, and if you don't attack quickly, they will level off and snicker at you as they take flight to a neighboring field. You are allowed to shoot three wild birds a day, and I can confirm that to get your limit, you better bring plenty of shells. At least for certain outlanders.

Walking the fields of South Dakota and seeing the beautiful cock pheasant take flight is a warming exercise. To observe dogs like Jett and Zeke come bounding through amber waves of grain with a ring-neck in their mouth is a rich experience. While I have South Dakota pheasant mounts from past trips, hunting with the Reinkes was so enlivening, I had to search for a taxidermist at the end of the day. When that ring-neck finds its way to the wall in my den, I will remember a balmy day in South Dakota, when the sky was filled with pheasant; when I had to work hard to bring home my bounty, but was blessed to enjoy an unparalleled landscape and uncommon fellowship.

My calendar is already marked for next year.

Visit with the Head of the Bulldog Club
in Cortona, Italy

CORTONA, Italy—As a young boy, Riccardo Bertocci became fascinated by the Americans who spent their summers studying abroad in the Tuscan hilltop town of Cortona, his hometown.

Riccardo learned to speak English by eavesdropping on their conversations in the *piazza* where they would hang out for coffee, beer, wine, and small talk. With the passing of time, he learned about the Bulldogs and American football and that the Dawgs represented the University of Georgia in the Southeastern Conference. That is when his unquenchable passion for Athens took root.

Today, if he is not the biggest American college football fan in Italy, he is without question the biggest Georgia fan in his country and the leading Bulldog aficionado and alumnus in this agricultural enclave, tourist mecca, and career-enhancing UGA outpost.

It became a dream of Riccardo's to enroll in the "classic city," and, as he says "identify with Bulldog lore, earn a degree, and admire the pretty girls on campus." "They were so beautiful in Cortona, but when I got to Athens, I discovered that there was a beauty queen in every classroom and one on every corner of every street."

Eventually, he met a coed named Amy, who had enrolled in the Cortona Program one summer. They began dating and eventually were married. However, she was an Ole Miss graduate whose family was emotionally linked to Auburn. "That she came from a War Eagle family," he laughs, "was not a problem at first, but because her family is as passionate about Auburn as I am about the Bulldogs, it was a problem on that one Saturday in November day if the Bulldogs did not win." Eventually they were divorced, but remain good friends.

Riccardo's passion for UGA only intensified along the way, in concert with his antipathy for Auburn. "But just that one Saturday," he smiles. "That is the one game which I want Georgia to win the most." With a son, Dante, also having graduated from Georgia, loyalty in the Deep South's oldest rivalry has a slight edge favoring the men in the family. His daughter Lia has no college affiliation. She is more concerned about the running of the Palio in Siena. Stay tuned.

With Riccardo hosting us and our neighbors, Mike and Jennifer Fitzgerald, it was easy to conclude after almost a week in his company that if he ventured into politics, he would easily be elected mayor of this city that dates back to Etruscan times. Everybody in Cortona knows Riccardo. They shout *ciaos* from flats above Via Nazionale, the main thoroughfare in the piazza, and in the restaurants and bars. Proprietors frequently wink and remind guests that they will be getting a "Riccardo discount."

He remembers the scores of Georgia games from his first year in Athens (1982) to the Rose Bowl two years ago ("Oh what a highlight in my life"), bars like "Sparky's," and "Cleve's," and friends such as the late Jack Kehoe, who helped make his impossible dream to enroll at Georgia come true. "Jack Kehoe made Cortona so relevant and both the city of Cortona and the University are better off today because of his visionary leadership," Riccardo says with elevated emotion.

A sentimentalist, Riccardo sells wine internationally and enjoys countless friendships, both in the US and Italy. On his last trip across the Atlantic, he rented a Ford pickup from Hertz, which made his day. Not just any pickup, mind you, but a "Georgia red" one.

He has made it his business to sample the wines of North Georgia wineries. He gives several of them (including Frogtown Cellars, Wolf Mountain Vineyards, and Tiger Mountain Vineyards) a "thumbs-up" rating. "Let me tell you, they make good wines in my adopted state," he says.

He enjoys a nice friendship with the introspective Svetlana at the Five Points Bottle Shop. He smiled and gave her a "thumbs-up," too. "She is very, very knowledgeable," he says. Spend a day with Riccardo as your host in Tuscany's esteemed wine country and you will find that he is well-connected, well-received, and well-liked; and as he says about Svetlana, the same can be said of Riccardo. He is very, very knowledgeable when in discourse about vino, regardless of the winery.

We made stops for wine-tasting and meals at some of the very best wineries, including Tenuta Casanova in the town of Castellina in Chianti; Tenuta Fanti in Montalcino; and Tenuta Falconiere in Cortona. All local guides are friends of his. At Montepulciano, where we visited the Tolosa Vineyards, we were ushered into an exclusive and private tasting room adjacent to a tunnel leading down to an Etruscan tomb. Riccardo deferred to the winery host as the tasting of wines gained momentum, but on the drive to the next stop, he gave us verbal CliffsNotes on the history of the mysterious Etruscans. If Chris Robinson, the current director of the UGA Cortona Program, were to need someone to lecture about the Etruscans—Riccardo is within arm's reach.

You conclude after time spent with Riccardo that there never was a provincial time in his life. He can discourse on history, geography, food, and wine with the greatest of ease and insight. If your car overheats, he can jury-rig a makeshift solution to get you on the road again. A jack-of-all-trades? Sì!

Riccardo makes you appreciate that in other cultures there are things that sports-minded Americans can relate to. The Palio, for example: the world-famous horse race, which takes place July 2 and August 16 in nearby Siena, has the anticipation and antipathy you might find at a Georgia-Auburn game. The city lays a foundation of dirt around the square. The city districts, or *contrade*, enter their horses, which are decorated in definitive and sacred colors. Win the three-lap race and the bareback-riding jockey is handsomely rewarded financially and receives the same reverence Herschel Walker gets when he returns to a game between the hedges.

From those days growing up in Cortona that segued into an international business career, there have been other memorable centerpieces in Riccardo's life. He has traveled the globe, having lived briefly in Australia, Venezuela, and Thailand while working for Air Alitalia. He speaks four languages.

"Working for the airline enabled me to see the Dawgs more often. I love Athens and I love Cortona. I feel very fortunate and say a little prayer of thanks every day in memory of Jack Kehoe," he smiles exuberantly and triumphantly.

Riccardo is making plans to cook for a friend for a Georgia game this fall. That is another thing this passionate Georgia alumnus is expert at—managing an oven. He will put his spaghetti up against any chef in Athens. When making plans for a cookout this fall, he informed a Georgia friend that he will be working for tips: "Two tickets to the Kentucky game," he laughed generously.

That is the best deal a Georgia home game host could ever want. Bravo for Riccardo Bertocci, the *magnifico* Bulldog.

Dinner with the Vince Lombardi
of Interior Design

LOS ANGELES—As we moseyed down from their home in Hollywood Hills to a restaurant that had the feel of a *hacienda*, the Hearth & Hound on Sunset Boulevard, Madeline Stuart, the accomplished interior designer, said to her writer husband, Steve Oney, a loyal Dawg fan, "We are not going to talk football all night, are we?"

It wasn't a threat, but I liked that Madeline was taking the conversational offensive. I preferred to hear her talk about herself and her work. The former was out of the question and the latter put me at a disadvantage. I don't know about her world, but when I read up on her, I was impressed that her credentials were major-league, perhaps a term of endearment for Steve but not necessarily in her professional lexicon. With no offense to her husband and his friend, sports are pedestrian in her domain.

For this country boy, who is proud of a bent for curiosity, I am at a disadvantage when it comes to the fundamentals of Madeline's timeless designs and her ability to create decors that blow away aficionados of up-scale interiors.

I had actually pined for this opportunity for some time. I knew a lot about Steve Oney, a Henry Grady College of Journalism graduate of the University of Georgia. He is a writer of distinction, the centerpiece of his resume being his book, *And the Dead Shall Rise* (now in its twelfth paper-back printing), which recounts the murder of Mary Phagan and the lynching of Leo Frank, two tragic and sensational murders of yesteryear.

Steve has other credits, including his latest book, *A Man's World*, a collection of his magazine articles, published by Mercer University Press. Oney is a fluent, cogent, and articulate writer whose way with words leaves you with a passion for more. His initial magazine bylines were with the old *Atlanta Journal-Constitution Magazine*, which was once read with the affection that many today hold for the *New York Times Magazine*, one of the few left standing.

To be truthful, I was pleased that Madeline didn't want our evening to be a boys' night out to rattle on about football. I was happy to be in the company of the Vince Lombardi of interior design and want to do my best to tell you more about the missus, if I can. I have warm journalistic feelings for Steve, but I am sure he is proud to yield to a unwashed treatise on his wife, who has signature credentials in her industry. "She is one of the best designers in the country," Steve says, and notes proudly that her dad, Mel Stuart, was a terrific movie director. "Among his films are *Willy Wonka and the Chocolate Factory.* Madeline had a small part in it."

Madeline was born in New York and raised in Beverly Hills, which tells you right off—she is not afflicted with provincialism. However, she had relatives in Waynesboro, Georgia, that allowed for a glimpse of life "down on the farm."

Today, when she is not designing something spectacular for one of her abundant clients, she and Steve retreat to their garden spot in Santa Barbara, California's Mediterranean-like coastal enclave that dates back to Paleo-Indian times. Joining them for any sojourn are their Jack Russell Terriers, "Beatrice" and "Mr. Peabody." Art, stimulating conversation, and local wine turn Steve and Madeline on, and there is no place like Santa Barbara to bring about emotional fulfillment.

The evening with Madeline and Steve was worthy of bucket-list rank. At the risk of sounding condescending, I am nonetheless moved to say that Madeline is charming and personable with regal good looks to match her exquisite designs. To say that she is accomplished is not enough. Among the elite publications in her business with which she is connected are *Elle Decor, Veranda,* and *Town & Country Magazine,* but let an internet expert confirm her exalted status:

> [She is] a leading member of the Los Angeles design community whose wide ranging clientele comes from the entertainment industry, and the world of business and finance. Equally at ease designing a 1920s Hollywood hacienda, a Fifth Avenue Manhattan apartment or a Rocky Mountain retreat, Stuart stresses, above all else, the fundamental marriage of integrity and beauty. Her projects reflect a collaborative relationship between architecture and furniture, function and form, client and designer.

In signing off, one concludes that it is appropriate to sound forth the notion that my writer friend Steve Oney, as Waynesboro vernacular would suggest, "out-married himself."

Tenuta Casanova
A Vineyard Visit to Savor

CASTELLINA in CHIANTI, Italy — To allow you to become familiar with a signature wine tasting in the heart of Italy's celebrated Chianti Classico region, we begin with verbiage from a flyer that my wife and I came in possession of while on a trip to North Palm Beach, Florida, several months ago:

In the heart of the Sienese countryside, nestled among the hilly vineyards and olive groves near the ancient town of Castellina-in-Chianti, lies the Tenuta Casanova. Our scenic landscape, where the romantic Valdelsa meets the hills of Chianti, is the happy result of nature's design and man's hard toil. Delicious rewards await you at Tenuta Casanova, Tuscany.

If you can't get enough of fulfilling food and wine, you should come this way for an extraordinary experience that takes place on a twelfth century family-run farm and vineyard, where you will be emotionally seduced by the hospitality of Silvano and Rita Cis, the proprietors and producers of extraordinary wines and balsamic vinegars that evolve from an organic farming operation that has a singular touch.

Everything is pristine and neatly organized to ensure that when you are on the premises, you will enjoy an invigorating and stimulating outing. In the cask rooms and cellars your senses become acutely sensitive as you hear Silvano connect you with both history and the wine-making process, which makes for the best dining option in a stirring and memorable setting.

When you are here in the heart of Chianti Classico vineyards, you know you are within arm's reach of the finest Italian wines when you see the label of the black rooster on the bottles on your table. Even with a cursory knowledge of the history of wine, you are aware that it pre-dates David and Bathsheba, which offers curious perspective.

We have been told that Noah became intoxicated once, causing one to suspect that it happened as a result of imbibing wine—we just don't know if it was red or white. And what about the water being turned into wine at the marriage feast at Canna? Historians have made us aware that the Egyptians and subsequently the Romans were devout wine aficionados. The Greeks even had a god of wine, Dionysus. In Psalms 104:15, we learn that "wine is good for cheer." This brings about a toast to the past.

Anteing up for a Chateau Rothchild or Chateau Pétrus is not within reach for most of us, but lunch at Tenuta Casanova—in the ambient atmosphere of olive trees overlooking the plains of Tuscany with colorful peacocks flashing their feathered cloaks-of-many-colors and sounding forth with intermittent squawks—is an experience that does not require a second mortgage on your house.

There has been a passion to visit Tenuta Casanova since meeting the owners at a dinner party at the Bear's Club in South Florida last winter. We were the guests of friends and were charmed not only by the food and wine, but the passion of Rita and Silvano, who make trips to the US each year to host wine-tasting dinners.

When you enter their picturesque property, which is as kempt and tidy as a Jaguar showroom, you are greeted by photos of Barbara and Jack Nicklaus and Peyton Manning, who have stopped here in the recent past. I am happy to confirm that if it is good enough for Barbara and Jack and Peyton, it is good enough for me.

When you venture their way, Silvano and Rita remind you that you are not dining in a restaurant, you are enjoying a meal in their home—an introduction to an organic wine estate and farm and how it functions. Rita hosts cooking classes. Silvano, a veterinarian, hunts with his "faithful dog" Mia for wild mushrooms for your table. They produce cheese for your meal, and honey from bees on the property, and meat from free-range pigs, "a special breed called 'Cinta Senese.'" Then there is Rita's savory bruschetta with arrabbiata sauce. When it is time for dessert, you are served ice cream that is graced with Silvano's balsamic vinegar that has been aged for thirty years.

Their highly regarded wines are from small vintages but of the highest quality. You should try a bottle of the host's signature wine, "Easy to Fall in Love." Jack and Barbara Nicklaus have. Peyton Manning has. Our neighbors Mike and Jennifer Fitzgerald have.

You will likely agree with TripAdvisor that "Tenuta Casanova ranks among the 10 best wine cellars in Europe."

The Macallan
Every Scotsman's Favorite Single Malt

TROON, Scotland—As the British Open Championship comes to a close, there are those who follow the leaders step for step; but there are also those who choose to watch the action on giant screens with restrooms and countless bars nearby.

If you partake of the national drink of Scotland, as you might find, as you expected, that there is an endless supply of scotch. There are, by my unofficial count, roughly 150 single malt brands of scotch. I would assume that there are that many or more of the blended variety, like Famous Grouse, which is a popular choice during the Open Championship.

To survey a sunset in a Scottish garden, with a single malt like the Macallan in reach, is a memorable experience. I learned to drink beer in college like most everybody else. Travel in France and an introduction to French wines became so fulfilling that it was easy to eliminate beer altogether.

Not sure what your experience might be, but while there *is* a lot of drinking going on in the land of the Picts, I don't recall seeing a drunk Scotsman. However, I have a Scottish friend who invited me to dinner one year—he lived a few miles out in the country—and hired a taxi to come pick me up. He barely registered a DUI, but lost his license for twelve months as I recall. There is, as it is everywhere, a difference in being over the limit and being drunk, but the British courts are not very lenient with those who drink and drive.

One summer at the airport in Edinburgh, with a long wait for a flight to London, I ventured into a spirits shop and asked the lady behind the cash register a question: if a Scotsman could have his choice scotch when ordering, what would it be?

She looked around the store, which was empty—I was the only customer—and said, "I am not supposed to tell you this, but any Scotsman I know, having a choice, would choose The Macallan." The prevailing view in Scotland is that the Macallan is the best single malt there is.

There is a story of an American sportswriter spending time at Royal Dornoch, the birthplace of the famous golf architect, Donald Ross. He was researching the early life of the architect and played golf every day with a caddie named Sandy, who up learning that he was looping for a magazine writer on expense account, would go to the bar after golf and start ordering The Macallan.

At the end of the week, after playing the last round, the writer and the caddie headed to the bar with the caddie asking for a Macallan. Said the writer: "Sandy, have you drunk Macallan all your life?" The reply, with an acute Scottish accent was, "Oh, noe, notchet."

While for many travelers a single malt is a must when they stop in Scotland, but for the equally famous dish, haggis, there is often more restraint in fulfilling their curiosity for the equally famous dish, haggis.

If you "look it up" as they say, you will find that haggis is a Scottish dish "consisting of a sheep's or calf's offal mixed with suet, oatmeal and seasoning and boiled in a bag, traditionally one made from the animal's stomach."

The first time I ever had haggis, the host suggested that to enjoy haggis, I should liberally sprinkle single malt scotch over it. That did help a little.

If you happen to be invited to dinner with a sheik and he serves goat brains, the proper thing to do would be to partake of what he might consider a delicacy. Goulash in Budapest, chicken mull in North Georgia, and Rocky Mountain oysters in Montana—there is always something different throughout the world at mealtime.

I once asked a Scotsman how to cook haggis. He said: first, take all the ingredients and put them on the stove and let them marinate in the open air. Then put everything in a pot and let it simmer for twenty-four hours. Then take it off the stove, and sprinkle with salt and pepper generously as it cools to room temperature. Then take it out and throw it in the dumpster.

Thomas Jefferson
Renaissance Man with Feet of Clay

MONTICELLO, Virgina—At a stop at a convenience store before moving onto the expansive property that accommodates the former home of Thomas Jefferson, our third president, I asked the lady behind the cash register if she had change for a quarter.

With a quizzical look, she exclaimed, "Haven't had that request lately!" She may have been thinking that there was nothing in stock that cost less than 25-cents, but I was not interested in making a small purchase. I wanted to survey the back of the nickel, which reflects the image of Jefferson's plantation home, before touring the impressive structure that Jefferson began building when he was twenty-six years old on five thousand acres in Albemarle County that he inherited from his father.

Since 1938, the "Jefferson nickel," which replaced the Buffalo nickel, has featured the former president on one side and his home at Monticello on the other. While this exercise did not reveal anything insightful, it enabled one to stand outside the Jefferson mansion and connect with a nickel that I occasionally pull out of my pocket and rub for good luck. I wanted to make sure I was in possession of a Jefferson nickel while touring Monticello.

Before he became controversial, I was fascinated with the genius of Mr. Jefferson, who emotionally connected with the French to the extent that there are several tributes to him in Paris. The statue that seems to be most prominent is the one by the Seine. When Jefferson was the ambassador to France, he admired the dome of the Hôtel de Salm (now a national museum), which was being built at the time. When he returned home, he had the roof of his residence at Monticello removed and replaced with a dome that reminded him of the Salm.

Jefferson was a farmer, a builder, a botanist, an architect, a writer, and more. He is most famous for writing the Declaration of Independence. He was proficient and efficient. He built his alcove bed so that he could get up and move just a few feet to his study and work at any hour of the day or night.

Having lived in Paris, he seriously studied French architecture. Throughout the house and grounds at Monticello, the Jefferson influence makes you realize that this founder of the University of Virginia in nearby Charlottesville was one of the most remarkable Renaissance men that our country has ever known.

He kept detailed records on everything, especially trees and plants. He swapped ideas with his friend and neighbor, James Madison. Montpelier, Madison's plantation, is twenty-nine miles away, but when the Madisons came to visit the Jeffersons, they stayed for weeks.

The Louisiana Purchase was one of the greatest decisions made by an American president, unless you consider Seward's Folly, the purchase of Alaska from the Russians, to be a better deal. Jefferson, as president, arranged to buy 530 million acres of Louisiana territory from France for $15 million. The Louisiana Purchase literally changed the face of America, doubling its size, and helped to further reduce the influence of the British on this side of the Atlantic.

Jefferson's best work, perhaps, came when he was the principal author of the Declaration of Independence. In this great work, there are references to all men having been created equal, which brought a sentiment that is clouded in retrospect by the fact that he was a slave owner.

In addition to that, there is DNA testing that became convincing that one of his slave women, Sally Hemings, was indeed his mistress who bore six children by him. The museum library here at Monticello is filled with accounts of the affair. Jefferson was, by many accounts, good to his slaves, but apparently given to the view that they were inferior human beings.

After a second trip here, there remains continued inspiration by Jefferson's brilliance, but frustration at the controversy around his character—a slave owner who did not live up to his poignant wording in the Declaration of Independence.

The history of slavery and its aftermath has troubled our great country for generations, and its effects often rest on our conscience to this day.

Yampa Fishing Yields Trophy Fish
in the Best Outdoor Setting

STEAMBOAT SPRINGS, Colorado—Big-time skiing began here in one of the most fascinating of states. I am intrigued by the history of Colorado, a state with a hardscrabble past but one that offers inspiration for those who have an affection for history and the great outdoors.

There is Native American history, there's mining history, there's Dust Bowl history, there's hunting, fishing, skiing, and Denver Broncos football, if you want to identify with the latest passion. Whatever you are attracted to, you can find it—from sporting opportunity to the great outdoors. There are mountains and prairies, rivers and creeks. Colorado! Damn hard not to love it.

> Oh beautiful for spacious skies,
> For amber waves of grain,
> For purple mountain majesties,
> Above the fruited plain!

This is America at its best, and you can find it most graphically in the electrifying West, a region I don't visit often enough. But when I do, I fall in love with every sojourn and can't wait to return. There is not a Western state for which I don't reserve the greatest affection, but Colorado is hard to beat. Its varied landscape and a past that is both illuminating and ignominious—many Japanese Americans were sent here in WWII, and Colorado was once home to seventeen thousand members of the Ku Klux Klan—are a reminder that people are forever at odds with ambition, ideals, money, and one another.

Today, Colorado is vibrant, green, and exciting. It functions with zeal, love of the environment, and appreciation for its early times—from the Pony Express and wagon trains to the railroad and Coors Light. Our 38th state is where people flock to vacation or choose a homestead.

My most recent trip had me heading West as a guest. I'm grateful for that. My friend, Bill Griffin, has a tie with the Windwalker Ranch near

Steamboat Springs. The dictionary might not disclose what a "windwalker" is, but I think it must have some connection to the Native Americans. There's plenty to do at Windwalker Ranch, from horseback riding to fly fishing. Every meal, organized by Tom Henninger, the ranch foreman, is an adventure. Filling and fulfilling. Love and laughter. This is where the heavens meet the earth.

The Yampa River—its plentiful trout: rainbow, brown, and brook—is lively and alluring. The 250-mile-long, north-flowing body of water is a tributary of the Green River. It has the second largest watershed in the state. It hasn't seen a small trout since Noah docked the ark. When you stand in the rock-strewn Yampa less than knee-deep, you find that nymph fishing here has to be the best imaginable.

However, it was a San Juan worm that made my day. The San Juan worm is not exactly a worm, but a nymph pattern, first developed on the San Juan River below the Navajo Dam in New Mexico to, as fishermen say, "imitate the river's large abundance of aquatic worms." Being inexpert, I had no reason to appreciate the use of the fly when Colin Taylor said, "Let's try this."

It had been only a few minutes as I swooned to the view of the Rocky Mountains and the captivating scenes that were fascinating to a sometime fisherman who believes that fly fishing is like golf—you don't have to be good at it to enjoy it—when a strike took my breath away. Little did I know that a 21-inch brown trout—tenacious, bold, and unrelenting—was on the line. He was as determined to spit my San Juan worm as I was eager to make him my signature trophy catch.

My arms became fatigued. My resolve was tested, but the trout, after a prolonged skirmish, reluctantly slid into Colin's net. It wasn't a walk in the park by any means, but I won the fight. "Gee," Colin said. "Good fly fishermen fish for years and don't catch a brown like that." I savored every moment, softly singing "America the Beautiful." I was humbled and felt like taking a knee, so I did, right on a big rock in the middle of the Yampa River.

"God bless America!" Colorado and the Yampa River confirm that He did.

PART IV

In Touch with the Greatest Generation

Although I had an uncle, a favorite, who served in the Pacific in World War II, and my mother's younger brother died mysteriously in training exercises near Pensacola, Florida, in preparation to join the war in the Pacific, I did not get attached to the "Good War" (what could be good about a war that resulted in more than eighty million deaths worldwide?) until traveling through Europe in the summers of the seventies and eighties.

With the good fortune of latching onto a light public relations job, I chose to be paid with an airline ticket to Europe instead of a monthly check, which enabled me to travel to the British Open every summer. A week spent in England or Scotland brought about the most rewarding and fulfilling experiences.

For years, I would spend a week bouncing around Europe and then the better portion of a week at the championship venue. In 1980, the Open championship took place at the Royal St. George's Golf Club, located in the village of Sandwich, which is a fraction more than twelve miles from Dover.

After starting out at Stratford, where I saw a live production of Shakespeare's *A Midsummer Night's Dream*, I found my way to Dover by train and crossed the English Channel via hovercraft. At Calais, I rented a car and drove to the Normandy beaches and was overwhelmed by the Normandy American Cemetery at Colleville-sur-Mer. I spent three days at Normandy before crossing back over the English Channel and winding up at a village called Elmstone for the Open.

Following that sojourn, I developed an insatiable desire to connect with the history of the Greatest Generation, and have not missed many of the major battle venues in Europe as well as a few in the Pacific. Early on, however, I always made an attempt to meet up with survivors—and not just the American heroes.

An opportunity came when I learned about the town of Oradour-sur-Glane, where following the D-Day invasion the Nazis attempted to murder the entire town of 642 inhabitants, including women and children. Women and children were expendable when the brutal Nazis held sway.

There were six survivors including a Frenchman named Robert Hébras. After invoking an assist from my daughter, Camille, who speaks French, an effort was made to contact him, but to no avail.

Finally, I called my friend Denis Lalanne, an internationally celebrated French sportswriter, who lived out his life in Biarritz, which is near the Spanish border. He took a train to Chartres and subsequently drove us through the French countryside to enjoy the farm scenes, food, and wine in the charming villages on the way to Biarritz.

The focal point of our journey was Oradour-sur-Glane. Being the expert reporter that he was, Denis got out the local phone book and tracked down Robert Hébras' son, who linked us to his father.

We went by Robert Hébras' house for a couple of hours one afternoon, with him telling us how he survived. Mr. Hébras is living today at the age of ninety-five. His story (see page 281) is stunning. In warm sunshine accompanied with a nice bottle of Bordeaux, he talked matter-of-fact about the heinous event that claimed the life of his sisters and mother.

It was a sobering moment that I shall never forget.

The WWII historian Stephen Ambrose became a friend, owing to a book he had written. Myrna and I extended our stay in France one summer following the British Open to take a pleasure cruise with our Parisian friends up the Seine to the Oise river, destination: Compiègne, where the "controversial little railway car" (facsimile) is the town's greatest attraction. The Compiègne wagon is where the armistice that ended WWI was signed, and later it was taken by Hitler to Berlin to humiliate the French when his blitzkrieg brought France to its knees in 1940. While in Compiègne, I read Ambrose's book *Pegasus Bridge*, which has to do with the Normandy invasion, British sector.

Following that summer trip, I found my way to New Orleans as soon as possible to meet Ambrose, who had been offered a scholarship by Coach Wallace Butts to play football at the University of Georgia. Ambrose would eventually become the foremost WWII historian.

We became casual friends. He was always generous with regard to introductions to many of the WWII heroes he knew and had interviewed. Because of Ambrose, I got to interview many of them, too: Major John Howard, the British commander who liberated the first French family of the war, and his glider pilot Jim Wallwork, who had migrated to Victoria, Canada (on a trip to Seattle, I rented a car and drove to his home. It was a delightful sojourn that offered the ancillary benefits of seeing the beautiful Northwest and spectacular Canadian countryside.

Ambrose also introduced me to Hans von Luck, who had served in the 7th Panzer Division and 21st Panzer Division in Germany. Luck, a protégé of Field Marshall Erwin Rommel, autographed his book *Panzer Commander* for me.

Ambrose organized a D-Day conference in New Orleans in the early eighties that included appearances by Tom Hanks, star of *Saving Private Ryan*, and Tom Brokaw of NBC News and author of *The Greatest Generation*. I met a number of WWII veterans, many of whom I later visited on their turfs, which were uplifting and resonating opportunities.

I even got to know a pettifogging, but delightful, imposter named Howard Manoian. He claimed to have jumped with the 82nd Airborne Division at Sainte-Mère-Eglise on D-Day. He had a home there and returned every summer, holding court in the local bars, notably "Le Stop." Howard not only duped me; he duped the French government, which awarded him its Légion d'Honneur. He was charming to talk to, nonetheless, and I was not in a position to vet his tales before writing about him. Live and learn.

The books I have read on WWII number in the dozens, and if somebody comes out with a new treatise on the war, I will be eager to ring up Amazon for immediate delivery.

In my basement office, I have a filing cabinet filled with information about Normandy and dozens of WWII and Normandy brochures. In my bar, you will find a bottle of Calvados, the apple brandy that Normans are delighted to serve before or after meals, or when just relaxing in the sun. Our servicemen who were a part of the Normandy breakout were quite pleased to tell you about Calvados.

À votre santé. To your health.

Admiral Nimitz
Truly a Great American

FREDERICKSBURG, Texas—German immigrants began arriving here in the 1800s during the time of Prince Frederick of Prussia and totaled more than three thousand by 1850. Some were political refugees, some fled religious persecution. Many simply saw opportunity.

They were, as you might expect, hearty, industrious, and extraordinarily adept at making do. Their influence is still prevalent in Fredericksburg, where you can walk down the street and buy German sausages and sample beer made from recipes that date back to the time of the early settlers. It should come as no surprise that there is a Biergarten on Main Street.

The main attractions in Fredericksburg are the National Museum of the Pacific War and the museum honoring Fleet Admiral Chester Nimitz, who grew up here. Visitors with a bent for World War II history, especially the Pacific theater, will find the Admiral Nimitz Museum inspiring. Chances are that one visit will make you want to return. The town, the inviting appeal of Texas Hill Country, and the Nimitz legend are alluring.

With more than a casual interest, I am an aficionado of the life and times of Chester W. Nimitz, a third-generation German who was born on February 24, 1885. Four years later, another man with Germanic influence, Adolf Hitler, was born in Braunau, Austria, during the days of the Austro-Hungarian Empire: one man, the latter, demented and given to horrific crimes against mankind; the other a hero in the epic struggle to rid the world of that dastardly dictator, Adolf Hitler.

Most of us are not schooled in the tenets of war. Most of us identify easier with the early hippie movement, "Make love, not war." Too often, young men must give up their lives to win battles against senseless odds so that vainglorious generals can write books, pin on more medals, and enjoy their day in the conqueror's sun. Patriotic feelings, however, have caused millions throughout history to be willing to give their lives for their country. The Greatest Generation, for whom we should be forever grateful, for example. Nimitz had compassion for those men. Hitler was a man devoid of compassion when it came to human life.

Nimitz was perhaps the most exceptional of leaders. He and Dwight David Eisenhower were different than most. They were given to gentlemanly traits. You think of them and then think of Patton, Montgomery, MacArthur, and Mark Clark. Doesn't matter the cost, get there first.

When Mark Clark, whose decisions have been negatively critiqued by historians, marched into Rome ahead of the British, he was chagrined and disappointed that the Normandy invasion gained worldwide headlines two days after his troops had captured Rome: "How do you like that?" Clark is quoted in several books. "They didn't even let us have the newspaper headlines for the fall of Rome for one day."

One of the most moving speeches for twentieth-century Americans came when Gen. Douglas MacArthur made his farewell speech to the United States Corps of Cadets at West Point on May 12, 1962. Look for it on the internet and you will likely be overcome with the prose and heartfelt reminisces of his military career—but this is the same MacArthur who waded ashore when he returned from Australia to the Philippines and proceeded to repeat the process so the photographers could get the "best shot" of his landing. With MacArthur it was "like father, like son." An officer who knew both men once said, "Arthur MacArthur was the most flamboyantly egotistical man I have ever seen, until I met his son." Dwight Eisenhower noted that MacArthur "....would like to occupy a throne room surrounded by experts in flattery."

For contrast, Admiral Nimitz was a real leader, giving credit to others and allowing his staff to work together effectively without the influence of an overbearing, egotistical superior who was more concerned about his image than sharing credit. Nimitz even forgave his subordinates if they made mistakes.

When Nimitz assumed command of the Pacific Fleet ten days after the Japanese attack on Pearl Harbor, there was a critical shortage of ships, planes, and supplies, but Nimitz inspired confidence in his staff and the sailors under his command, which would bring about a halt to the Japanese dominance in the Pacific, aided by a most valuable contribution in materiel production back home.

As the rearmed and resupplied navy began to inflict serious losses on the Imperial Japanese Navy, US forces gained momentum and remained on the offensive, which helped hasten the end of the war. It was a personal thrill to stand before a photo of Admiral Nimitz in his hometown of

Fredericksburg, Texas, and salute a modest war hero who gave of him-self—a rare and selfless leader who was without ego and vanity.

Bobby Bell
Some of Our Heroes Rest In Peace
on International Soil

HENRI-CHAPELLE, Belgium—Meeting Bobby Bell brought about one of those serendipitous moments to savor—the result of a referral. Enterprise and referral can foster the most delightful experiences, connecting you with someone who has something to offer, something to say—something of substance that is resonating and uplifting.

"Tomorrow," Miranda Prevaes had said over drinks with her husband, Bas, and their energetic young son, Sebastian, at the Hotel Beaumont in Maastricht, a charming and delightful city, "They will be waiting for you at Henri-Chapelle."

Miranda had organized an illuminating tour of the Netherlands American Cemetery at Margraten and was now connecting a visitor with officials of other American cemeteries in the region.

Upon arrival at Henri-Chapelle, I was greeted by the aforementioned Bobby Bell, the superintendent, who hails from the Florida Panhandle. He is an affable, hospitable, and informative type. If you are taking notes as you walk the grounds of the cemetery with him, it is nearly impossible to keep up.

Bobby knows the history of this cemetery like Bacchus knew wine. He knows about those who rest here in honored glory. He has a cogent grasp of the history of World War II. He is an expatriate who connects visitors to facts they would not otherwise be introduced to. He constantly toasts the Greatest Generation. He is a proud American.

Effusive and accommodating, he wants all visitors to appreciate the contributions of the Americans who paid the ultimate price for victory in battlefields on this side of the Atlantic. We were at a disadvantage, but with uncommon valor and enduring commitment we were able to take the measure of an enemy who was better prepared, better equipped, and blessed with the advantage of waging war on familiar soil. Hitler viewed the "citizen-soldiers" of America without the resolve to measure up to the task at hand. Happily, history confirms he was wrong. Our citizen-soldiers gave a sensational account of themselves.

In order to prove Hitler wrong, 405,399 Americans gave their lives to the Allied cause. There are three Medal of Honor recipients buried here at Henri-Chapelle. The three Tester brothers, natives of the New Victory community in Tennessee, are buried side by side, and their story offers this poignant historical vignette. The Testers' father, a humble and austere farmer, was notified that a telegram awaited him at the Western Union office in town. Not once, which would have been bad enough, but thrice, he drove a horse and buggy to town to learn that another son had been killed in battle. Overcome with grief, he cried all the way home every time. Surely heaven awaits this everyday American. He, too, is a member of the Greatest Generation.

We often consider the sports figures who blaze athletic trails while making millions of dollars as heroes. They are not, but the parents of the Tester brothers are. They gave up their sons for America's cause.

Unspeakable tragedy of a different nature is affiliated with Henri-Chappelle. Here lie buried the seven of the eleven black men who were massacred at Wereth, Belgium, during the Battle of the Bulge. The "Wereth 11" happened on the farm of a Dutch family who took them in and befriended them. They fed the black soldiers and provided shelter. Somehow or other, as such tragedies take place, the Nazis learned their story. They came and captured the unit and took them out into the woods and tortured them to death, mutilating their bodies.

This was just prior to the Allied advance into Germany, which is worth noting. Had time been on the side of the Nazis, the Dutch family who befriended the black US soldiers would have suffered a similar fate. All of which brings front and center this question. How could anybody be as brutal and inhumane as the Nazis?

If you think about it, the Nazi mentality is no different from yester-year's Ku Klux Klan, which still has sympathizers. Taking the life of another whom you deem to be unworthy requires no conscience.

The biggest despots in history were also the biggest cowards.

D-Day Ranger, UGA Matriculate,
Wants to Set the Record Straight

POINTE DU HOC, France — A trip to the Normandy beaches allows for an opportunity to absorb as much as possible. Your briefcase bulges with brochures, maps, and useful printouts that help one try to relive the D-Day experience.

If any reference to home—meaning the state of Georgia—surfaces, you latch on to it like gold. That is why it made my chest stick out button-popping proud when I found a booklet that told the Pointe du Hoc story of a Georgian, "L-Rod" Petty, wiping out thirty enemy soldiers on D-Day.

The booklet noted that he was from Cohutta, the North Georgia hamlet near Dalton, which gets its name from the Cherokee Indian word that means "frog." So, a search began to see if he was still living. A series of calls to strangers in Cohutta led to a nice lady who knew about L-Rod Petty and she politely explained that this World War II hero lived in Carmel, New York.

Telephone Information provided his number, and a call went out to a man who is really named William L. Petty, a University of Georgia matriculate who for years has run an underprivileged boys' home an hour or so from Manhattan.

"I came here after the war," he says, "fell in love with the kids and never left," this reluctant hero told me by phone one spring afternoon.

It turns out that he had been a maverick in school in Cohutta, which had only 138 kids in the entire student body. A mumps and measles epidemic kept a lot of students and teachers away from school at one point. When a substitute teacher passed around the roll one morning, Petty signed in as L. Rod McGee. This meant that he could play hooky and get away with it, which he did, but only briefly. The principal, when the "L. Rod" business came to his attention, knew exactly what was up. And who the imposter was.

Petty's name became L-Rod with his classmates, however, and it stuck throughout his life. War historians have referred to him that way for years, but he has been upset since D-Day about his invasion reputation.

He simply does not like what has been written about him. He says that the accounts of his personal heroics are an "embarrassment."

What upsets Petty is that he is not sure how many enemy soldiers he killed at Normandy. He insists that the box score of 30 is an exaggeration and that is what troubles him. "What damn fool," he says, "would actually keep count?" Killing another man, even in war, is nothing to celebrate.

The way his reputation came about was that a couple of days after D-Day, a writer from the Atlanta papers looked him up at the pointe and said, "I'm looking for a hero and they say you are it." With that, Petty began to complain that the men around him were heroes as much as anybody. Then one member of his company yelled out, "Don't let him fool you, he killed at least thirty Germans." Petty tried, in vain, to disclaim what was said, "but that figure made every headline in Georgia," he said.

That is the way it has been for years, and he can't seem to set the record straight.

He has fought with writers for years to get it right. He even fought with the Ranger historian, who he says is a self-serving plagiarist. "That ground [Pointe du Hoc] is sacred ground," Petty says. "A lot of men died there with distinction. There is no need to dramatize things. There is no need to exaggerate."

He fought *Reader's Digest* editors to make sure that any reporting on his experience was accurate.

> We lost a lot of men from machine gunfire on our flanks, but even so, some of the stories have been so dramatic that you realize what has been written has been an exaggeration. Naturally I did shoot enemy soldiers. I jumped in a ditch once with a bunch of Germans. Another time, several Germans jumped in a ditch where I was. What are you going to do in that situation? But to keep count would be ghoulish as hell, and it embarrasses me that accounts of my involvement have been exaggerated. I owe it to those who are buried over there to tell the truth.

Petty says that he normally doesn't talk about the invasion that much, except with family and fellow Rangers who get together for reunions. This time around, he has talked with someone who has called for one reason. "I would like to set the record straight," he says.

L-Rod Petty is one of World War II's reluctant heroes.

French Woman Remembers Liberation
of First French Family in WWII

LISIEUX, France—Georgette Verhaeghe was ten years old at the time of the D-Day invasion. She will never forget the liberation of her country from the Germans. She will always remember how her mother loathed the Nazis and how frightened her family was of the occupation troops. She will never forget the happiness the Allied invasion brought her family, particularly her mother who had grown up in the Alsace-Lorraine area of France where she had first learned about German occupation troops as a girl.

Georgette's parents, Georges and Theresa Gondree, ran a café at the Bénouville Bridge near Caen.

The bridge was later named the Pegasus Bridge for the mythological Greek horse whose image had become the emblem of the British paratrooper unit that captured the bridge intact on D-Day.

The Gondrees were members of the French Resistance, and being from Alsace-Lorraine, Madame Gondree understood German. Whatever she and her husband learned about the German military they passed on to the underground.

They learned where the explosives that were meant to blow up the bridge in case of an Allied attack were kept. They knew where the gun emplacements were located, the calibers and working conditions of the guns. They knew how long and how deep the trenches and bunkers were. They knew the location of the pillboxes. They knew how many troops were guarding the bridge. Whatever they learned they passed onto the underground, which relayed it immediately to Allied contacts in England.

On the 50th anniversary of the D-Day invasion, Georgette Verhaeghe wants the world to not forget the heroic French Resistance. German executions of suspected Resistance members took place daily and publicly. But the French refused to give in.

Fishermen would cast nets close to German positions but in those nets would be Kodak cameras. Spies in laundries removed name tags from German underwear. Carrier pigeons with valuable information were released to fly home to England, much to the constant irritation of the Germans. Radio transmissions took place nightly throughout Normandy, even though discovery of such equipment meant instant death.

When the British airborne units arrived by glider in the night at the Pegasus Bridge, Georgette's mother heard the crash. "Mommie," Georgette says, "was disturbed by the noise of the landing but was not sure what was happening. She awakened Daddy and told him, 'The invasion has begun.' 'You dream,' he said. 'No,' she told him. 'Something is not normal on the other side of the canal.'"

Madame Gondree became such a fan of the British 6th Airborne Division that no one from that unit who was there on D-Day ever had to pay for a drink at her café afterwards.

The Gondrees were the first French family to be liberated on D-Day, making their liberators fully aware of how appreciative they were.

Her parents, Georgette realizes today, could have experienced the alternative fate of many Normans, who were as courageous as the D-Day invaders, by giving their own lives working with the French Resistance fighters.

George Poschner
An Immigrant Story that
Leaves you Weak-Kneed

While I continued to soak up the ongoing replay of Georgia's Rose Bowl defeat of Oklahoma on New Year's Day and subsequently took a second trip to Pasadena, I was reminded of what was taking place in Athens seventy-five years ago.

The many country boys, who enjoyed the thrill of Georgia's 9-0 victory over UCLA, had traded in their gridiron regalia for rifles and bullets. They had swapped their leather helmets for military headgear made of magnesium and steel, weighing just under three pounds, that would hopefully resist an enemy bullet.

The National Football League existed, but all able-bodied would-be players were bunking on ships or in foxholes. The Bulldogs had, for the most part, come home from the Rose Bowl and went straight off to war. Some would never return home.

One of the more remarkable stories was that of George Poschner, the All-American end who enrolled at UGA, owing to his friendship with superstar Frank Sinkwich. In high school, Poschner was such a skinny, lightweight kid that he was not allowed to play football. He became a cheerleader.

At UGA, Poschner was the beneficiary of three ample meals a day (as a kid, the best his widowed mother could do was provide two daily meals) and he began to put on weight until soon he weighed in at 175 pounds—certainly not imposing, even for that era, but with other assets, he became an exceptional player. The coaches learned that Poschner, as the late Bill Hartman often said, "had the guts of a burglar."

Against Alabama in 1942, a game that was played at Grant Field in Atlanta because of wartime gas rationing, Poschner had one of the greatest days of any Bulldog pass receiver. He and his hometown buddy, Sinkwich, fueled a comeback victory, 21-10, that caused the Rose Bowl to begin seriously tracking Georgia. The game attracted regional and national sportswriters, who had wanted to observe Sinkwich in action but came away dazzled by the performance of Poschner, Sinkwich's roommate. Poschner's play in that game influenced *Look* magazine to select him for All-America honors.

Down 10-0 at the half, one of the Bulldogs players sarcastically remarked, "How do you think Tommy Witt feels about us now?" Witt, a teammate, had lost his life in military action in North Africa. The remark electrified the team as Sinkwich then led the Bulldogs to a pair of touchdowns that won the game. Poschner was the receiver on both tosses, one a sensational fingertip catch and the other a spectacular grab that was described as follows by Bulldog historian John Stegeman: "From the Alabama 14, Sinkwich fired toward Poschner, at the goal line, but two Alabama defenders got to him at the same time as the ball—one hitting him high and the other low, causing him to turn a flip and land on his head. A moan went up from the stadium, but suddenly the officials' arms were in the air. Poschner had somehow held on to the football and incredibly Georgia was ahead."

A second-generation Hungarian, Poschner remembered that his family received a letter from an old country official, exhorting him to return home and fight for the fatherland (then under Nazi control). Even though Poschner experienced a hard life, as it turned out, he would have never considered taking up arms for anybody except America.

He did just that, and the consequences were debilitating. During a battle in France at the time of Battle of the Bulge, Poschner charged a German machine-gun nest and was severely injured. He was left for dead, which brings about an interesting story. A medic, Robert Taylor, from Shaker Heights, Ohio, actually saved his life.

Poschner, who had met Taylor after the war, had lost contact with his fellow Ohioan when I visited Poschner at his winter home in Ft. Lauderdale in the early eighties. I made a call to Hal Lebovitz, columnist for the *Cleveland Plain Dealer*, who wrote a note in his column that Poschner was interested in contacting Taylor, who then read the reference, subsequently responded, and went to see Poschner in Youngstown in August of 1982.

In my conversation with Taylor, following his reunion with Poschner, he recalled the battle and the aftermath. "We made an attack and Poschner was part of the attack, very, very effectively on a German position. The weather was bitter cold, probably five or ten degrees above zero. On the counterattack, he got hit and in the process I used up two aid kits trying to staunch the wound, which was from a bullet right down from the front of his eyes and out the back of the head. The probabilities of living through that were one in a million. I patched him up the best I could.

"I took a coat off a dead German as we were being forced out. I covered him [Poschner] with the coat over his American coat so he would be as warm as possible. We did not get back to where he was for at least three days. We had counterattacked and took the position back.

"The first thing I did when we came back through, was to check George for a pulse. There was none. I checked his eyes and throat and there was still life there. I used morphine on him before leaving him. I did all the checks a medic would do and one of the things I checked was his eyelids. There was action there [his eyelids flickered just a bit] and he still had a pulse in his throat.

"We called for the aidmen and they came and took him to the rear. The next thing I heard was that George had recovered. When I returned to Cleveland there was an article about him in the newspaper and I identified myself as the medic who had worked with him.

"The only reason that he wasn't picked up by the Germans was because they must have thought he was dead and were going to call their grave registration service to pick him up."

Poschner was honored with the Purple Heart, the Distinguished Service Cross, and the Bronze Star Medal. However, he had both legs amputated below the knees, lost all the fingers on his right hand (he had to learn to write left-handed), and was partially paralyzed on his right side. When he was elected to the Georgia Sports Hall of Fame in 1982, Poschner refused assistance and somehow rose up from his seat, wobbling on his crutches, and made it to the podium where he expressed gratitude for being an American.

George Poschner's story is one of the most amazing and compelling in Georgia football history.

Glider Pilots Achieved the Improbable, If Not Impossible

LADNER, British Columbia—Jim Wallwork flew the Horsa glider that delivered Major John Howard's unit right on target, where they captured the Bénouville Bridge–later known as Pegasus Bridge—and the Ranville bridge intact on D-Day.

Capturing the bridges before the Germans could blow them up was a key development for the British invasion objective to move men and equipment over those bridges for the attack on the German communication center of Caen.

Major Howard knew that the element of surprise was in his favor, but only if the glider put down in an appropriate proximity of the bridges.

By the time of the the the 50th anniversary year of the Normandy invasion, allied pilots were finally getting proper credit for their spectacular flying feats.

Jim Wallwork and his copilot, Johnnie Ainsworth, achieved the improbable, if not the impossible. They made a bullseye landing, delivering Howard and his men within fifty yards of the Pegasus Bridge.

Wallwork was typical of the British glider pilots trained for D-Day.

They had been recruited from regular army units. Air Vice-Marshal Arthur Harris, Chief of Air Staff, had said: "The idea that semiskilled unpicked personnel could, with a maximum of training, be entrusted with the piloting of these troop carriers is fantastic. Their operation is equivalent to force-landing the largest sized aircraft without engine aid—than which there is no higher test of piloting skill."

Air Chief Marshal Leigh Mallory, who commanded the Allied Forces on D-Day, called it the greatest flying feat of World War II.

Wallwork and his fellow glider pilots had practiced Operation Deadstick, the name of the glider operation, forty-two times by D-Day. "We were bloody good at it [flying and landing the gliders]," he says.

On the perfect landing of his glider, Wallwork says, "We were not the least bit surprised. Not that I am arrogant about it. It was the training, and it gave us confidence. We used a stopwatch and followed precise procedures. There was the temptation to fly by the seat of our pants, but we knew what we had to do. Coming in, I could see the river, the canal in the bridge out of the corner of my eye."

Now that his story is the subject of widespread interest on both sides of the Atlantic, Wallwork is not altogether comfortable with what is taking place.

I feel that I am a bit of a fraud," he says. "I don't like being singled out for a praise, even in my late years. It is very simple. I left so many friends behind when I came home. My assignment was a comfortable way to go into war. It was a short commitment and I never think about the war without thinking about the poor infantrymen who went through four years of hell in the worst conditions. You never want to be in the bloody infantry.

How it worked out that I lived to tell my experiences is something that I have often thought about. Why was I one of the lucky ones? There are so many who didn't make it. Young boys who weren't so fortunate.

D-Day is something that I can talk about since it was a victory for us, but the landing later at Arnhem [Holland] where we lost so many men is something that I never talk about. We took a terrible thrashing there. That is one we lost.

Wallwork flew his glider into Holland, and as it was in Normandy, the fighting was intense but he survived once again. Wallwork can still see the faces of his buddies who gave their lives in the war. He has thought often of them and why they were not smiled on by fate. A clever, cynical-speaking man with a warm dose of humor punctuating every conversation, Wallwork always becomes sentimental when he talks about his experience. He never forgets his buddies.

They had no chance to start a postwar life. To choose a mate, raise a family. To own a home and a boat, as he does for pleasure-cruising and scenic Western Canada. To enjoy good health and the good life. To bounce grandchildren on their knees.

Wallwork talks about the mission today for one reason. "They," he says of his friends who never came home, "deserved better. You know they all had one thing in common. They were all willing to die for their country. I was too, I just wasn't called on. Why was it different for me? It is a question I think of often."

"Here Rests In Honored Glory,
A Comrade In Arms"

OMAHA BEACH, France—Having been here before, there is the immediate impression that you suddenly know more about what went on during the D-Day invasion of June 6, 1944. It's like getting a second chance, a second look—a second opinion.

You are also keenly aware that it doesn't matter how many times you return to these beaches; emotionally, nothing can compare to the first visit.

In my case, my first visit came late in the afternoon on a calm and casual weather day as the sun was setting over the English Channel. I was alone in the Normandy American Cemetery by Omaha Beach, and was overwhelmed by the sheer majesty, dignity, and serenity of the cemetery. Nothing was unkempt, not a single chewing gum wrapper drifting about. Not a sprig of grass needed shearing away. Everything was as orderly as a plebes' quarters at West Point.

The sun glistened off the acres of grave markers, which are so perfectly aligned that they seem to have been placed by a surveyor who allowed for no margin of error. You look straight ahead, and the alignment is perfect. You look diagonally and the alignment is perfect. Flowers abound. Trees and shrubs dot the landscape, fittingly nestled among the tombstones as if there could be some order with death.

Then you search the names on the markers, and you realize that while seasoned veterans from the North African campaign died here, many teenagers also died here. Farm boys, city boys. Kids raised during the Great Depression. Well-to-do kids, privileged kids. Poor kids. Protestants, Catholics, and Jews.

Years later, you recall over and over again that first Normandy cemetery experience. It rests indelibly in your mind, even if there were no family members who took part in the Great War and were too old for WWII. I had an uncle who went through some difficult fighting in the Pacific. Most of my rural Middle Georgia relatives were past draft age for the second World War..

With a fair amount of research on the events at Normandy, I began to better understand the invasion from a fabulous model of the D-Day invasion at a museum a few miles from here at Arromanches-les-Bains. Spending the afternoon at the museum resulted in arriving at the Normandy American Cemetery—which is just east of Saint-Laurent-sur-Mer and northwest of Bayeux in Colleville-sur-Mer, 170 miles west of Paris—at sunset.

The cemetery is the biggest I have ever seen. The initial sweep of the several plots with your eyes is a breathtaking experience. There are just under ten thousand Latin crosses and Stars of David here for the eye to behold. (This doesn't account for the fourteen thousand bodies that were sent home.)

If a cemetery can be beautiful, the American Cemetery is. Even inspirational.

My sundown experience stirred emotions even more. The setting sun added to the dignity and serenity of the moment, but all you could think about was that young men in their late teens and early twenties had experienced the sunset of their lives.

Then you walk by the marker that says, "Here rests in honored glory, a comrade in arms, known but to God." The Unknown Soldier.

You feel as though you are going through an emotional and spiritual cleansing. It is too difficult to comprehend how war could be so unfair, so brutal. How can a human being indiscriminately take another's life? Why cannot swords be turned into plowshares and spears into pruning hooks?

I had the urge to discover a marker of a Georgian who died here. I knew of no one who had given their life at Normandy, but then one marker caught my eye: Private Julian E. Smiley.

"It can't be," I thought, "but it says 'Georgia' on his marker."

I first thought that this had to be the father of Julian E. Smiley, who had lettered for Vince Dooley at Georgia in 1969–70, but a call to the former Bulldog running back revealed that it was his uncle.

"I am named for him," Julian says. "He was the youngest of five boys, and as I recall was not yet twenty-one years old. He was on a landing craft which was hit by a German shell as it was coming into the beach. There were only three survivors, and ironically one of them lives in Savannah."

You walk the rows and rows of markers and you are overcome with emotion. You pay your respects for those you never knew, and you say a "thank you" to them for the price they paid for your freedom. You can't walk this cemetery and not become emotionally affected. People come here and cry unashamedly, even those who have no relatives quietly resting in peace.

That first trip here, I remember walking down to the beach and looking back up at the cliffs and trying to imagine what it must have been like to have been pinned down on the beach under murderous enemy fire. Like so many others, I had read about the horror of the invasion and tried to envision what it could have been like. For a few fleeting seconds, I could hear the big guns from the battleships roaring and the enemy's machine gunfire strafing the beaches.

The invasion statistics boggle the mind today. The armada was the biggest in the history of the world: 10,500 aircraft; 9,000 vessels, including 4,000 landing craft; and six battleships and ninety-three destroyers. Supplies included 450,000 tons of ammunition; 50,000 tanks, Jeeps, and other vehicles; 1,000 locomotives; 20,000 railroad cars; and 124,000 hospital beds. At the end of the day, the number of Allied troops landing on D-Day totaled 154,000; 23,000 airborne troops flew across the English Channel.

The fighting was so brutal that in many instances it was safer to stay in the water. No progress was being made until those leaderless troops became the leaders themselves and took charge.

One of the most famous quotes came from Colonel George Taylor, who said, "There are two kinds of people staying on this beach, the dead and those who are going to die. Now let's get the hell out of here." And they did.

For years, I have always understood that if a man went through serious fighting, he does not talk about it. The ones who talk may not be trustworthy with the facts. I have generally found that to be exactly the way it was and is. However, D-Day veterans are now talking, brought about by the encouragement of Stephen Ambrose, the New Orleans-based historian.

Conversation with British World War II Hero

GUILDFORD, England—Six miles from here is a place called Albury Park, which is where you will find a retirement home in a peaceful setting with ring-necked pheasants walking about in view of meadows and meandering streams.

The peaceful setting makes you think of a fairy-tale life, one in which nobody suffers—conflict is absent; goodwill toward mankind eliminates strife, avarice, and greed. The setting was probably the same a little more than fifty years ago—until Adolf Hitler overran Europe and began a vicious bombing assault on England.

Here, in this serene environment, John Howard, a British war hero, lives out his last years with hope that what the Allies accomplished at Normandy fifty years ago will serve to remind us that a heavy price was paid for the world to remain free and that we should never forget.

Major Howard is an accommodating and selfless man who has spent much of the last year recalling his experience on D-Day, June 6th, 1944. His airborne unit captured the Bénouville Bridge and the Ranville Bridge near Caen. The capture of these bridges was a key development in the war, and the story of the taking of the heavily guarded canal bridge can be found in historian Stephen Ambrose's book *Pegasus Bridge*. The name Pegasus comes from the winged horse of Greek mythology. The British airborne division had taken the Pegasus image for its emblem prior to the battle.

The British military personnel, who had invaded the Sword, Gold, and Juno beaches, needed to capture the Bénouville and Ranville bridges in order for troops and equipment coming ashore to have access to the routes leading to Caen, the focal point of the British objective. There was fear that the Germans would blow up the bridges and hamper the invasion objective.

Howard had trained his restless men for weeks with the idea that nothing could go wrong, yet he understood that training exercises, no matter how well-simulated, are never the real thing.

He had one particular advantage working for him. Howard knew every detail of the area where he and his group would land. He had a relief model of the area where his unit would put down, and no attention to detail was spared. This was because the French Resistance would immediately send England any developments on the landscape. "If the Germans cut down a tree on Monday," Howard says, "it was taken down on my model the next day."

"It was so bloody good," says Howard's glider pilot, Jim Wallwork, "we could almost see the Germans working at it."

Howard knew where the pillboxes were, how deep bunkers and trenches were. "Whatever I needed in training I got," Howard adds. "The intelligence was out of this world. I was flabbergasted at the detail they accumulated." Howard asked for a German tank and received it. He knew there was such a tank at the bridge and he and his men had to know how to operate it if they captured the tank.

On the glider flight, coming in for the landing, Howard remembers the lush French countryside below and cows grazing peacefully although Caen was ablaze from Allied bombing. Yet the tranquility of the scene was a great source of confidence and relief. "It was overwhelming," he says, "but it also confirmed we were on course perfectly."

The landing went off without a hitch—no loss of men or supplies, but most significantly, they had achieved complete surprise. They were able to take out the German sentries and the nearby pillbox. Soon English radios were crackling with the code words "Ham and Jam." This meant that they had taken both the heavily guarded canal bridge and the nearby bridge over the Orne River.

When he lectures today, Howard always brings out a whistle that he blows, which is the shrill sound his men heard soon after the midnight landing. That meant that the two bridges had been taken intact. They had done their job.

His next big worry would be what to do about the German tanks. "We were not equipped to deal with tanks," Howard says. "Our anti-tank equipment was not reliable."

The German high command gave him an assist with that problem. Berlin had decreed that no tanks could be released for counterattack until they were sure that the Normandy invasion was not a feint.

Against all odds, the Allies had gotten ashore at Normandy; but it would be just as challenging to break out and oust the Germans from France. The first objective, however, had been realized. Momentum would come next.

One Man's Recall of Iwo Jima's Death Trap

Seventy years ago this year, the Allies had gained the momentum in World War II. The war was not over, but Hitler was in his bunker refusing to yield while the Japanese were poised to fight to the last man as the United States prepared to invade Japan.

We were squeezing the Nazis' jugular. We had a death grip. On May 8, 1945, the war came to a conclusion; V-E Day victory in Europe was celebrated worldwide. In the Pacific, it was different. The Allies had the upper hand, but the Japanese mentality had the US War Department concerned about the casualties that would result from invading the Japanese home islands.

The battle of Iwo Jima, which began on February 19, 1945, reflected what would likely face the US if it invaded Japan. Admiral Chester Nimitz sent 70,000 marines, navy corpsmen, and U.S. Army airmen to Iwo Jima. It was a bloody battle, the U.S. suffering 6,821 killed while the Japanese saw 18,844 of its 22,060 personnel lose their lives. It took almost five weeks to rout the Japanese from the bunkers and caves in which they were entrenched.

One of the 70,000 who joined the invasion party was Winfield "Skeets" Baldwin, native of Wilmington, North Carolina, and longtime chemistry professor at the University of Georgia. He was on the beaches for only two days and two nights, but never rested easy in his foxhole, knowing that the Japanese were famous for attacking in the middle of night, bent on slitting the throats of their adversaries. Baldwin went ashore on the 20th to relieve those who had landed first, as the rotation was a Godsend for some, eternity for others.

"I was only eighteen years old," Baldwin says. "Naturally, I was one of the fortunate ones since I wound up on Guam a few days later. It was a miserable experience. We stacked marines up on the beach five and six deep. Although I was eager to sign up for military duty, I had no idea what I was in for. Still, I am proud to have been a member of the Greatest Generation. My initial objective was to become a pilot but knew that I likely would not pass the physical.

"You could join the military when you were seventeen years old, but to enter officer training, which I had planned to do, you had to be eighteen. I didn't want to wait a year so I took the enlisted man's route. I am proud to have served my country, but am disappointed that we seem to have lost some of the patriotic emotion in this country. After Pearl Harbor, the tone in this country was to sign up and fight for America. Our country truly was great back then, and I am not sure we will ever regain the attitude which prevailed in the forties."

After the war, Baldwin enrolled at the University of North Carolina where he later earned a PhD. In 1967, he joined the faculty at the University of Georgia, where he taught for twenty-seven years. When he arrived, his brother-in-law, Ken Rosemond, was the Bulldogs basketball coach.

Entering the war at such a tender age, and surviving after brief combat, Baldwin realizes his good fortune but has never wanted to return to Iwo Jima, where many veterans have journeyed for reunions over the years. However, he is emotionally moved when he sees the historic photo of the marines raising the U.S. flag on Mt. Suribachi. Skeets left a couple of days before Joe Rosenthal took the famous photo on Jan. 23, 1945.

"For the many who return for reunions, I understand their motivation, but it is not something that I have wanted to do, especially now. I simply want to enjoy retirement. But, let me say this, I admire those guys who fought at Iwo Jima and survived. We should remember the sacrifice that they made," Baldwin notes.

"Even though I was anxious to enlist, I still went through a tough emotional experience with only two days on Iwo Jima. I knew what could have been in store for me if I had stayed longer."

Had President Truman not made the decision to drop atomic bombs on Hiroshima and Nagasaki, Baldwin would have likely stormed the shores of Japan. Fortunately, he lived to tell a different story.

Margraten
Where the Dutch Remember Our Military

MARGRATEN, The Netherlands—This is about World War II. I can't ignore the statistics that remind us how many gave their youthful lives to end Nazi tyranny. They never had an open discussion in a classroom or at a bar or at the family dinner table. They were never asked whether they should go or not. They all eagerly volunteered, imbued with faith and love of country and flag. That is why they were called the "Greatest Generation." Nobody can get enough of their stories.

Every year, there is a fresh introduction or a new vignette causing one to feel fortunate to be able to connect with people who are in some way linked to those who made the ultimate sacrifice. We should never allow the world and successive generations to forget. For sure, the Dutch haven't forgotten.

I have stopped at a lonely plot of ground, near a foundation that supports a flagpole where the American flag waves in the breeze every day of the year. I am in the company of Miranda Prevaes, a knowledgeable Dutch woman who has brought me to the grave of James Lee Cole, one of the 8,301 Americans buried here in Margraten.

Most of them lost their lives in Operation Market Garden, which was a failure and a reminder that generals often scheme out plans that go awry. The British General Bernard Montgomery thought this battle would allow the Allies to gain a quick entry into Germany and make him a hero. It was, history reminds us, not a good decision.

This brings about an aside that requires a disclaimer. I am not a historian, merely an enthusiast. However, when it comes to the history of WWII, any curious advocate of the war's enduring history comes away more humbled than when he arrived. I am fascinated with the major headlines but the obscure details as well.

This grave in Margraten is the final resting place of the aforementioned Lee Cole, a paratrooper who lost his life in Operation Market Garden. He had survived the Allied landings at Normandy, but his luck ran out on him in the Netherlands. I am here to pay my respects on behalf of his daughter, Lee Cole Wright, who lives in Athens and has never been to her father's grave. I am her surrogate.

So many emotions crowd your consciousness when you visit an Allied cemetery in Europe. These were men, some kids, who volunteered to fight across borders they, in so many cases, would not have known had it not been for war. James Lee Cole was one of them.

However, it is Dutch nationals like Luc Amkreutz, who are ensuring, even three-quarters of a century later, that those who are buried here will never be forgotten. Even if we don't remember, the Dutch remember. Can you believe that every single grave at Margraten has been adopted by a Dutch family? And get this—there is a waiting list. They bring flowers on the deceased's birthday, the anniversary of D-Day, and Christmas, among other occasions. Over coffee in Leiden, a suburb of Amsterdam, Luc and I talk about his commitment to the ongoing honoring of Americans who "gave us our freedom." He has never met Lee Wright or her husband, Bill, but they correspond via email. "I hope," Luc said, "they will come here someday. I would be honored to take Lee to her father's grave at Margraten."

You cannot know Luc and the thousands of Dutch families who honor members of the "Greatest Generation" with their acts of respect without it crossing your mind that perhaps the Dutch care more than we do! Except for the Revolutionary War and Civil War, we have never experienced the ravages of war on our soil. Hitler, lest we forget, came very close to winning World War II. Even so, he not only made girls like Lee Wright grow up without a father, but he brought unnecessary grief to millions.

This brings me to a note left at the grave of a German soldier at the German cemetery at La Cambe in Normandy. The German soldier had gotten his wife pregnant before leaving for Normandy and getting killed in battle. The following is the poignant, written message his daughter would someday leave at her father's grave: "On my third trip here, I cannot meet you. How many more daughters will never know their fathers because of war?"

Ex-Panzer Commander Offers a Different D-Day Perspective

NEW ORLEANS—Hans von Luck is an octogenarian: slender and erect; a deliberate sort of man with penetrating eyes and a story of World War II that offers a different viewpoint—that of a German colonel who fought bravely and did his duty, but not without compassion for the plight of those suffering from the ravages of military battle.

That is in contrast with the view Allied citizens would have likely held for a German officer fifty years ago.

Luck was like a son to the great German general Erwin Rommel. He rode with Rommel's troops into Poland, France, and Russia. Luck tasted defeat for the first time in North Africa and then again when the Allies landed at Normandy on D-Day. He wound up in a Russian POW camp in the Caucasus Mountains.

When I met him here a few weeks ago, I was struck not only by his recall of details from the D-Day invasion, much of which he has written in his autobiography, *Panzer Commander*, but his human side as well. His memoirs, his publisher says "...reproduce the events and experiences that a young German had to go through in a period that changed Europe and almost the whole world. The Second World War stands at the center. It shows, along with the preceding years, how intolerance, a false ideology, and propaganda can mobilize whole peoples against each other and plunge them into misery."

Early in the Poland campaign, Luck was asked to befriend the German wife of a Pole, and it turned out that she was a distant relative of Luck. He says poignantly, "It struck me how senseless the war was, and yet there was no escape from it."

In his moving story, Luck asks the question that many of us would ask about Hitler's ability to fanatically sway an entire nation. "How could a people," he asks, "from whom a Goethe and a Beethoven had sprung become blind slaves of such a leader and fall into hysteria when he made a speech?"

Luck, who lives in Hamburg today, cites four key reasons in his book that led to the unbridling of Hitler and the Nazis:

The army of 100,000 men to which we were entitled under the Treaty of Versailles was deliberately trained not to be political. As a result, the officer corps lacked perspective.

Hitler's initial successes—the elimination of unemployment and the communist threat, as well as the reparation of former German territories to the greater German Reich—restored self-confidence to the German people and their growing Wehrmacht.

The young people who were called up for military service were re-cruited mainly from Hitler youth and other national socialist organizations and were correspondingly motivated if not fantasized.

Most decisively, it seems to me: the oath of allegiance was the creed of the officer corps. Hitler knew this and exploited it shamelessly.

Luck's closeness with General Rommel gave him the opportunity to critique Hitler's mistakes throughout the war. Rommel knew that Hitler's decision to control the panzer units and their movements in Normandy was suicidal. Rommel knew that field commanders could best make on-the-spot combat decisions involving troop and armor movement.

"Hitler's command," Luck explains, "felt that the invasion would come either at Calais or further south near Cherbourg. They wanted the panzer units inland so they could move quickly to the point of attack. Hit-ler was constantly bothered by constant Allied deception and became con-vinced the Normandy beach invasion was a diversion tactic with the real invasion to follow at a deep-water port like Calais or Cherbourg.

"Rommel often told me that we must throw the enemy back into the sea in the first twenty-four hours or it will be the beginning of the end," Luck said.

The old general was right, and felt so strongly about his feelings that he, according to Luck, had left Normandy by June 5, 1944, to meet with Hitler about changing his policy. Also, Rommel had been advised that the English Channel was too rough for an invasion and took the opportunity to return home to celebrate his wife's birthday. When Rommel learned of the invasion, he said of his ill-advised absence, "How stupid of me!" "How stupid of me!" he repeated.

"With Rommel away," Luck says, "We had no division commander. When the invasion came, we were under strict orders to do nothing. We could make no move without orders from the higher commands, and the higher command insisted that the Normandy invasion was a diversion attack."

When the order to counterattack came, some eight and a half hours after the start of the invasion, the Allies had overcome serious fighting and logistical complications to get ashore. They could not be thrown back into the sea.

"Once the orders to counterattack came," Luck says, "confusion ensued. There were crippling delays, and the delay was costly."

Rommel had told Luck in March of 1943 that the war was lost. In the book *Pegasus Bridge*, Luck quoted Rommel for author Stephen Ambrose: "We lost Stalingrad, we will lose Africa, with the body of our best trained armored people. We can't fight without them. The only thing we can do is ask for an armistice. We have to give up all this business about the Jews, we have to change our minds about the religions, and so on, and we must get an armistice now at this stage while we have something to offer."

Luck, who has a keen insight into history, is very familiar with the mistakes of the German high command. He has a great appreciation as to how the German soldier was developed into a seasoned and battle-hardened fighter. He understands why Hitler's propaganda machine was so effective. Most of all, he has a perspective that puts into focus how we should look at those events of fifty years ago.

"To forget is great," he says. "To forgive is better. Best of all is reconciliation. As a professional soldier I have to take responsibility for what happened, but as a human being, I have no hate."

Remembering Oradour

In the past week, we experienced the 76th anniversary of the D-Day invasion, except this time it was quiet and understated when compared to past celebrations.

While I have never been to Normandy on June 6 in any past summer, I have made a few trips to those historic beaches. Returning would be another sobering experience to graphically connect with the courage and resolve that brought about Allied victory.

It actually *was* a race against time, given Nazi Germany's proximity to developing superweapons beyond the devastating V-1 missiles and V-2 rockets that rained down on London. It was a critical juncture for the free world.

Adolf Hitler's micromanaging the war turned out to be a plus for the Allies—along with his arrogance, insanity, and stupidity. His defiance of his generals became a godsend. Going into Russia in the midsummer of 1941 gave his army its greatest challenge in the face of an impactful winter that was one of the worst on record.

The Allied invasion of Normandy will forever be remembered for the bravery of the American and British forces, but there was also an element of luck, along with Hitler's arrogance and personal habits, that was helpful. Hitler steadfastly clung to the notion that the Normandy action was a feint, certain that the real invasion would come 250 miles north at Calais. As a result, the panzer units could not be released to the point of attack without Hitler's approval. That approval did not come until he awakened at noon, and nobody dared disturb him and bring about his uncontrolled wrath.

There are countless books, movies, and documentaries that have chronicled and analyzed both the war and Hitler, including the unthinkable tragedies that the Nazis engendered.

We know about Auschwitz and the other death camps, but there were other scenes of abject brutality that are a reminder of what evil dictators are capable of. On June 10, 1944, four days after the Allies established a beachhead in Normandy, the citizens of an entire French town, Oradour-sur-Glane, were massacred.

The raw statistics acutely overwhelm. A total of 642 died, including a half dozen visitors who had ridden their bicycles into the village. Of the victims, 247 women and 205 children were brutally murdered. Only a handful survived.

In the summer of 2006, I made a second trip to Oradour. I had discovered the name of a survivor of the massacre and had tried to contact him by phone—to no avail. An alternate plan was successful, however. A call went out to a French journalist and good friend Denis Lalanne, who took a train from his hometown of Biarritz to Chartres to meet me. We then drove to Oradour, which is near Limoges.

With a reporter's instincts, Denis took the local phone directory and searched until he identified Robert Hébras, the survivor we wanted to meet. Denis located Hébras' son who connected us with his father.

We arrived at Hébras' home in the early afternoon for conversation and wine. He explained what happened. On the fateful day, the Nazis rang the town bell for the residents to report to the center of the village. They organized the residents into two groups, sending the men and teenage boys to the stables at the foot of the village and herding the women and children into the cathedral.

At the stables, they began shooting at the legs of the males, causing them to fall over, and then they set about executing everybody. Hébras fell to the ground, with dead and dying bodies falling around him. The guards then set fire to the stables, creating a funeral pyre. Hébras was able to extricate himself and escape to cover.

The women and children were locked in the cathedral. The SS soldiers placed an incendiary device beside the church and ignited it, causing a stampede for the doors and window. They were then met with machine-gun fire. One of the victims was Hébras' sister.

On the day I interviewed Hébras, with my friend Denis translating, sixty years had passed. Hébras was no longer bitter and had participated in reconciliation conferences between French and German groups.

The officer who gave the orders for the atrocity was arrested years after the war and defended his actions, arguing that he was only following orders. He bewailed imprisonment, saying that he was an old man and that incarceration meant he would be unable to enjoy his grandchildren.

All I could think about was that bullets from his thugs kept a great number of innocent people from someday having grandchildren. And what about the grandchildren that they murdered? Having spent time in Oradour, I had a sensation that the victims were begging the world to never forget this repugnant moment in history; lest it happen again.

About the Author

Loran Smith has spent most of his professional life at the University of Georgia as former assistant sports information director, business manager, and executive director of the Georgia Bulldog Club, and as a member of the Athletic Association development office. A past chairman of the State of Georgia Sports Hall of Fame, he currently serves as a fundraiser and historian for University of Georgia Athletics. Smith holds a Journalism degree from UGA and is a writer and author or co-author of eighteen books. He maintains daily and weekly radio shows that air statewide.

Index

Index